PROVERBS, ECCLESIASTES *and* the SONG OF SONGS *for* EVERYONE

Also available in the Old Testament
for Everyone series by John Goldingay

Genesis for Everyone, Part I

Genesis for Everyone, Part II

Exodus and Leviticus for Everyone

Numbers and Deuteronomy for Everyone

Joshua, Judges and Ruth for Everyone

1 and 2 Samuel for Everyone

1 and 2 Kings for Everyone

1 and 2 Chronicles for Everyone

Ezra, Nehemiah and Esther for Everyone

Job for Everyone

Psalms for Everyone, Part I

Psalms for Everyone, Part II

PROVERBS, ECCLESIASTES *and the* SONG OF SONGS *for* EVERYONE

JOHN GOLDINGAY

Published in the United States of America in 2014
by Westminster John Knox Press, Louisville, Kentucky

Published in Great Britain in 2014

Society for Promoting Christian Knowledge
36 Causton Street
London SW1P 4ST
www.spckpublishing.co.uk

British Library Cataloguing-in-Publication Data
A catalogue record for this book is available from the British Library

ISBN 978–0–281–06135–8
eBook ISBN 978–0–281–06785–5

First printed in Great Britain
Subsequently digitally printed in Great Britain

eBook by Graphicraft Limited, Hong Kong

Produced on paper from sustainable forests

CONTENTS

Acknowledgments		ix
Introduction		1
Proverbs 1:1–19	Wisdom's Dictionary	7
Proverbs 1:20–2:22	Students in Four Flavors	11
Proverbs 3:1–35	On Trust	15
Proverbs 4:1–27	On Discipline	19
Proverbs 5:1–23	Crazy for Love (1)	23
Proverbs 6:1–34	On Safeguarding Concord	26
Proverbs 7:1–27	Let Me Tell You a Story	30
Proverbs 8:1–36	Let Me Tell You Another Story	33
Proverbs 9:1–18	The Two Voices	38
Proverbs 10:1–32	The Mouth of the Faithful Person Is Fruitful	42
Proverbs 11:1–31	With Modesty There Is Wisdom	47
Proverbs 12:1–28	Anxiety and a Good Word	52
Proverbs 13:1–25	Discipline Your Teenagers If You Can	56
Proverbs 14:1–35	Even in Laughter a Heart May Hurt	61
Proverbs 15:1–33	A Gentle Response Turns Back Wrath	66
Proverbs 16:1–33	Arrogance Goes before Shattering	70
Proverbs 17:1–28	Yahweh Tests Minds	75
Proverbs 18:1–24	Yahweh's Name Is a Refuge	80
Proverbs 19:1–29	Does God Have a Wonderful Plan for Your Life?	84
Proverbs 20:1–30	Drink Is a Brawler	90
Proverbs 21:1–31	The Way of a Man Can Be Strange	95
Proverbs 22:1–16	Rich and Poor Meet	100

Proverbs 22:17–23:21	Don't Let Your Nap Go On Too Long	105
Proverbs 23:22–24:22	Acquire Truth, Don't Sell It	110
Proverbs 24:23–25:22	On Heaping Coals	115
Proverbs 25:23–26:28	Things Complicated and Back to Front	121
Proverbs 27:1–27	Faithful Are the Wounds of a Friend	127
Proverbs 28:1–28	For Lenten Thought	132
Proverbs 29:1–27	You Could Suddenly Break, and There Could Be No Healing	138
Proverbs 30:1–14	I'm Just a Weary Sojourner, but I Have Some Words from God	143
Proverbs 30:15–33	Creation and Numbers	147
Proverbs 31:1–9	The Demon Drink	151
Proverbs 31:10–31	The Strong Woman	153
Proverbs by Topics		157
Ecclesiastes 1:1-11	Under the Sun, Where Randomness Rules	175
Ecclesiastes 1:12–2:11	The Secret of Life Is ...	179
Ecclesiastes 2:12–26	What Legacy?	182
Ecclesiastes 3:1–15	Everything Has Its Time	186
Ecclesiastes 3:16–4:3	There's No Justice	189
Ecclesiastes 4:4–16	If Two People Lie Together, They Can Be Warm	193
Ecclesiastes 5:1–7	Sell Your Tongue, and Buy a Thousand Ears	196
Ecclesiastes 5:8–6:9	It's Not Enough, but It's Not Nothing	198
Ecclesiastes 6:10–7:22	Be Realistic	202
Ecclesiastes 7:23–8:15	I Have Not Found a Woman	205
Ecclesiastes 8:16–9:12	Remember You Are Going to Die	208
Ecclesiastes 9:13–10:20	The Distressing Dynamics of Wisdom and Power	212
Ecclesiastes 11:1–12:7	Enjoy Your Life Mindful of Your Creator	216
Ecclesiastes 12:8–14	One Ecclesiastes Is Good, but One Is Enough	219
Song of Songs 1:1–17	Alone Together	222
Song of Songs 2:1–17	My Love Is Mine, and I Am His	227
Song of Songs 3:1–11	Nightmares and Dreams (1)	231
Song of Songs 4:1–5:1	Crazy for Love (2)	235

Song of Songs 5:2–6:10   Nightmares and Dreams (2)   238

Song of Songs 6:11–7:13 I Belong to My Love, and His Desire Is
                         toward Me   242

Song of Songs 8:1–14   Love Is as Fierce as Death   246

Glossary   251

ACKNOWLEDGMENTS

The translation at the beginning of each chapter (and in other biblical quotations) is my own. I have stuck closer to the Hebrew than modern translations often do when they are designed for reading in church so that you can see more precisely what the text says. Thus although I prefer to use gender-inclusive language, I have let the translation stay gendered if inclusivizing it would obscure whether the text was using singular or plural—in other words, the translation often uses "he" where in my own writing I would say "they" or "he or she." Sometimes I have added words to make the meaning clear, and I have put these words in square brackets. At the end of the book is a glossary of some terms that recur in the text, such as geographical, historical, and theological expressions. In each chapter (though not in the introduction or in the Scripture selections) these terms are highlighted in **bold** the first time they occur.

The stories that follow the translation often concern my friends or my family. While none are made up, they are sometimes heavily disguised in order to be fair to people. Sometimes I have disguised them so well that when I read the stories again, I was not sure initially whom I was describing. My first wife, Ann, appears in a number of them. A few months after I started writing The Old Testament for Everyone, she died after negotiating with multiple sclerosis for forty-three years. Our shared dealings with her illness and disability over these years contribute significantly to what I write in ways that you'll be able to see but also in ways that are less obvious.

Then, a year or so before I started writing this particular volume, I fell in love with and married Kathleen Scott, and I am grateful for my new life with her and for her insightful comments on the manuscript, which have been so careful and illuminating that she practically deserves to be credited as coauthor.

I am also grateful to Matt Sousa for reading through the manuscript and pointing out things I needed to correct or clarify and to Tom Bennett for checking the proofs.

INTRODUCTION

As far as Jesus and the New Testament writers were concerned, the Jewish Scriptures that Christians call the "Old Testament" *were* the Scriptures. In saying that, I cut corners a bit, as the New Testament never gives us a list of these Scriptures, but the body of writings that the Jewish people accept is as near as we can get to identifying the collection that Jesus and the New Testament writers would have worked with. The church also came to accept some extra books such as Maccabees and Ecclesiasticus that were traditionally called the "Apocrypha," the books that were "hidden away"—a name that came to imply "spurious." They are now often known as the "Deuterocanonical Writings," which is more cumbersome but less pejorative; it simply indicates that these books have less authority than the Torah, the Prophets, and the Writings. The precise list of them varies among different churches. For the purposes of this series that seeks to expound the "Old Testament for Everyone," by the "Old Testament" we mean the Scriptures accepted by the Jewish community, though in the Jewish Bible they come in a different order, as the Torah, the Prophets, and the Writings.

They were not "old" in the sense of antiquated or out-of-date; I sometimes like to refer to them as the First Testament rather than the Old Testament to make that point. For Jesus and the New Testament writers, they were a living resource for understanding God, God's ways in the world, and God's ways with us. They were "useful for teaching, for reproof, for correction, and for training in righteousness, so that the person who belongs to God can be proficient, equipped for every good work" (2 Timothy 3:16–17). They were for everyone, in fact. So it's strange that Christians don't read them very much. My aim in these volumes is to help you do so.

My hesitation is that you may read me instead of the Scriptures. Don't fall into that trap. I like the fact that this

1

series includes the biblical text. Don't skip over it. In the end, that's the bit that matters.

An Outline of the Old Testament

The Christian Old Testament puts the books in the Jewish Bible in a distinctive order:

Genesis to Kings: A story that runs from the world's creation to the exile of Judahites to Babylon

Chronicles to Esther: A second version of this story, continuing it into the years after the exile

Job, Psalms, Proverbs, Ecclesiastes, Song of Songs: Some poetic books

Isaiah to Malachi: The teaching of some prophets

Here is an outline of the history that lies at the books' background (I give no dates for events in Genesis, which involves too much guesswork).

1200s	Moses, the exodus, Joshua
1100s	The "judges"
1000s	King Saul, King David
900s	King Solomon; the nation splits into two, Ephraim and Judah
800s	Elijah, Elisha
700s	Amos, Hosea, Isaiah, Micah; Assyria the superpower; the fall of Ephraim
600s	Jeremiah, King Josiah; Babylon the superpower
500s	Ezekiel; the fall of Judah; Persia the superpower; Judahites free to return home
400s	Ezra, Nehemiah
300s	Greece the superpower
200s	Syria and Egypt, the regional powers pulling Judah one way or the other

100s   Judah's rebellion against Syrian power and gain of independence

000s   Rome the superpower

Proverbs, Ecclesiastes, and Song of Songs

The three books we cover in this volume come together in the Old Testament because they are all associated with Solomon. His name appears in the first verse of Proverbs and of the Song, and he's just under the surface of Ecclesiastes (as we'll see when we look at Ecclesiastes 1–2). As is the case with the association of Psalms with David, the link with Solomon doesn't imply that he personally wrote the books (despite the nice rabbinical saying that Solomon wrote the Song with the naiveté of youth, Proverbs with the maturity of middle age, and Ecclesiastes with the disillusion of old age). Indeed, sayings such as the ones that appear in Proverbs don't exactly have authors; the sayings somehow emerge. Further, Proverbs 25, 30, and 31 explicitly refer to other authors or collectors of the material in Proverbs. Ecclesiastes doesn't name Solomon, and its use of Hebrew shows that it doesn't belong to his day— it would be as if Shakespeare wrote in modern English. And Solomon's story in Kings shows that he was clueless about love and is an unlikely author for love poetry. The point about the link with Solomon is that he's the patron saint of wisdom as David is the patron saint of psalmody. First Kings 3 does speak of his asking God for wisdom, and God gives him a wise and discerning mind; he becomes the model of a wise king (for a while). So all wisdom can be seen as Solomonic.

The nature of the sayings in Proverbs likely means they accumulated over centuries. Many will go back before Solomon's day and have their background in family life and the teaching of children by parents. Thus, when sayings speak like a father and mother teaching children, they are not speaking wholly metaphorically. Other passages in Proverbs relate especially to questions such as the relationship of a king's staff to the king, and teaching of this kind in other Middle Eastern countries belongs in the context of the court college where people were prepared for the life of politics and administration. In contrast, other material in Proverbs and Ecclesiastes relates more to questions that would be asked in a theological college or seminary, questions about the meaning of creation, the nature of God's relationship with the world, and the possibility of having answers to life's big questions. It was during the Second Temple period that theological schools, the kind of places where rabbis would be trained, were developing in Israel; this might be the background of such elements in Proverbs and Ecclesiastes.

Proverbs and Ecclesiastes explicitly focus on the nature of wisdom. The Song, in expounding the nature of sexual love, doesn't do so; but what it has in common with the other two Solomonic books is its focus on everyday life. The unique feature of the three Solomonic books is that they make no reference to the exodus or the covenant or the Torah or prophecy or the Day of the Lord. They do speak of God as Yahweh, and their teaching can parallel the teaching of the Torah; they are clearly Israelite. But they don't teach by telling us that their teaching comes from God's speaking or forms a response to God's acting. The basis of their teaching is the way life actually works. They look at life and reflect on experience and encourage people to live on the basis of how life works. They don't just leave people to live on the basis of their own experience; they assume that we can learn from other people's experience, and they seek to pass on the reflection of wise men and women that arises from their experience. They assume that we learn from other people and learn from the past. We don't have to keep reinventing the wheel. These books appeal to experience, which links them with equivalent works produced in countries such as Babylon and Egypt. These books don't emerge from Yahweh's special dealings with

Israel that enabled Israel to know things about God's purpose in the world that other people didn't know. They emerged from the awareness about life of which any people can know something through being made in God's image and living in God's world.

Proverbs and the Song have in common that they are poetic books through and through; Ecclesiastes includes one of the best-known poems in all Scripture, but its poetic sections appear in a prose framework. In terms of form, the main characteristic of Hebrew poetry is that it is composed in short lines of about six words each, such that the second half of each line reexpresses, completes, clarifies, illustrates, or contrasts with the first.

> Listen to your father's discipline, son,
>> don't abandon your mother's teaching.
>>> *(Proverbs 1:8)*

> Kiss me with the kisses of your mouth,
>> because your love is better than wine.
>>> *(Song 1:2)*

These two examples illustrate how Proverbs' poetry tends to be down-to-earth, while the Song's poetry is more lyrical. All poetry uses imagery so as to make more profound statements, and the Song is full of imagery—some of it rather obscure to us in our different cultural context.

Proverbs and the Song also have in common a fundamentally hopeful attitude to life. They think life can be understood and appreciated. Ecclesiastes belongs with Job in raising more questions than it answers. Proverbs and the Song on one hand and Ecclesiastes and Job on the other thus fulfill a complementary role in Scripture. Proverbs and the Song remind the worried, the uncertain, and the cynical of positive insights and of possibilities to reframe their attitudes. Ecclesiastes and Job remind the confident, the trusting, and the naive, of questions they need to take into account rather than thinking they have the truth all buttoned up.

Ecclesiastes and the Song also belong to the same group of books—known as the "Five Scrolls"—within the Hebrew Bible's different orderings of its books. The other books in the Five Scrolls are Ruth, Lamentations, and Esther. These books were read at five different festivals each year—the Song at Passover (on the basis of its being understood as an allegory of God's history with Israel) and Ecclesiastes at Sukkot (perhaps because of its stress on joy and on God's giving, even in the context of its acknowledging the transience of life). It was the Greek translation of the Old Testament that located these books with the other poetic books in a way that draws attention to their being not books that tell a story about the past (like Genesis through Esther) or books that announce what God will do in the future (like Isaiah through Malachi) but books that relate directly to everyday life in the present.

PROVERBS 1:1–19
Wisdom's Dictionary

1 Sayings of Solomon son of David, king of Israel,
2 for knowing wisdom and discipline,
   for understanding words that express understanding,
3 for getting the discipline to act sensibly,
   faithfulness, the exercise of authority, and uprightness,
4 for giving judiciousness to the naive,
   knowledge and discretion to the young person,
5 so that the wise person may listen and increase in his grasp,
   the discerning may acquire skill,
6 for understanding a saying and a parable,
   the words of the wise and their puzzles.
7 The first principle of knowledge is awe for Yahweh;
   stupid people despise wisdom and discipline.

8 Listen to your father's discipline, son,
   don't abandon your mother's teaching,
9 because they are a graceful garland for your head,
   a chain for your neck.
10 If offenders entice you, son, don't be willing,
11 if they say "Go with us.
   Let's lie in wait for blood,
   let's ambush an innocent person, for nothing.
12 Let's swallow them alive, like Sheol—
   whole, like people going down to the Pit.
13 We'll find every sort of valuable wealth,
   we'll fill our houses with plunder.
14 Cast your lot in the midst of us;
   there will be one purse for us all."
15 Don't go on the road with them, son;
   keep your foot from their path.
16 Because their feet run to evil,
   they hurry to shed blood.
17 Because it is for nothing that a net is spread
   in the sight of any winged creature.
18 But those people lie in wait for their own blood,
   they ambush their own lives.

¹⁹ Such are the ways of everyone who gets wrongful gain;
    it takes the life of its owner.

I turned onto the freeway near our house, built up speed down the ramp, noticed as I reached the main lanes that there was a gap in the traffic but that a bunch of cars was on its way, so I built up speed to 80 or so to get ahead of them. Unfortunately they included a highway patrolman who pointed his radar gun at me. On went his lights and his siren. When we had stopped, he asked me, "Sir, do you know what the speed limit is on this road?" I said yes; I knew it was 65. But if we had been in Israel and we had been speaking Hebrew, I might have been less sure how to answer, because in biblical Hebrew, at least, the verb for "know" often denotes not merely knowing something in your head but knowing something in your actions. To know the law or to know God implies not merely knowing what the law says or knowing God in a personal way but acknowledging the law or acknowledging God by one's behavior—submitting to and obeying what one knows.

The opening paragraph of Proverbs thus comes to a climax by declaring that the first principle of knowledge is **awe** for **Yahweh**, whereas stupid people despise wisdom and discipline; the opening chapter of Proverbs refers to knowing or knowledge six times. But the knowing isn't expressed merely in achieving a high IQ or a high score in the Standardized Admissions Test (SAT). The point runs through the opening paragraph, which introduces many of Proverbs' key words. The connection between what goes on in the head and what goes on in the life immediately appears in the link between wisdom and discipline. Increasing in wisdom is tied up with increasing in discipline. It's linked with the idea of "getting" discipline or "getting" wisdom—the word is the Hebrew verb that means to take. Getting hold of wisdom involves action. We speak of "grasping" things, and the word for "grasp" here is related to the word for "getting." Grasping is an activity. In substance, gaining wisdom is related to understanding words that express understanding—the Hebrew word for understanding is related to the word for "between," so it hints at the capacity to distinguish between things or to see behind the surface of things.

The Hebrew word for judiciousness is often translated "shrewdness"; it's the capacity attributed to the snake in Genesis 2. It suggests being able to get people to do what you want them to do. It can have a bad connotation or a good connotation. Similarly "discretion" suggests skill in thinking things through and formulating plans, which in other contexts can be evil plans. That ambiguity points toward the significance of some other motifs in this opening paragraph. Alongside the references to wisdom and knowledge comes a sudden reference to **faithfulness**, the exercise of **authority**, and uprightness. The first two expressions appear frequently in the Prophets and also in the **Torah**; they are usually translated something like justice and righteousness, but they denote something more like faithfulness in making decisions. Appearing here, they imply that knowledge, judiciousness, and discretion need to be in the service of these moral qualities.

Together, the references to these moral qualities and to awe for Yahweh make a double point. It can be tempting to treat questions about economics, business, education, counseling, or foreign policy as issues in their own right that should not be mixed up with questions about religion or ethics. In particular cultural contexts (such as that of the United States with its separation of church and state), people such as Jews and Christians may have no alternative to living with that assumption in some areas of life. But we need to see how unnatural and unbiblical it is to consider policy questions, ethics, and God as separate spheres. Proverbs begins by urging its readers to let them interweave. Christians and Jews cannot adopt from the world theories or practices of business or counseling or education without setting them in the context of what we know about ethics and about God. Proverbs thus models how to go about learning from the secular world: we are open to such learning, but we set the secular world's theories and findings into a framework that includes God and ethics.

Maybe that fact links with the further promise that Proverbs' teaching is designed to help people understand parables and puzzles. Parables are straightforward-sounding stories whose real meaning is rather enigmatic; puzzles are the mysterious topics that the wise seek to understand, such as the nature of creation and the problem of evil. We'll never understand everything about such topics, but we'll gain more understanding if we take ethics and God into account.

The subsequent paragraph of teaching on a specific topic offers a correlative take on these questions. Parents are naturally concerned about their children getting into company that will lead them astray. The topic the paragraph raises makes clear that Proverbs' references to children should not be assumed to concern little children. It's a better starting assumption that they have in mind teenagers and adults. Proverbs assumes that father and mother continue to be the heads of the family as long as they are alive. Even if the middle-aged children are running the family farm, their parents are still the repository of wisdom.

The opening paragraph has made the positive point that ethical living will also be wise living (live ethically and you'll get on in life OK). The teaching about avoiding bad company makes the correlative negative point that unethical living is stupid. If you spread a net in the open to catch a bird, you'll fail; it will not be so silly as to fall into the trap. But the gang's proposed kind of behavior suggests it's trying to get caught. It's like setting an ambush for yourself.

PROVERBS 1:20–2:22

Students in Four Flavors

20 Wisdom resounds out in the open,
   in the squares she gives her voice,
21 at the head of the noisy places,
   at the entrances of the gates.
   In the city she speaks her words:
22 "How long will you naive people give yourselves to naiveté,
   arrogant people delight in their arrogance,
   stupid people repudiate knowledge?—
23 turn at my rebuke.
   Here I pour out my spirit to you,
   I let you know my words.
24 Because I called but you refused me,
   I stretched out my hand but there was no one paying
       attention.
25 You have spurned all my counsel,
   and you were not willing for my rebuke.
26 I myself in turn will laugh at your calamity;
   I'll mock when what you dread comes about,
27 when what you dread comes about like a disaster
   and your calamity arrives like a whirlwind,
   when trouble and disaster come upon you.
28 Then they will call me, but I won't answer,
   they will search urgently for me, but they will not find
       me,
29 because of the fact that they repudiated knowledge,
   did not choose awe for Yahweh.
30 They were not willing for my counsel,
   they spurned every rebuke of mine.
31 They will eat the fruit of their way,
   they will have their fill of their own counsels.
32 Because the turning of the naive will kill them,
   and the complacency of stupid people will destroy them.
33 But the person who listens to me will dwell trustingly,
   safe from the dread of evil."

2:1 My son, if you take my words,
   store up my commands with you,
2 making your ear attend to wisdom,
   inclining your mind to understanding,

11

³ if you indeed call for understanding, raise your voice for
   understanding,
⁴ if you seek it like silver, search for it like treasure,
⁵ then you'll understand awe for Yahweh,
   find knowledge of God.
⁶ Because Yahweh gives wisdom;
   from his mouth comes knowledge and understanding.
⁷ He stores up skill for the upright;
   [he is] a shield for people who walk with integrity,
⁸ guarding the paths of authority,
   protecting the way of people committed to him.
⁹ Then you'll understand faithfulness and the exercise of
   authority,
   and uprightness, every good track.
¹⁰ Because wisdom will come into your mind,
   knowledge will delight your spirit.
¹¹ Discretion will protect you,
   understanding will guard you,
¹² rescuing you from the way of the evil person,
   from the one who speaks things that are crooked,
¹³ people who abandon upright paths,
   following the way of darkness,
¹⁴ who are glad to do evil,
   rejoice in the crooked actions of the evil person,
¹⁵ people whose tracks are crooked,
   who are devious in their paths;
¹⁶ rescuing you from the other woman,
   from the alien woman whose words are charming,
¹⁷ who abandons the partner of her youth,
   disregards her covenant with God.
¹⁸ Because her household goes down to death,
   her tracks to the ghosts.
¹⁹ Anyone who comes to her does not return;
   he does not reach the paths of life—
²⁰ so that you may walk in the way of the good people,
   keep the paths of the faithful.
²¹ Because the upright will dwell in the country,
   the people of integrity will remain in it.
²² But the faithless will be cut off from the country,
   the treacherous will be ripped up from it.

My students come in several flavors. Some begin their papers with an apology for the fact that before the class they had never read the Pentateuch or the Prophets (or whatever is the subject). Some have done enough study to hit the ground running with sharp questions and sharp observations. Some have been told by their Sunday school teacher what the Old Testament is about and are resistant to reading it for themselves and finding that it's other than what they expected. Some are intrigued by that discovery. Some just want to get a passing grade and will spend part of their class time answering emails rather than taking part.

Proverbs has four related target audiences. There are the naive, young people, the people who might be literally addressed by their mothers and fathers. They need to acquire insight for life. Yet this doesn't mean its teaching is irrelevant to older people who have already gained some such insight. Proverbs believes in lifelong learning and believes that the people who are already wise need to continue to increase in wisdom; the opening paragraph has already made that point. We sometimes wonder what new truths we need to learn, but as often as not we need to get a securer or fresher grasp of things that in theory we know already.

For both the naive and the wise, Proverbs has some hope. Of the other two groups, it's more despairing. Wisdom's antithesis is stupidity. Stupid people are not people with academic learning difficulties but people who turn their backs on the kind of wisdom that has moral implications. Stupidity thus overlaps with arrogance. The arrogant are the people who mock the teaching of the wise. They think they know everything already. Their mouths are always open, but their ears are closed.

Proverbs pictures Ms. Wisdom as a personification of its teaching and imagines her like a prophet standing in a public square where merchants and other preachers might assemble to sell their wares. Like a prophet, Ms. Wisdom urges people to pay attention, warns them of the consequences of their stupid lifestyle, and urges them to turn from it. Wisdom's teaching is very similar to that of the **Torah** and the Prophets, though it argues its point on a different basis. Instead of saying "Listen, because I say so," like Moses, or "Listen, or God will intervene in judgment," like a prophet, Ms. Wisdom says "Listen, or you'll find your life ends up in a mess as a natural result of the choices you're making. And don't think that I shall be weeping when it does. I shall be thinking that it's just what you deserved." As my mother used to say, "Don't come crying to me when it happens." But she didn't really mean it, and neither I imagine did Ms. Wisdom: like a mother, she knows that actually she'll be weeping and will respond to her child. But she's willing to try anything to get through her child's thick skull, to get her to take some notice.

In the second paragraph, Proverbs becomes even more like Moses or a prophet in speaking of God's involvement in our lives in a personal way. Life isn't simply a matter of natural cause and effect, as if God had set the world going at the beginning with its inherent cause-and-effect system and could then leave it to its own devices. **Yahweh** is one who gives, speaks, stores up, shields, guards, protects.

The transition to talk about adultery at the end of the chapter seems sudden. We will note several possible reasons for its being a focus in Proverbs 1–9. This passage makes one of the few explicit biblical references to marriage as a covenant, a key element in the theological and ethical reasoning that sees adultery as wrong. Further, the phrase "alien woman" may indicate that the woman is a foreigner and thus a worshiper of some other god than Yahweh, the God of Israel, so that marital unfaithfulness and unfaithfulness to Yahweh are related. It's easy to imagine that there were women in Israel who walked out on their marriages (and maybe fled to another country) because of abuse or because of their husbands' adultery, and in the cultural context it would be more or less impossible for them to have a home and have access to something to eat except in the context of a family (a birth family or a marital family). The pressures were perhaps not so different from ones in the modern world that drive women into the sex trade. But the passage doesn't give us the woman's side to the story, because its focus lies elsewhere, in teaching men about the need to be sensible and not stupid in the way they relate to sexual temptation. In almost any culture, getting into illicit sexual relationships is inclined to ruin a person's life, a possibility of which the section's closing lines give another hyperbolic portrayal.

PROVERBS 3:1–35

On Trust

¹ Don't disregard my teaching, son;
   your mind is to safeguard my commands.
² Because length of days and years of life
   and well-being is what they will add to you.
³ Commitment and truthfulness must not abandon you;
   bind them on your neck, write them on the tablet of your
      mind.
⁴ Thus find grace and good sense,
   in the eyes of God and of people.
⁵ Trust in Yahweh with all your mind,
   don't lean on your own understanding.
⁶ In all your ways acknowledge him,
   and he himself will keep your paths straight.
⁷ Don't be wise in your own eyes;
   be in awe of Yahweh and depart from evil.
⁸ It will be health for your body,
   a tonic for your bones.
⁹ Honor Yahweh with all your wealth,
   with the first of all your revenue.
¹⁰ Your barns will fill with plenty,
   your vats will overflow with new wine.
¹¹ Don't reject Yahweh's discipline, son,

don't despise his correction.
12 Because the one Yahweh gives himself to, he corrects,
just like a father the son he favors.

13 The blessings of the person who finds wisdom,
the person who obtains understanding!
14 Because her profit is better than the profit of silver,
her revenue than gold.
15 She is more valuable than rubies;
nothing you delight in equals her.
16 Length of days is in her right hand;
in her left hand are riches and honor.
17 Her ways are pleasant ones;
all her paths are [full of] well-being.
18 She is a tree of life to people who take hold of her;
the person who holds onto her is blessed.
19 It was by wisdom that Yahweh founded the earth;
he established the heavens by understanding.
20 By his knowledge the deeps split,
and the skies would drop dew.

21 They must not depart from your eyes;
guard skill and discretion.
22 They will be life for your spirit,
and grace for your neck.
23 Then you'll go your way with trust,
and your foot will not trip up.
24 When you lie down, you won't be fearful;
you'll lie down and your sleep will be sweet.
25 You won't be afraid of a sudden terror
or of the disaster for the wicked that will come,
26 Because Yahweh will be your confidence
and will keep your foot from being snared.

27 Don't withhold good from the person to whom it's due
when it's in your hand to act.
28 Don't say to your neighbor, "Go, and come back,
and tomorrow I'll give [it to you]," when it's with you.
29 Don't devise evil against your neighbor,
when he's living trustingly with you.
30 Don't contend with someone for no reason,

when he hasn't done you any wrong.
31 Don't envy a person of violence,
and don't choose any of his ways.
32 Because a devious person is abhorrent to Yahweh,
but his friendship is with upright people.
33 Yahweh's curse is on the household of the faithless person,
but he blesses the home of faithful people.
34 If he himself behaves arrogantly to the arrogant,
to the lowly he gives grace.
35 Wise people will possess honor,
but fools get disgrace as their recompense.

A senior member of our congregation died last week. Joe had fought in the Second World War and was then one of the first African Americans to graduate from the Art Center College of Design in Los Angeles. A number of his paintings hung in the family lounge. One was a slightly mysterious portrayal of two arms, neither joined to a body; the hand of one held the other arm. His son explained to me that it represented a vision God had given his father when he had a stroke fifteen years before he died. He had seen God's arm reaching out to grasp his arm and help him get up; and God had done so. He had recovered to live a normal life for most of those years. He fought the good fight of faith, his son commented.

Joe embodied this section of Proverbs, not least the part about trust. Specifically it's about trust in **Yahweh**. You could say that these early chapters of Proverbs are about trust in wisdom, not about trust in Yahweh, but the wisdom that they urge is Yahweh's wisdom, and paying attention to wisdom is Proverbs' equivalent to paying attention to Yahweh—Moses speaks of paying attention to **Torah** and the Prophets speak of paying attention to Yahweh's word, and they are all referring to the same thing.

The Torah and the Prophets would agree that the opposite of trusting Yahweh is trusting in oneself, or leaning on one's own understanding. The Hebrew word for "lean" can refer to someone literally or metaphorically leaning on someone else's hand or arm, and it reminds me again of Joe's painting. Proverbs invites us to lean on the arm of Yahweh that grasps us.

To put it another way, trusting in one's own understanding is to be wise in one's own eyes. Proverbs 26:12 will declare that making this mistake puts someone into a worse situation than simply being a fool. Admittedly, one may not realize that one is falling into this trap. The phrase refers to people who have acquired a little wisdom, and know it, and think they have arrived. There's at least the possibility that a fool may "come to his senses," as we say, and seek wisdom, but someone who thinks that they have already found it may have less chance to do so.

The chapter refers twice more to trust. It declares that people who pay attention to wisdom will go their way with trust. Their trust will not turn out to have been misplaced; their foot will not trip. It makes the same point in different words when it promises that Yahweh will be your confidence and will keep your foot from being snared. The Hebrew word for "confidence" is also one of the words for being stupid—it's related to the word for "fools" in the last line. Trust in God can look stupid, but actually it's the most sensible thing in the world. Trusting in yourself and following your hunches can seem sensible, but it may be stupid. Urging people to trust in a crucified Jew looks really stupid, but it's the most sensible thing in the world, whereas the world's wisdom is actually stupid (so Paul will note, nuancing Proverbs' point).

The other reference to trust comes when it talks about the neighbor who is living trustingly with you; you're not to make some plan against him. One definition of love is making the world safe for the other person, who can then know it's possible to count on you to do so. So trust isn't only key to our relationships with God but key to relationships with other people. My father was a trusting person, and my mother

18

sometimes despaired at the risks he would take in connection with other people. I follow my father, whereas my wife is like my mother. The complementarity in both marriages is good; Proverbs has already given good reason for discernment about whom you trust. It would be possible for an unprincipled person to take advantage of a sucker like my father or me, and Proverbs urges people not to do so. Taking advantage of people's trust undermines the possibility of trust. An implication is that deviousness and wisdom are incompatible. In the worlds of politics and business, parsimony with the truth if not downright lying may seem necessary if you're to get on or to achieve ends you know are good. In the long run it's a destructive view.

Proverbs can't find enough spectacular ways to exalt Yahweh's wisdom in the eyes of its audience. Wisdom is a tree of life, it says. The phrase recurs in other Middle Eastern works. In an Old Testament context, it's a striking promise. You know how Adam and Eve could have gained eternal life if they had eaten the tree of life? Well, paying attention to wisdom can give you a really fulfilled and fulfilling life. Proverbs goes further. You know God created the world? How do you think he did so? He used his wisdom. Just look at the world and how amazing it is. It's the kind of thing you can achieve if you pay attention to wisdom.

PROVERBS 4:1–27

On Discipline

1 Listen to a father's discipline, sons,
   attend in order to know understanding.
2 Because I give you a good grasp;
   don't abandon my teaching.
3 Because I was a son to my father,
   tender and the only one to my mother.

19

4   He taught me and said to me, "Your mind is to take hold of
        my words;
      keep my commands and you'll live."

5   Acquire wisdom, acquire understanding;
      don't disregard and don't divert from the words of my
        mouth.
6   Don't abandon her and she'll guard you;
      give yourself to her and she'll protect you.
7   The first principle of wisdom is, acquire wisdom,
      and in all your acquiring, acquire understanding.
8   Exalt her and she'll elevate you;
      she'll honor you if you embrace her.
9   She'll give a graceful garland for your head,
      she'll present you with a beautiful diadem.
10 Listen, son, and grasp my words,
      and the years of your life will be many.
11 I am teaching you in the way of wisdom,
      I am directing you in upright tracks.
12 As you go, your step will not be hindered;
      if you run, you won't stumble.
13 Hold onto discipline, don't let go,
      guard it, because it's your life.
14 Don't enter on the path of faithless people,
      don't walk in the way of wrongdoers.
15 Avoid it, don't pass through it;
      turn from it and pass your way.
16 Because they will not sleep if they don't do evil;
      they are robbed of their sleep if they don't make someone
        stumble.
17 Because they eat bread that comes from faithlessness
      and drink wine that comes from violent acts.
18 But the path of the faithful is like dawn light,
      getting more light until the fullness of the day.
19 The way of faithless people is darkness itself;
      they don't know what will make them stumble.

20 Pay attention to my words, son,
      turn your ear to what I say.
21 They must not depart from your eyes;
      keep them within your mind.

22 Because they are life to the people who find them,
     health for a person's whole body.
23 Above everything that you guard,
     protect your mind.
24 Keep away from you crookedness of mouth;
     put deviousness of lips far away.
25 Your eyes must turn forward,
     your gaze be straight ahead of you.
26 Weigh the track for your foot;
     all your ways must be firm.
27 Don't turn right or left;
     keep your foot way from evil.

We were talking about what makes people change. My wife asked me if I had changed over the years, and if so how it had happened. I know I'm mellower than I used to be and find it easier to get up in the morning. Those differences may be partly the result of getting older, but the biggest factor in making me change over the years was dealing with the long years of my first wife's illness. In effect those were years of discipline, a bit like the discipline people impose on themselves when they do weight training. In my case, the discipline came from outside. I could have refused to accept it; sometimes I did so. But on the whole I submitted myself to learning to lift the weights, and the discipline strengthened my muscles. Maybe it was mostly that imposed discipline that made me mellower, more easygoing.

Proverbs is keen on discipline. It is vital that we impose discipline on ourselves, though Proverbs also makes clear the assumption that life and God provide us with most of our sources of discipline. So this chapter begins with an exhortation to pay heed to the discipline that the father figure offers. While a literal father can *impose* discipline, a father-teacher cannot do so. The discipline has to be accepted and internalized by the pupil, the disciple. You could say that a disciple is someone who accepts someone's discipline. The Greek word for "disciple" means more literally a pupil, a learner, which also fits with Proverbs. Learning involves submitting yourself to someone else's discipline, not "making up your own mind."

We prefer to make up our own minds, so we need the exhortation to hold onto discipline and not let it go, to guard it, because it's our life. The teacher in Proverbs has some anxiety about getting his disciples to see the point and live by it. When my students look at the stress on discipline in Proverbs, they ask whether the New Testament speaks in these terms, rather hoping that it might be a feature of the Old Testament that they can see as superseded in Christ. I am amused to be able to point out that Hebrews 12 takes up this motif from Proverbs and emphasizes the way God relates to us like a father in imposing discipline. It quotes from Proverbs 3, then takes up the exhortation from Proverbs 4 about weighing the track for your foot. The Sermon on the Mount implies accepting discipline as a disciple, too.

Linked with the connection between discipleship and discipline is Proverbs' assumption that learning should be embodied in life as well as embraced in the head. Western education has traditionally dissociated theory and practice; you can get a degree in theology by studying and going to school but without actually doing anything "theological" and without being changed as a person. Proverbs wouldn't see such study as real education. The course in ethics that my wife is taking involves her in some community service; there was no such requirement when I studied ethics decades ago. How scary it would be if the professor had to certify that her students "knew" something on the basis of how she saw them living or saw them change in their habits as a result of acquiring new knowledge. How scary it would be if the professor had to be an embodiment of ethics and not merely well-informed about the subject.

PROVERBS 5:1–23

Crazy for Love (1)

1 Pay attention to my wisdom, son,
   incline your ear to my understanding,
2 so as to keep discretion,
   and so that your lips may protect knowledge.
3 Because the lips of an alien woman drip honey,
   her mouth is smoother than oil.
4 But her end is as bitter as gall,
   sharp as a two-edged sword.
5 Her feet go down to death,
   her steps get hold of Sheol.
6 Lest she weigh the path to life,
   her tracks wander, though she doesn't acknowledge it.
7 So now, sons, listen to me,
   and don't depart from the words of my mouth.
8 Keep your way far from her,
   don't go near the door of her house,
9 lest you give your honor to other people,
   your years to someone harsh,
10 lest strangers eat their fill of your strength
   and [the fruit of] your toils be in the house of a foreigner.
11 You'll groan at your end,
   when your flesh and body are spent.
12 You'll say, "How I repudiated discipline,
   and my mind spurned rebuke.
13 I did not listen to the voice of my teachers,
   I did not incline my ear to my instructors.
14 I was soon in every kind of evil
   in the midst of the assembled congregation."

15 Drink water from your own cistern,
   running water from within your own well.
16 Should your fountains gush outside,
   your streams of water in the squares?
17 They should be for you alone,
   so that there is none for strangers with you.
18 May your spring be blessed,
   may you rejoice in the wife of your youth.
19 She is a doe to love,

23

> a graceful deer.
> Her breasts should satisfy you all the time;
> be crazy on her love always.
> 20 So why be crazy on a stranger, son,
> and embrace the bosom of a foreigner?
> 21 Because one's ways are in front of Yahweh's eyes;
> he weighs all your tracks.
> 22 One's wayward acts ensnare the faithless person;
> he gets caught up by the ropes of his offense.
> 23 That person dies for lack of discipline;
> he's crazy on the greatness of his stupidity.

A married couple who are both pastors whom I know and love have just separated. The wife had confronted the husband about his close relationship with another woman. There had been no physical adultery, but it was a close relationship that compromised their marital relationship. The confrontation had led him to tell his wife that he had been addicted to pornography for many years. His wife now feels doubly betrayed, and the crisis has led to their giving up their joint ministry. I have some hope that the separation may not be permanent and that the relationship may find healing, but they are less hopeful than I am. I have to admit that the man's sexual activities outside his marriage threaten the death of the marriage and the end of the ministries and of much of the promise of the lives that each of these individuals had.

Proverbs addresses just such situations—or rather, seeks to anticipate it. It knows that men get into sexual messes, and it seeks to forestall this process. One can sometimes wonder whether the church and society are excessively preoccupied by sexual sins, but actually that preoccupation reflects the huge, deep, far-reaching importance of sex to humanity. When sex goes wrong, it has profoundly disturbing and disruptive effects on personal relationships and on the family.

Proverbs analyzes the sexual politics of its society only in terms of male sexual activity; it wants men to follow their heads rather than some other part of their anatomy. In most societies it has been easier for men than for women to get away with sexual unfaithfulness. Further, one of Proverbs' functions is to train men for service in government and administration (such service brings its own opportunities for sexual dalliance). In Western culture the opportunities and the pressures are more gender-inclusive, so a woman reading Proverbs will have to reverse the way it portrays the sexual roles. It's the alien man who becomes the tempter.

The expression "alien" or "strange" in these exhortations might have a number of backgrounds. Comparison with Ezra and Nehemiah would suggest getting involved with foreign women; we noted in connection with Proverbs 2 that foreign women are in some contexts a particular temptation. But English parlance has often referred to the person with whom a man had an adulterous relationship as "the other woman," which might be an equivalent expression to the ones Proverbs uses. Either way, she's a woman who longs for a new love relationship, which can bring a temptation to a man. Maybe she has understandable reasons for that longing—maybe her own husband has been unfaithful, maybe he has thrown her out, maybe she's alone and needy. In a Western context, she might be a dedicated career woman who eventually realizes her aloneness and whose emotional needs make her vulnerable as well as unintentionally a temptation. Proverbs' concern isn't to understand her story but to get its male audience not to be vulnerable to it. Typically, Proverbs doesn't focus on the fact that having an affair is wrong (though it will presuppose that this is so) but on the fact that it's really stupid. Falling for her will ruin your life.

Uniquely in these opening chapters of the book, Proverbs goes on to provide a positive approach to the peril it describes, to accompany the negative warning. The key to not being vulnerable to this temptation is cultivating your marital relationship. Proverbs expounds this positive approach by means of imagery in the second paragraph. The general point is clear, though the detail of the imagery is less so, perhaps because Proverbs is trying to be a bit delicate. If a man is to confine his sexual activity to his own wife, he needs to cultivate his relationship with her and his appreciation for her. By all means be crazy for love, Proverbs urges, but make sure it's your wife you're crazy for, otherwise you'll end up being simply crazy and paying the penalty for it.

PROVERBS 6:1–34

On Safeguarding Concord

1 Son, if you have given a guarantee for your neighbor,
   shaken hands for a stranger,
2 trapped yourself by the words of your mouth,
   caught yourself by the words of your mouth:
3 do this, then, son,
   and rescue yourself.
   When you have come into your neighbor's power, go,
   lower yourself, press your neighbor.
4 Don't give sleep to your eyes
   or slumber to your eyelids.
5 Rescue yourself like a gazelle from the hand,
   like a bird from the hand, of a hunter.

6 Go to the ant, lazybones,
   look at its ways and get wise.
7 One that has no commander,
   officer, or ruler,
8 produces its food in summer,
   gathers its provisions at harvest.
9 How long will you lie down, lazybones,
   when will you get up from your sleep?
10 A little sleep, a little slumber,
   a little folding of the hands to lie down,
11 and your poverty will come walking in,
   your want like someone with a shield.

12 A worthless person, an evil individual,

    going about with a crooked mouth,
[13] winking his eyes, gesturing with his feet,
    pointing with his fingers,
[14] crookedness in his mind, planning evil,
    all the time he unleashes arguments.
[15] Therefore suddenly calamity will come on him,
    in an instant he'll break, with no healing.

[16] These six Yahweh repudiates,
    seven are abhorrent to him:
[17] haughty eyes, a lying tongue,
    and hands that shed innocent blood,
[18] a mind devising wicked plans,
    feet hurrying to run to evil,
[19] a false witness who breathes out lies,
    and someone who unleashes disputes among brothers.

[20] Son, guard your father's command
    and don't turn your back on your mother's teaching.
[21] Fasten them into your mind always,
    bind them onto your neck.
[22] When you're going about, it will lead you,
    when you lie down, it will keep watch over you,
    when you wake up, it will talk to you.
[23] Because the command is a lamp and the teaching is a light,
    and the rebuke that disciplines is the way to life,
[24] to keep you from the evil woman,
    from the smoothness of the tongue of an alien woman.
[25] Don't desire her beauty in your heart;
    she must not capture you with her gaze.
[26] Because on account of a whore—as far as a loaf of bread,
    but the wife of [another] man will snare the very life.
[27] Can a person put fire in his pocket
    and his clothes will not burn?
[28] If a person walks on coals,
    will his feet not burn?
[29] So it is with someone who has sex with his neighbor's wife;
    no one who touches her will go free.
[30] People don't despise a thief when he steals
    for the sake of his appetite, when he's hungry.
[31] But if he's found out, he'll pay back sevenfold;

> he'll give all the wealth of his household.
> 32 The person who commits adultery with a woman is lacking in sense;
>   one who so acts is destroying himself.
> 33 He'll meet with injury and disgrace;
>   his reproach will not be wiped away.
> 34 Because jealousy [arouses] a man's fury;
>   he won't pity on the day of redress.
> 35 He won't have regard for any compensation;
>   he won't agree, even if the inducement is great.

The pest control man came the other day to check that we had no termites or other unwelcome guests. It reminded me of an experience a few weeks after we moved to California, when another Old Testament professor who was in town came for afternoon tea. He watched me proudly opening the storage tin where I had put our homemade scones, on which I was about to put jam and cream, and we shared the horror of seeing that they were covered in ants (though only I felt the embarrassment). Admittedly you would be less surprised to find ants in your house in California, where they are endemic, than in Britain. You can see them scurrying in a neat line from some miniscule space between the floor tiles and the wall to some crumbs on the countertop and then scurrying back again. Those ants knew what they were doing.

So learn the lesson from them, Proverbs says. It presupposes a different attitude to poverty from one that appears elsewhere in the Old Testament. The Prophets speak of poverty as a bane that the haves (people like us who can afford to buy books) bring on the have-nots. The **Torah** focuses on what people like us can do for the have-nots. Proverbs makes the complementary point. Not every person who loses his family farm can blame bad luck or injustice. It can be laziness. So laziness is an example of stupidity, while ants are an embodiment of wisdom. Someone with a shield is a person you can't overcome.

In the opening paragraph, Proverbs points to another way to get into an economic mess. The Torah and the Prophets assume one has an obligation to help a family whose harvest fails, but in doing so, one could compromise the viability of one's own farm (for instance, by surrendering the portion of this year's harvest that would be the seed for next year). God sometimes inspires people to such wild and risky action, but Proverbs issues the complementary warning about irresponsibility. So if you realize you have committed yourself beyond what is wise, maybe because you wanted to look like a hero, do your best to get out of the overcommitment.

Proverbs as a whole recognizes the points the Torah and the Prophets make; the third paragraph gives an instance. It can be human deceitfulness that brings ruin on a family, making it possible to rob it of its farm and its livelihood. Like the Torah and the Prophets, Proverbs promises that deceivers will pay for their destructiveness. It here thinks in terms of wrongdoing receiving its reward by a kind of natural process built into the way God created the world. No divine intervention is required to bring about the fall of people who try to stir things up in the way Proverbs describes.

Numerical sayings like the one in the fourth paragraph often come to the climax with the last in the sequence of phrases. That understanding makes sense here. The first six are meant seriously, but they are commonplaces of Old Testament teaching. The condemnation of someone who incites quarrels among brothers is more distinctive; it follows the similar reference in the third paragraph. The brothers might be literally family members or the members of the community more broadly. Either way, encouraging disputes undermines its life. Neither the family's work nor the community's work can be done if they are torn apart by arguments. In a Western urban context we can be more isolated than people in a traditional society, all having our own jobs, changing employers, living alone, and not dependent on other people in a meaningful way that is reinforced by love but dependent only on functional relationships. It makes it easier to hang onto resentments and quarrels instead of resolving them.

The further exhortation about marital faithfulness links with this concern. Adultery can destroy families and communities. The line about the whore might concern a prostitute or simply an immoral woman, and the loaf of bread might be the cost of her hire or might more likely be what you're reduced to through involvement with her. Either way, Proverbs isn't implying that recourse to a prostitute or having an affair with an unattached woman is simply fine; it's rather pointing out that an affair with someone else's wife will cost much more than that kind of dalliance. It can mean shame, disgrace, and reproach in the community, and physical violence from the woman's husband, who is unlikely to have his wrath ameliorated by the offer of compensation. Sex and marital faithfulness are too big a deal for such an offer to work.

PROVERBS 7:1–27

Let Me Tell You a Story

1 Keep my words, son,
    store up my commands with you.
2 Keep my commands and live,
    and [keep] my teaching as the apple of your eye.
3 Fasten them on your fingers,
    write them on the tablet of your mind.
4 Say to Wisdom, "You are my sister,"
    and call understanding "Friend,"
5 to keep you from the alien woman,
    the foreign woman whose words are charming.

6 Because through the window of my house,
    by way of my lattice, I looked out,

7 and saw among the naive, perceived among the young
      men,
    a youth lacking in sense.
8 He was passing along the street by her corner,
    he was walking by the way to her house,
9 at dusk, in the evening of the day,
    at the approach of night and darkness.
10 There: a woman [comes] to meet him,
    dressed like a whore but guarded in heart.
11 She is bustling and rebellious;
    her feet don't rest in her house.
12 Now in the street, now in the squares,
    and near every corner, she lurks.
13 She takes hold of him and kisses him,
    emboldens her face and says to him,
14 "Fellowship sacrifices [were incumbent] on me,
    today I've fulfilled my pledges.
15 Therefore I've come out to meet you,
    to look eagerly for your face, and I've found you.
16 I've spread my couch with coverlets,
    colored Egyptian linens.
17 I've perfumed my bed,
    with myrrh, aloes, and cinnamon.
18 Come on, let's fill ourselves with love until morning,
    let's enjoy ourselves in lovemaking.
19 Because the man of the house isn't here,
    he has gone on a journey a long way.
20 He has taken a bag of money in his hand;
    he'll come home [only] at the middle of the month."
21 She has swayed him with the abundance of her
      persuasiveness,
    with the charm of her lips she forces him.
22 All at once he walks after her,
    like an ox that goes to the slaughter,
    like a deer stepping into a noose
23 until an arrow pierces its liver,
    like a bird rushing into a snare
    when it doesn't know it will be at the cost of its life.

24 So now listen to me, sons,
    pay attention to the words of my mouth.

25 Your mind isn't to turn into her ways;
   don't wander into her paths.
26 Because she has made many fall wounded;
   numerous are all the ones slain by her.
27 Her house is a highway to Sheol,
   going down to death's chambers.

Last Sunday we said Psalm 62, which includes the line "put no trust in extortion," but the person who led the psalm read it as "put no trust in exhortation." It struck me that the misreading was rather profound (it reminded me of an occasion when someone read the line in Romans 8 about being "freed from the shackles of mortality" as "freed from the shackles of morality"). How do you get people to change? Maybe it's the pastor's most far-reaching question. It's always tempting to assume that change comes about because we exhort people to change, and to operate on that basis, but a moment's reflection reminds us of the uncomfortable truth that it's not so.

Proverbs 7 implies this awareness. It has issued a series of exhortations to young men not to get involved with a married woman. Now it moves to painting a picture or telling a story, in seeking to get them to write its teaching on the tablets of their mind. It wants it always to be in front of them like something on a whiteboard, or to be inscribed into the neural patterns that shape their behavior. Once again the woman is compared with a whore, but the description that follows implies that the word is used in the loose sense. She's not someone in the sex trade but a woman who is lonely. She would settle for any lover but will give him the impression he's the only one. The point about her reference to offering sacrifices may be that she has been purifying herself after her period and therefore is in a position to make love. Who could resist an offer like the one she makes?

Proverbs knows she's inviting him to his death. Previous chapters have implied two reasons why this is so. Adultery tends to get found out, and the woman's husband will then come after the young man; within the terms of this story, it would be wise to allow for his coming back from his business trip earlier than expected, a recurrent motif in fiction and in real life. Lying behind this reason is the fact that the very nature of the universe's moral order means that wrongdoing tends to get its reward.

Why does Proverbs 1–9 keep coming back to young men and their sexual involvements? It's the section of Scripture that gives most sustained attention to sexual faithfulness. Maybe one reason is that cultural contexts can put special pressure on people, as is the case with the context in California in which I work. Proverbs 1–9 comes from a social context after the exile where within God's people old certainties had gone (as Ecclesiastes illustrates) and old social structures no longer prevailed. The multiethnic, multicultural, multireligious circumstances of Judahite life in the Second Temple period could encourage openness to other ways of thinking that could be positively broadening but also wrongly broadening. Proverbs 1–9 suggests an audience involved in studying deep theological questions, and it sees insight embodied as a woman, Ms. Wisdom. It implies a desire for its addressees to be open to learning from women. One can see that its young men might let a right kind of openness become a wrong kind of openness.

PROVERBS 8:1–36

Let Me Tell You Another Story

1 Doesn't wisdom call,
   understanding give voice?
2 At the highest point along the way,
   at the crossroads, she takes her stand.
3 At the side of the gates at the town's entrance,
   at the entryway of the doors, she resounds.

4 "People, I call to you,
   my voice [comes] to humankind.
5 Understand judiciousness, you who are naive;
   understand sense, you who are stupid.
6 Listen, because I speak honorable things;
   the opening of my lips [speaks] upright things.
7 Because my mouth utters truth;
   faithlessness is abhorrent to my lips.
8 All the words of my mouth are characterized by
         faithfulness;
   there's nothing crooked or twisted in them.
9 All of them are right to the person of understanding,
   upright to people who find knowledge.
10 Accept my discipline and not silver,
   knowledge more than choice gold.
11 Because wisdom is better than rubies,
   and no delights can compare with her.

12 I, wisdom, dwell with judiciousness;
   I find knowledge of discretion.
13 Awe for God
   is repudiation of evil.
   Superiority and self-importance and the way of evil,
   and a crooked mouth, I repudiate.
14 Mine are counsel and skill;
   I am understanding, I have might.
15 By me kings reign and rulers legislate what is right;
16 by me officials govern, leaders, all who decide what is right.
17 I give myself to people who give themselves to me;
   people who seek me keenly find me.
18 Riches and honor are with me,
   enduring wealth and faithfulness.
19 My fruit is better than gold, even fine gold,
   my revenue than choice silver.
20 I walk in the way of faithfulness,
   in the midst of the paths of authority,
21 bestowing wealth on people who give themselves to me,
   and I fill their treasuries.

22 Yahweh acquired me at the beginning of his way,
   before his works of old.

34

23 Long ago I was formed,
  at the beginning, before earth's origins.
24 When there were no deeps I was birthed,
  when there were no springs rich in water.
25 Before the mountains were settled,
  before the hills I was birthed,
26 while he had not yet made the earth
  and fields and the first of the world's dirt.
27 When he established the heavens, I was there,
  when he fixed the horizon on the face of the deep,
28 when he made the skies above firm,
  when the deep's fountains were strong,
29 when he set its limit for the sea,
  so that its waters might not transgress his mouth.
  When he fixed earth's foundations,
30   I was a child by his side.
  I was full of delight day by day,
  playing before him all the time,
31 playing in his inhabited world
  and full of delight with humanity.

32 So now, sons, listen to me:
  the blessings of people who keep my ways!
33 Listen to discipline and become wise, don't disregard it;
34 the blessings of the person who listens to me!–
  seeking my gates keenly day by day,
  watching at the posts of my doors.
35 Because one who finds me finds life,
  and obtains favor from Yahweh.
36 But one who offends me does violence to himself;
  all who repudiate me give themselves to death."

On the way out of chapel yesterday, we bumped into the
provost (his position stands midway between being the
principal and the vice-principal in U.K. terms). Before he
became provost a few months ago, we had dinner with him
and his wife, but we have hardly seen them since he took
office. I can't remember the precise words he used to describe
how things had been, but I knew he had been dealing with a
series of big issues. In the context of a global financial crisis,

the seminary had to rework its budget, and the librarian had left so we needed to find a new one. And because the provost had been promoted from being a dean, we needed a new dean; and he had been heading up the search for such a person. We are also in the midst of a major rethink of how we seek to facilitate students' spiritual formation. Who has the wisdom to fulfill such responsibilities?

Here, the second paragraph picks up the question of a leader's responsibility and notes how wisdom is key to fulfilling it. Proverbs 1–9 is concerned throughout to get people in general to take wisdom seriously, and it's for this reason that it refers to the leader. Ms. Wisdom declares, "It's by me that kings reign, that rulers legislate what is right, that leaders govern, that sovereigns and others decide what is right." Solomon's story illustrates the point. First Kings 3–4 relates how God asked Solomon what he wanted to pray for. Solomon asked for wisdom, God granted it, and Solomon then exhibited it in adjudicating between two prostitutes disputing which was the mother of a baby, and then in setting up his administration. He thus illustrates wisdom's claim that she **gives** herself to people who give themselves to her; "people who seek me keenly find me." The chapter also reaffirms the link between the wisdom that enables you to get things done and **awe** for God or submission to God, along with commitment to **faithfulness** in the exercise of **authority** and also with resistance to the temptation to be deceptive or to take oneself too seriously.

Proverbs wants leaders to exercise such wisdom, but its point is at least as much to get ordinary people to live their lives on that basis; this concern is the implication of the chapter's frame, its opening and closing paragraphs. So it is backing its exhortation to ordinary people by saying, "leaders rely on wisdom—so shouldn't you?" In the third paragraph it tops that argument by another, even more impressive one: "As

God's wisdom, I was involved in the world's creation—so shouldn't you rely on me too?"

The chapter here picks up the personification of wisdom that has featured a number of times and pushes even further the boundaries of what can be said by means of the personification. Proverbs 3 made the point that God used his wisdom in creating the cosmos; he could hardly have undertaken this task without doing so. Here, Ms. Wisdom doesn't explicitly reassert that point but focuses on other aspects of her involvement in creation. First, the chapter points out that God had his wisdom from the beginning. It's as if Ms. Wisdom was there at creation as a person distinguishable from God, while being an aspect of God. It's as if God had given birth to his wisdom at the beginning of everything. God thus "acquired" his wisdom back then (Proverbs uses the verb that Eve used of her "acquiring" Cain as her son in Genesis 4). So Ms. Wisdom was able to be there when God created the cosmos. Wisdom is the design principle that made and makes things work in the world; Ms. Wisdom is a member of the divine cabinet that God consults and that takes part in the decision making about the world and keeps watch over the world.

There is a further aspect to her testimony. Wisdom sounds like something rather serious, but it turns out to be something rather playful. It's not certain that Ms. Wisdom describes herself as a "child"—different translations have "confidant" or "craftworker." But it's clear from the lines that follow that she was having a playful, enthusiastic, animated, childlike time when God was creating the world. You could infer that creation was itself an outworking of joy; that joy created the world. Ms. Wisdom was excited in the creation that God was bringing into being, and not least with humanity itself. Genesis 1 describes each element of creation as good, but does so rather solemnly. Ms. Wisdom claps her hands and dances.

The chapter is playful, though serious, as the last paragraph shows when it returns to solemnity and sobriety.

When early Christians needed to speak about Jesus as existing before becoming a human being and as divine yet distinguishable from the Father, they picked up the idea of God's Wisdom, which a passage such as Proverbs 8 describes as divine yet pictures as distinguishable from God in person (of course in the context of Proverbs this picture is more metaphorical than it is when we speak of Jesus as the embodiment of God's Wisdom). The description of Jesus as God's Word in John 1 picks up the terms that describe God's Wisdom in Proverbs 8. The implication isn't so much that we should read Jesus into Proverbs but that we understand Jesus in light of Proverbs. Jesus' teaching is an expression of the wisdom written into creation.

PROVERBS 9:1–18

The Two Voices

1 Wisdom has built her house;
      she has hewn her seven pillars.
2 She has slaughtered her animals, mixed her wine,
      indeed set her table.
3 She has sent her girls so that she can call,
      on the town's high elevations,
4 "Whoever is naive should turn in here";
      the person who is lacking in sense,
      she says to him,
5 "Come, eat my food,
      drink of the wine I've mixed.
6 Abandon naiveté and live,
      walk in the way of understanding."

7 One who disciplines an arrogant person gets disgrace for
         himself;
      one who reproves a faithless person gets hurt.
8 Don't reprove an arrogant person or he'll repudiate you;

reprove a wise person and he'll befriend you.
⁹ Give [a word] to a wise perso,n and he'll get yet wiser;
  make something known to a faithful person, and he'll
    increase in his grasp.
¹⁰ Awe for Yahweh is the beginning of wisdom;
  understanding lies in acknowledgment of the Holy One.
¹¹ Because through me your days will be many
  and the years of your life will increase.
¹² If you're wise, you're wise for your benefit;
  if you're arrogant, you'll carry it alone.

¹³ The Stupid Woman bustles about [in] naiveté,
  and doesn't acknowledge anything.
¹⁴ She sits at the door of her house,
  on a seat at the town's heights,
¹⁵ calling to passersby,
  people making their paths straight:
¹⁶ "Whoever is naive should turn in here";
  the person who is lacking in sense, she says to him,
¹⁷ "Stolen water is sweet,
  secret food is tasty."
¹⁸ He doesn't acknowledge that the ghosts are there;
  the people she summons are in the depths of Sheol.

I've just come back from a workshop on sexual exploitation at church, which included DVD presentations incorporating testimonies by victims and exploiters (some actual, some actors). One troubling feature was one exploiter's comment about how he had fooled himself concerning the propriety of his action. It brought happiness to both parties (in the short term), so could it be wrong? Another troubling feature was the interpretation of expressions of repentance. How can one know whether such expressions indicate actual repentance in the Old Testament sense, where the word most often translated "repent" literally means "turn" and thus indicates a change of behavior? One could be fearful both of failing to rejoice in genuine repentance and of colluding with mere remorse. In the past, two voices have been addressing the exploiter, one voice declaring that the action is wrong and another declaring it to be an expression of love. The two voices are both internalized; both will continue to make their view known. Everything depends on how the exploiter responds when addressed by those voices in the future.

Proverbs 9 speaks of these two voices—or rather, it articulates them. It's the last of the nine opening chapters of Proverbs comprising a series of homilies interweaving talk about wisdom and marital faithfulness. Here, sexual promiscuity and stupidity are closely identified. Sexual unfaithfulness is the ultimate folly, and both unfaithfulness and folly are associated with failure to live in **awe** of **Yahweh** —that is, in obedience to Yahweh. The prominence of sexual exploitation and sexual wrongdoing in the Western church makes it especially troublesome to consider that link, and even more troublesome not to consider it. It can be a subject that churches avoid because it's uncomfortable; a young person in our workshop was troubled to have to think about the possibility that a minister might be involved in exploitation (most of the presentations' examples of exploitation involved ministers). It's easier to avoid thinking about the issue. It's therefore a great gift of God to have a book like Proverbs that gives such concerted attention to sexual temptation.

Ms. Wisdom has featured prominently already. Here in the last paragraph Ms. Stupidity is constructed as her imagined negative counterpart. They are two prophet-like beings, a true prophet and a false prophet. As happens with prophets, it's easy to confuse the two, especially if you're willingly inclined to do so, and especially when they are both voices inside your own head. Both take their stands in prominent positions and call out to naive people, people who are lacking in sense (it's not a fault to be naive and lacking in sense, but you have to grow beyond this position toward maturity). Both invite such people to come and listen, to come and enjoy the feast they offer.

Wisdom's house has seven pillars; it contains all the wisdom anyone needs. Ms. Stupidity is the antithesis of Ms. Wisdom because Ms. Stupidity is the very embodiment of naiveté, even though she thinks of herself as the embodiment of sophistication; she lives in denial and/or justifies the teaching that embodies her lack of wisdom. How would she know she was doing so? Her own naiveté is a reason why it's important to let others and the **Torah** discipline us and hold our behavior up to something for comparison. She's also the embodiment of confident, busy arrogance (another antithesis to wisdom in Proverbs) in that she doesn't acknowledge anything outside herself. She seeks to divert people who know where they are going—people who are making a straight path (it's the word that can also be translated "upright"). Like a sexual exploiter, she seeks to divert them into something about which they will have to be secretive. When we are contemplating action that might count as wrong, we are not inclined to check it out with others first. She seeks to divert people into a relationship that will have the thrill that can accompany an affair, something that will initially seem life-giving but will ultimately have the odor of death. The naive person who yields to her blandishments doesn't see that her house opens up the road to death's realm.

What do you do when you suspect that someone in your church is involved in sexual exploitation? How do you talk to the person about it, or who do you talk to? The middle paragraph of Proverbs 9 offers some sobering comments that speak to those questions. There may be a cost to be paid, though not as high a price as the price paid by the person who accepts Ms. Stupidity's invitation.

PROVERBS 10:1–32

The Mouth of the Faithful Person Is Fruitful

1 Solomon's proverbs.

A wise son brings joy to a father,
but a stupid son brings grief to a mother.

2 Treasures that come from faithlessness don't profit,
but faithfulness rescues from death.

3 Yahweh doesn't let the faithful person go hungry,
but he thwarts the desire of faithless people.

4 A slack hand causes poverty;
the hand of determined people enriches.

5 One who gathers during summer is a sensible son;
one who sleeps during harvest is a disgraceful son.

6 There are blessings on the head of the faithful person,
but the mouth of faithless people conceals violence.

7 The mention of the faithful person becomes a blessing,
but the name of faithless people rots.

8 One who is wise of mind accepts commands,
but one stupid of lips comes to ruin.

9 One who walks in integrity walks in security,
but one who makes his ways crooked gets found out.

10 One who winks an eye gives hurt,
but one stupid of lips comes to ruin.

11 The mouth of a faithful person is a fountain of life,
but the mouth of faithless people conceals violence.

12 Animosity stirs up strife,
but giving oneself conceals all acts of rebellion.

13 Wisdom is found on the lips of the person of insight,
but there's a club on the back of the person lacking in
sense.

14 Wise people store up knowledge,
but the mouth of a stupid person is ruin drawing near.

15 The wealth of the rich person is his strong city;
the poverty of the poor is their ruin.

16 The earnings of the faithful person make for life;
the revenue of the faithless person makes for offense.

17 One who heeds correction is on the way to life,
one who abandons reproof goes astray.

18 The person who conceals repudiation [with] lying lips
and the one who issues charges, he is stupid.

19 Where there is a multitude of words, rebellion isn't lacking,
       but one who restrains his lips is sensible.
20 The tongue of a faithful person is choice silver;
       the mind of faithless people is worth little.
21 The lips of a faithful person pasture many,
       but stupid people die for lack of sense.
22 Yahweh's blessing—it enriches,
       and toil doesn't add to it.
23 Real fun for a stupid person is implementing a scheme,
       but for a person of understanding, it's wisdom.
24 The dread of a faithless person—it comes to him,
       but the desire of faithful people is granted.
25 When a storm passes, the faithless person isn't there,
       but the faithful person is a lasting foundation.
26 Like vinegar to the teeth, like smoke to the eyes,
       so is the lazy person to the people who sent him.
27 Awe for Yahweh prolongs life,
       but the years of the faithless shorten.
28 The hope of faithful people is joy,
       but the expectation of faithless people perishes.
29 Yahweh is a stronghold for someone of integrity in his way,
       but the ruin of people who do wrong.
30 The faithful person never collapses,
       but the faithless will not dwell in the country.
31 The mouth of the faithful person is fruitful with wisdom,
       but the crooked tongue will be cut off.
32 The lips of the faithful person know what finds favor,
       but the mouth of the faithless [knows] crooked things.

I rode to my mother's funeral with our rector, who told me a funny, poignant story about her. Being a mother, she had an exaggerated sense of her son's significance. One day she asked the rector whether he thought I had wasted my life being a priest and theological teacher. I guess he swallowed any realization that she had insulted him by implying either that he had also wasted his life or that he had not wasted his life, which would imply that his life was less significant than mine. We enjoyed the unintentional humor of the story. In return I described the day I apprehensively told my parents that I felt called to the ministry. I was eighteen. I can still remember that September Sunday, with the late afternoon sun streaming into our lounge. My father's response was, "Well, it's not what we would have chosen for you, but we only want you to do what you want to do."

Notwithstanding both their comments, I hope and think I was a son who brought joy rather than grief to his father and his mother, even though they might have thought there was a sense in which I was stupid to have spent my life as I have. In Proverbs' understanding, wisdom lies in **awe** before **Yahweh** and obedience to what he says; stupidity expresses itself in ignoring Yahweh's expectations (v. 27). All being well, God's wisdom is expressed in the teaching of parents; hence Proverbs' expectation that one will take note of them, too (and when it was a matter of my parents' moral teaching, I hope I did so). So it doesn't matter so much that Proverbs is ambiguous about whose commands one is to accept (v. 8) and whose correction and reproof to heed (v. 17). The point is that stupidity lies in the assumption that one has nothing to learn and in a preference for having one's mouth rather than one's ears open (vv. 8, 19). Stupidity is a sign of rebelliousness (v. 19), not of limited mental ability, and it will bring down a bludgeon on one's back (v. 13), invite ruin into one's house (v. 14), and mean losing one's way in life rather than finding life (v. 17). Conversely the words of the wise are valuable, nourishing, and fruitful (vv. 20, 21, 32).

Before sensing that call to the ministry (which was more surprising to me than to them), I was planning to study economics, which could have showed more wisdom in leading me into a life that made more money. But Proverbs would not view that life as wiser than the one into which I felt pushed by God. Not that Proverbs is unrealistic about money and about poverty (v. 15). But its opening observation (v. 1) leads neatly into consideration of the fact that in the end you don't really gain from making money through **faithlessness**

(v. 2). In the end **faithfulness** pays, sees its desires fulfilled, issues in joy, stands firm, whereas faithlessness "makes for sin" (that is, is sinful and gets treated as such), finds its expectations frustrated, loses its land, and receives its reward (vv. 2, 16, 24, 28, 30). To put it less financially, such blessing comes to the faithful that their name is used in blessings, as people pray, "May God bless you as God blessed *x*," whereas the opposite is true of the faithless (v. 7). Integrity generates security; crookedness gets found out (v. 9). The faithless person is like a wooden house that gets carried away in a tornado, whereas a faithful person is like a proper house made of brick (v. 25).

How does faithfulness rescue from death (v. 2) and make for life (vv. 16, 27)? Proverbs implies several ways; sometimes just one factor may be operative, and sometimes more than one is operative. A first is that there's a cause-and-effect linkage built into the way life works. That conviction is explicit in the observation that laziness means people don't have enough to eat; diligence means they do (v. 4).

A second is that faithfulness builds up the community, and when the community is functioning well, it works well for faithful individuals. One aspect of the link between individual and community emerges in the way failure to take action to make the most of the harvest and put enough away to last you through the next year not only indicates stupidity but also brings shame on you and on your family (v. 5). The sayings have a converse concern for faithfulness within the community, which is what will undergird the way the community works well for individuals. Deception or plotting (v. 10), animosity or **repudiation** (vv. 12, 18), lying or slander (v. 18), scheming (v. 23), and dishonesty (vv. 31, 32) undermine the community and will backfire (vv. 18, 31, 32). Being unreliable has the same effect (v. 26). On the other hand, honesty (v. 11) and **self-giving** build up the community

(v. 12); speech that is backed up by faithfulness means a person is widely accepted in the community (v. 32).

A third way is that God makes it work thus, sometimes via those first two, sometimes by intervening to ensure that it does so. Whether the faithful go hungry and whether the faithless fulfill their desires come from **Yahweh's** being involved (v. 3). Speaking of blessings on the head of the faithful implies this involvement, because it's Yahweh who blesses (v. 6). It's because Yahweh is the source of blessing that you cannot add to it by your own effort (v. 22), even if you can forgo it by putting no effort into life. Yahweh is a stronghold or a cause of ruin according to which group you belong to (v. 29).

Things don't always work out in such a way that faithfulness rescues from death. Sometimes people pay for their faithfulness with their lives, or poverty comes from other people's oppression. But Proverbs assumes that its generalizations work out often enough to be worth heeding and likely assumes that it would be a pretty weird world that God had made if its generalizations were not broadly true. It will also expect people to be faithful even when faithfulness doesn't rescue from death. It wouldn't expect people to be faithful simply because faithfulness pays.

Proverbs 10 is different from Proverbs 1–9, because Proverbs 10 comprises a series of one-liners that cover a broad range of subjects rather than a connected exposition of a theme. Most of Proverbs 10–31 takes the form of Proverbs 10. Sometimes there are little sequences of sayings on related themes. Sometimes the order of the one-liners is less random than it looks because there are verbal links in the Hebrew that are not evident in English. But in terms of subject they mostly jump from one issue to another. The chapter divisions are random, and in reading you may want to browse your way through them until you alight on one that strikes you and stick with that one for a while. At the end of the comments on

Proverbs there is list of the sayings on some of its topics, organized by subject.

PROVERBS 11:1–31
With Modesty There Is Wisdom

1 False scales are an abomination to Yahweh;
  a true weight is what he favors.
2 Arrogance comes, then humiliation comes;
  with modest people there is wisdom.
3 The integrity of the upright guides them,
  but the deviousness of treacherous people destroys them.
4 Wealth doesn't avail on the day of wrath,
  but faithfulness rescues from death.
5 The faithfulness of a man of integrity makes his way
    straight,
  but the faithless person falls by his faithlessness.
6 The faithfulness of the upright rescues them,
  but the treacherous are taken by desire.
7 At the death of a faithless person hope perishes;
  the expectation of wealth perishes.
8 The faithful person escapes from trouble;
  the faithless person comes [into it] in his place.
9 With the mouth the impious person destroys his neighbor,
  but through the knowledge of the faithful, people escape.
10 When things are good for the faithful, the town exults;
  when the faithless perish, there is resounding.
11 A town rises up by the blessing of the upright,
  but by the mouth of the faithless it breaks down.
12 One who despises his neighbor lacks sense;
  a person of understanding keeps quiet.
13 Someone who goes about as a slanderer reveals a
    confidence,
  but someone trustworthy of spirit conceals a matter.
14 When there is no steering, a people falls;
  deliverance comes with an abundance of counselors.
15 Evil will come about when someone stands surety for a
    stranger;
  the person who repudiates pledges will be secure.

¹⁶ A woman of grace attains honor;
     violent men attain wealth.
¹⁷ A person of commitment benefits himself;
     a cruel person harms himself.
¹⁸ A faithless person makes a deceptive profit;
     someone who sews faithfulness [makes] a reliable wage.
¹⁹ The person who is steadfast in faithfulness [goes] to life,
     the person who pursues what is evil, to his death.
²⁰ The crooked in mind are an abomination to Yahweh;
     people of integrity in their way are the ones he favors.
²¹ Hand to hand, the evil person will not go innocent,
     but the offspring of the faithful will escape.
²² A gold ring in a pig's nose
     is a beautiful woman turning away from discernment.
²³ The longing of the faithful is only good;
     the expectation of the faithless is wrath.
²⁴ There is one who scatters and gets still more;
     one who holds back beyond what is upright, only to be in
        want.
²⁵ A person of blessing will be made fat;
     someone who refreshes—he'll also be refreshed.
²⁶ One who withholds grain—the community will curse him;
     but blessing will be on the head of one who sells it.
²⁷ The person who urgently aims for what is good seeks favor,
     but the one who looks for what is evil, it comes on him.
²⁸ One who trusts in his wealth—he falls,
     but the faithful flourish like foliage.
²⁹ The person who ruins his household comes to possess
        wind;
     the stupid person is a servant to one who is wise of mind.
³⁰ The fruit of a faithful person is a tree of life,
     but a wise person takes lives.
³¹ If the faithful person is recompensed on earth,
     how much more the faithless person and the offender.

In an earlier volume of The Old Testament for Everyone I referred to the fact that I'm inclined to think that nothing I do as a teacher or writer or pastor makes any difference to anyone. Last week I had a message from someone who read that volume and wrote to rebuke me, which I appreciated. I was amused that he referred to another writer on the Old Testament whom I admire who had expressed the same conviction, and he told me how he had rebuked him, too. So I feel duly chastised, but I probably won't stop feeling that way, and I don't think it does much harm that I don't take myself too seriously. My wife's version of the rebuke is to tell me not to underestimate the way other people take me seriously; my casual and half-meant words and overstatements can have a greater effect than I think.

Proverbs 11 supports me and challenges me. It warns about the danger of taking oneself too seriously (v. 2); as the English saying puts it, pride comes before a fall. On the other hand, like chapter 10, it notes the importance and the power of words. You can destroy someone with words (v. 9). People in the United States value politeness, and students are deferential to professors. I can hurt students by a casual remark that I don't intend too seriously. I can inhibit them from asking questions in case I joke and laugh about their question. To me it's a sign that their question is interesting and that they are cute, but it comes across to them as disrespectful or insensitive, the action of one who despises his neighbor and lacks sense, in contrast to the person of insight who is more restrained (v. 12) and can also keep a confidence (v. 13).

Proverbs knows that words can be harmful in more urgent ways. If you lie about your neighbor in the elders' assembly at the city gate, it could literally mean his or her death, unless there are some **faithful** people to use their wisdom on the neighbor's behalf (v. 9). Such events threaten the very being of the community. So words are important to the community itself—both lying words and words of blessing (v. 11).

Like the Prophets, Proverbs is thus interested in honesty, and it urges the importance of not cheating in business (v. 1). It promises that honesty pays and that dishonesty isn't as profitable as swindlers expect (v. 18). More generally, in the end integrity pays (vv. 3, 5, 6), partly because **Yahweh** is involved in the way human affairs work out (vv. 20, 31). It may look as if **faithlessness** pays and the faithful lose out, but in the end the faithless and the faithful will change places (v. 8). To put it more sharply or paradoxically, living in a selfless way may be in your own interests, while living in a self-focused way may rebound (v. 17). A concrete example is holding onto your surplus grain when there's a shortage, expecting that you'll do better by selling it later (v. 26). Ironically, while the longing of the faithful does result in good things, the "expectations" of the faithless are fulfilled differently from the way they expect (v. 23). The generous can end up better off despite their generosity, while the stingy can end up worse off despite their carefulness (v. 24). So a by-product of blessing others (here blessing likely means something concrete rather than words that express good wishes) can be gaining something for oneself, and a by-product of giving refreshment can be receiving it (v. 25).

Once again, one reason for making such statements is that the exceptions to the rule may make more of an impression on us than the instances of the rule; the community needs the encouragement to believe the rule even though it often looks otherwise (v. 10). Its general reliability is vital for the community's well-being, even for its continuing in being at all (v. 11). The comment about steering or giving direction (v. 14) makes a more general point about the community, about its need of collective leadership. Several heads are better than one. In the context of Proverbs' later comments about kingship, it implies both that the community needs strong leadership and that a leader is unwise to go it alone. A leader may be gifted to inspire and communicate, but such abilities aren't necessarily accompanied by the insight that can discern the right action or by the personal qualities that provide safeguards against wrong action. (The KJV for v. 14 has "where there is no vision the people perish," which is an edifying comment, though hardly what the saying denotes:

the Hebrew word for "steering" refers to skill in steering a boat.)

Gaining wealth will not help you in a life-threatening crisis (v. 4). The day of wrath may be when God acts to punish you (maybe by early death), especially if the punishment relates to your gaining that wealth by dishonest means. Or it may be a day when human wrath falls upon you. The same possibilities arise later (v. 23). Similarly (v. 21), the judge who will not acquit the evil person may be God, or the saying may be a statement of confidence in the integrity of the court at the city gate, or an implicit exhortation to its members. ("Hand to hand" may imply "you can shake hands on it"; it's guaranteed.) One way or another justice will be done. A similar ambiguity occurs in the saying about seeking what is good for oneself (v. 27), which advises us to seek favor—it may refer to God's or other people's. The second half of this line uses "evil" in two senses; if you seek what is morally and socially evil, you'll experience something evil.

It's tempting to use violent means to obtain wealth (v. 16): the saying provocatively stimulates reflection on the different priorities that can characterize men and women (Proverbs recognizes that women have their own temptations: see v. 22). The faithless are then trapped by their desire (v. 6). Faithless people may think that wealth will be their security from whatever threatens them, but such expectations are exposed as false, and they perish when death comes (v. 7). Trust in wealth leads to disaster, while faithfulness leads to flourishing (v. 28). Proverbs knows that it's important to have enough wealth to keep your family alive and to be generous to people in need, and it urges you not to be silly and irresponsible with such resources (v. 15)—the stranger will be an outsider to the village who may disappear as quickly as he came. You could ruin your household and end up with nothing and in servitude to someone less stupid than you are (v. 29). It's better to be a faithful person who is a tree of life to his

household than one who gives a wiser person chance to take
control of other people (v. 30: but this is an obscure saying).

PROVERBS 12:1–28

Anxiety and a Good Word

1   One who befriends correction befriends knowledge,
        but one who repudiates reproof is stupid.
2   A good person obtains favor from Yahweh,
        but he regards a man of schemes as faithless.
3   A person cannot stand firm through faithlessness,
        but the root of the faithful will not collapse.
4   A strong woman is her husband's crown,
        but a shameful one is like decay in his bones.
5   The plans of the faithful are the [right] exercise of
            authority;
        the steering of the faithless is deceit.
6   The words of the faithless are a deadly ambush,
        but the mouth of the upright rescues them.
7   Overturn the faithless and they are not there,
        but the household of the faithful stands.
8   On the basis of his good sense an individual is praised,
        but one who is crooked in his thinking comes to
            contempt.
9   Better one who is of little account and is his own servant
        than one who looks honorable but lacks food.
10   A faithful person knows his animal's spirit,
        but the compassion of the faithless is cruel.
11   One who serves his land will have his fill of food,
        but one who follows empty pursuits lacks sense.
12   The faithless person covets the snare of evil people,
        but the root of the faithful gives [fruit].
13   In the rebellion of lips is the trap of someone evil,
        but someone faithful gets out of trouble.
14   From the fruit of an individual's mouth he has his fill of
            good things,
        and the dealing of a person's hands returns to him.
15   The way of a stupid person is upright in his eyes,
        but the wise person listens to counsel.

16 A stupid person—his vexation makes itself known at the
     time,
        but a shrewd person conceals a humiliation.
17 The person who testifies truthfully speaks with faithfulness,
        but a false witness with deceit.
18 There is one who rants like sword-thrusts,
        but the tongue of the wise person is a healing.
19 A truthful lip stands firm forever,
        but a lying tongue lasts for the blink of an eye.
20 Deceit is in the mind of people who devise evil things,
        but for people who plan peace, there is joy.
21 No wickedness befalls the faithful person,
        but the faithless are full of evil things.
22 Lying lips are an abomination to Yahweh,
        but people who act truthfully are his favor.
23 A shrewd person conceals knowledge,
        but the mind of stupid people proclaims denseness.
24 The hand of determined people rules,
        but slackness leads to subjection.
25 Anxiety in a person's mind weighs it down,
        but a good word makes it rejoice.
26 A faithful person shows the way to his neighbor,
        but the way of the faithless leads them astray.
27 Slackness will not roast game,
        but the wealth of a person is valuable—determined.
28 In the path of faithfulness there is life,
        and [on] the way of its track, no death.

As usual, I got to sleep fine last night, but awoke after a couple
of hours as I sometimes do, and I stayed awake for about
three. I had an ache in my arm that wouldn't worry me if I was
fully awake; but in the middle of the night the ache aroused a
vague awareness that such a pain can be a sign of having a
heart attack. In addition, I'm coming to terms with the fact
that (after being out of town for nine days) I am behind with
various obligations and am not catching up fast enough.
Those are the anxieties I'm prepared to tell you about; there
are one or two others that I'm not. But over breakfast my wife

asked me what I was thinking about, and I told her, and she had a word or two to say, and I felt slightly better.

She is thus my crown rather than the arthritis in my bones (v. 4), and I trust I'm the same to her. "Anxiety in a person's mind weighs it down, but a good word makes it rejoice" (v. 25). Proverbs has already shown its interest in the fruitfulness of words (e.g., 10:11, 21); it knows that what we say, and what we don't say, is important. It is also interested in what goes on in the heart and mind, not just in outward lives. That saying about anxiety brings those two concerns together. The tongue of a wise person can bring healing (v. 18). That saying's reference to ranting makes one think of Job's friends who spoke much and brought no healing. It also points to the paradox that the tongue may heal by not saying too much, and by listening first and only then speaking. After all, shrewd people say less than they know, but stupid people proclaim their denseness by their loquacity (v. 23). Proverbs values words in inverse proportion to their number. The chapter again recognizes the broader importance of true words (v. 17) and the positive and negative power and effect that can attach to words, which can rebound on their speaker (vv. 13, 14). The false speaker lasts no longer than a tree with shallow roots (v. 19; compare v. 7). More broadly, people who lead others astray instead of showing them the way end up astray themselves (v. 26) instead of finding the path to life (v. 28).

No one enjoys being put in their place, but Proverbs knows that correction and reproof are keys to growth (v. 1). To put it in Proverbs' way, they are keys to wisdom. So people who want to be wise don't accept them merely grudgingly or reluctantly. They befriend them or **give** themselves to them. Proverbs uses the words for **love** and **hate**, which denote not merely emotions but expressions of the will—giving oneself as opposed to **repudiating**. Stupid people simply assume they know what they are doing, but the wise person looks for advice (v. 15). Conversely, when they are put down, the stupid person reacts, but the shrewd person avoids doing so (v. 16). Wisdom is thus key to having a respected place in the community (v. 8).

On the other hand, it's better not to have much status in the community and to look after yourself than to pretend to have status yet actually not have enough to eat (v. 9). Verses 10–12, 24, and 27 are linked in theme in their concern with the lives of ordinary farming people and with the way faithfulness expresses itself there. It's OK, indeed good, to work hard and to work the ground hard, rather than squandering your energy on projects that get you nowhere, but it's not good to work your animals too hard (vv. 10, 11). It's also a bit pathetic to envy the outcome of other people's hunting instead of paying attention to your own faithfulness and proving that it produces results (v. 12). Slackness will mean you don't have game to roast or don't get around to roasting it (v. 27), but determined people acquire resources. Indeed slackness leads to losing your farm and ending up as the servant of someone else who is more determined in the way he goes about his work (v. 24).

The chapter talks much about planning. The opposite of being a good person is being a scheming person (v. 2). **Faithless** people plan to ambush others, though faithfulness offers some protection (v. 6). Proverbs takes up the image of steering from the previous chapter, applying it now to the devious way faithless people exercise governmental **authority** as they guide the ship of state (v. 5). The parallelism in the saying about people who devise evil things (v. 20) suggests an irony of a kind that Proverbs likes. They are planning evil things for other people. But the contrast with the joy of people whose planning aims at peace suggests that the faithless end up generating evil things for themselves. Ironically but appropriately, evil things come to faithless people as they become the victims of other faithless people's wickedness (v. 21).

In ensuring that scheming gets its reward, the activity of God and the inbuilt order of things come together. On one hand, a good man gets **Yahweh's** favor, whereas Yahweh treats a schemer as faithless (v. 2); truthfulness gains God's favor, but God treats lying as it deserves (v. 22). On the other hand, in a way analogous to nature, a faithful person will be like a tree that stands firm rather than one whose root collapses. In our city we had a gargantuan windstorm a few months ago that caused seventeen million dollars' worth of damage to the city's corporate budget alone and felled hundreds of trees that you would have thought were securely rooted. "Overturn the faithless and they are not there, but the household of the faithful stands" (v. 7).

PROVERBS 13:1–25
Discipline Your Teenagers If You Can

1. A wise son [listens to] a father's discipline,
   but an arrogant person doesn't listen to a rebuke.
2. From the fruit of his mouth a person eats what is good,
   but the appetite of the treacherous is for violence.
3. One who guards his mouth preserves his life,
   but one who opens his lips wide—ruin is his.
4. The lazy person—his appetite desires, but there is nothing;
   the appetite of the determined is enriched.
5. A faithful person repudiates a lying word,
   but someone faithless stinks and shames.
6. Faithfulness guards integrity of the way,
   but faithlessness overturns a wrong.
7. There is one who acts rich but there is nothing,
   one who acts poor but there is much wealth.
8. The ransom for someone's life is his riches,
   but the poor person doesn't listen to a rebuke.
9. The light of the faithful is joyful,
   but the lamp of the faithless goes out.
10. Only by means of arrogance does someone produce strife;
    wisdom is with people who take advice.

11 Wealth gained from emptiness can dwindle,
      but the person who gathers by hand makes it grow.
12 Hope deferred sickens the heart,
      but desire that comes about is a tree of life.
13 One who despises a word, it will be evil for him,
      but one who is in awe of a command, he'll be rewarded.
14 The teaching of a wise person is a fountain of life
      to turn one away from deadly snares.
15 Good sense brings favor,
      but the way of treacherous people endures.
16 Every shrewd person acts with knowledge,
      but a stupid person spreads denseness.
17 A faithless aide falls into evil things,
      but a trustworthy envoy—healing.
18 Poverty and humiliation—one who rejects discipline,
      but one who heeds correction is honored.
19 Desire that comes about is sweet to the appetite,
      but turning from evil is the abomination of the stupid.
20 One who walks with the wise gets wise,
      but the friend of stupid people experiences evil things.
21 Evil things pursue offenders,
      but good things reward the faithful.
22 A good man endows grandchildren;
      the strength of the offender is stored up for the faithful
        person.
23 The fallow ground of the poor—abundance of food,
      but it's swept away for want of the [right] exercise of
        authority.
24 The person who is sparing with his club repudiates his son,
      but one who loves him gets him up early with discipline.
25 The faithful person eats to fill his appetite,
      but the stomach of the faithless lacks.

A mother recently told me how Christian parenting experts had urged her to start spanking her children; some said to continue only until the children become verbal, others at any sign of willful rebellion regardless of age. In not doing so, she was disobeying God's command. The comments were fleshed out with tales of woe about parents who had ignored God's command, with unfortunate results. If you parent in the disciplinary way, your child will turn out great; otherwise, they said, you're in for a load of trouble. She went on to ask with a grin whether I thought she would have a less rebellious spirit if she had been spanked as a child, but also whether the New Testament had anything to say on this subject.

Proverbs indeed affirms that the father who is sparing with his baseball bat **repudiates** his son, while the one who **gives** himself to his son gets him up early to discipline him (v. 24); the verbs are again the ones conventionally translated **love** and **hate**. We noted in connection with Proverbs 4 that the New Testament doesn't let us off the hook in connection with sayings such as this one. But another woman suggested a way of relieving parents. If we take such sayings in Proverbs as commandments like ones from the **Torah**, we will also beat stupid people, mockers, and impure people (19:25; 20:30; 26:3), cut off the tongues of treacherous people (10:31), conscript lazy people (12:24), cast lots to resolve disputes (18:18), and slice our throats if our appetites are too large (23:2). In other words, many sayings in Proverbs look as if they are figurative and hyperbolic, like Jesus' exhortation to gouge out your eye (or for that matter the Torah's own saying about an eye for an eye). Further, in passages such as Proverbs 1 the Hebrew words for "discipline" or "correction" often refer to instruction. They don't always suggest physical chastisement, even metaphorically.

It's also significant that other sayings about disciplining a son (e.g., in Proverbs 22) describe him as a youth. While the term can be used of a small child, it more often refers to someone older, though unmarried; in Israel I was once referred to by this term when I was thirty. The word for a child as opposed to a youth never comes in Proverbs. Further, when the Old Testament elsewhere raises questions about discipline by parents and rebellion by their offspring, it concerns the relationship of parents to their grown-up children, such as Samson's relationship with his parents or

David's with Amnon and Absalom. So Proverbs is urging the middle-aged heads of households to get a grip of their teenage and young adult sons, not their four-year-olds.

Proverbs' expectations are thus even more worrying for parents. Its expectations suggest a certain poignancy about observations concerning the attitude of these young adult or adult children to their parents (v. 1). Parents know what it's like to be mocked when they attempt to discipline or rebuke. They rejoice when their children speak well and thus eat well, but grieve when their appetite is for violence and their mouths get them into trouble (vv. 2, 3). They long for them to take advice (not least the parents' advice!) rather than being arrogant troublemakers (v. 10). They know that peers can be of more influence than parents (v. 20). They long for their children to listen to commands (not least the parents' commands!) rather than go their own way and get into trouble (v. 13). They want them to see that wise teaching (not least their parents' teaching!) is thus the way to life and to other people's favor and to avoiding life's traps, avoiding a fate they can't escape, and avoiding advertising their stupidity or drawing other people into it (vv. 14, 15, 16, 21). They rejoice when their children speak the truth and grieve when they deceive and make an evil smell in the community, bringing shame on themselves and on their parents (v. 5). They rejoice when their children are committed to hard work and thus do well, but grieve when they don't (v. 4). They rejoice when their children are people the community and its leaders can rely on to undertake a task on its behalf (v. 17). They rejoice when they embody how **faithfulness** means a life of integrity, but grieve if their **faithlessness** ruins their lives because they are sinners (v. 6)—the saying uses abstract terms but refers to the people who embody these abstractions. There's hardly anything that matters more to parents than their children growing up as faithful people whose life works out well, so

59

some poignancy again attaches to statements about this dynamic (v. 9).

We might treat the saying about the connection between accepting discipline and avoiding poverty (v. 18) as a link between the concern for parental instruction and the chapter's talk about wealth. If you do pay heed to discipline, you're more likely to do well and to gain honor in the community rather than being humiliated by it. There's maybe further poignancy in the chapter's statements about wealth. Wealth can enable you to buy your way out of a fix; but if you lack wealth you can be more cavalier when people threaten you, because you have nothing to lose (v. 6). Paradoxically, there are people who pretend to be doing well when they are not, maybe because their own estimate of themselves and their standing in other people's eyes have come to depend on their being successful (v. 7). There are also people who are doing well but hide the fact, maybe because other people will then be looking to them for a loan or because they are afraid their success may be only temporary or because of the possibility that they will be open to that pressure to buy their way with people (v. 7). Either way, don't take people at their face value. It can be tempting to seek wealth by projects that seem to generate money for nothing, but these are unlikely to work in the long run; slow but steady is wiser (v. 11)—gathering by hand is perhaps an image from the way farmers go about harvesting (we might contrast it with using a combine harvester). One may then have wealth to bequeath, when wealth gained dishonestly ends up in the estate of the faithful person (v. 22).

A corollary of the way wealth can be acquired dishonestly is that poverty may come about through the wrongdoing of others and the failure of people in power to do something about that wrongdoing (v. 23). Such experience on the part of ordinary people would then illustrate how the deferring of hope that has been cherished by the head of a household, the hope that he'll see his family fed, sickens the heart; whereas when he sees that desire fulfilled, it's a life-giving experience (v. 12). Seeing your longings fulfilled is sweet in more senses than one, and it's a hope worth holding onto rather than that one should persist in an evil lifestyle that leads to an evil end (v. 19). Proverbs doesn't want to give up the idea that faithfulness and faithlessness do get their deserts (v. 25).

PROVERBS 14:1–35

Even in Laughter a Heart May Hurt

1   The wisest of women builds her house,
        but stupidity tears it down with her own hands.
2   One who is in awe of Yahweh walks uprightly,
        but one who despises him is devious in his ways.
3   In the mouth of the stupid person there is a shoot of
            arrogance,
        but the lips of wise people guard them.
4   When there are no oxen the stall is clean,
        but there's abundance of revenue through the strength of
            a bull.
5   A trustworthy witness doesn't lie,
        but a false witness testifies lies.
6   An arrogant person seeks wisdom and there is none,
        but knowledge is easy for the person of understanding.
7   Get away from the presence of the stupid person;
        you won't have known knowledgeable lips.
8   The wisdom of someone shrewd means understanding his
            way,
        but the denseness of stupid people is deception.
9   Reparation is arrogant toward stupid people,
        but between upright people there is favor.
10 The heart knows its inner bitterness,
        and in its joy a stranger doesn't share.
11 The house of the faithless will be destroyed,
        but the tent of the upright will flourish.
12 There is a way that is upright before a person,
        but its end is the ways of death.

13 Even in laughter a heart may hurt,
   and celebration—its end may be grief.
14 Someone who turns back in his heart will be full from his
         ways,
   and the good person from his deeds.
15 A naive person trusts in anything,
   but a shrewd person understands his step.
16 A wise person fears and turns from what is evil,
   but a stupid person rages and is confident.
17 One who is short-tempered will do stupid things;
   a person of schemes will be repudiated.
18 The naive gain possession of stupidity,
   but the shrewd wear a crown of knowledge.
19 Evil people bow down before good people,
   and the faithless [bow down] at the gates of someone
         faithful.
20 Even by his neighbor a poor person is repudiated,
   but the friends of a wealthy person are many.
21 One who despises his neighbor is an offender,
   but one who is gracious to the lowly: his blessings!
22 People who plan evil things, do they not go astray?—
   but people who plan good things [find] commitment and
         truthfulness.
23 In all toil there will be profit,
   but [in] the [mere] word of lips [there will be] only being
         in want.
24 Their wealth is the crown of the wise,
   but the denseness of stupid people is denseness.
25 A truthful witness saves lives,
   but one who testifies lies, deceit.
26 In awe for Yahweh [there will be] strong security,
   and for one's children one will be a refuge.
27 Awe for Yahweh is a fountain of life,
   to turn from deadly snares.
28 The glory of a king lies in the abundance of a people;
   in the absence of a nation lies the ruin of a ruler.
29 Long-temperedness is abundant in understanding,
   but shortness of spirit exalts stupidity.
30 A healthy heart is life for the flesh,
   but passion is rot for the bones.
31 One who oppresses a poor person insults his maker,

62

but one who is gracious to a needy person honors him.
32 In his misfortune a faithless person is thrown down,
     but a faithful person is secure in his death.
33 In the mind of a person of understanding wisdom rests,
     and in the midst of stupid people it makes itself known.
34 Faithfulness exalts a nation,
     but wrongdoing is a shame to peoples.
35 The favor of a king [will be] toward a servant of good
     sense,
     but his rage will be [toward] a shameful one.

A friend of mine told me last week about a dinner he and his wife had had with another couple. The other wife was my friend's ex, but both couples are happily married so it seemed that this piece of history would not be a problem, and the couples had a jovial evening during which my friend and his wife gave their well-rehearsed joint account of the unusual circumstances in which they met, with much laughter. But when they got home my friend's wife told him how upsetting she had found the evening because it was so difficult meeting someone who had a longer history with him than she did, and because he seemed so glad to spend time with her. Actually (he told me), he himself didn't enjoy the occasion anywhere near as much as he seemed, and he would have preferred to avoid the event but didn't feel they could do so.

"Even in laughter a heart may hurt, and celebration—its end may be grief" (v. 13). There are lots of senses in which it may be so. It's always unwise to assume that the emotions people show are the ones they feel. I'm often surprised when someone describes another person as sharing how he or she "honestly" feels, as if verbal expressions of joy or sorrow are bound to be genuine. People can be good actors. Even more thought-provokingly, even if you do know the true nature of someone's feelings of sadness or joy, don't think you actually share them (v. 10). There's perhaps a sense in which each of us is alone with our inner experiences; there are limits to empathy. Or at least, there's no cheap empathy. Sharing

63

someone's experience involves costly effort and a resistance to the temptation to say, "I empathize with you." It's the other person who needs to decide whether you have done so.

"A healthy heart is life for the flesh, but passion is rot for the bones" (v. 30). It's another saying that sounds as if it's declaring an unvarying truth when it's a generalization that works by and large. Sometimes a person's inner being may be in good shape, but he or she may contract a devastating illness. Sometimes passions such as jealousy and anger are correct reactions to situations and make people take action that needs taking. On the other hand, bottling up such strong feelings rather than owning them may indeed be hurtful to the whole person, body as well as spirit.

Biblical usage matches English usage in referring to the heart in various connections. We often refer to the heart in speaking of the emotions, while the Bible often refers to it in speaking of the mind or the will. Both usages see the heart as the center of a person's inner being, the wellspring of who a person is. That last usage will overlap with the others. When a person's heart turns back from the right way rather than continuing to walk in a good way, it results in experiencing the fruit of one's action (v. 14). The turning directly involves the will, but it reflects something that has happened deeper in the inner being. Wisdom's residing in the heart implies residing in the mind (v. 33), but it also permeates the inner being more broadly. It makes itself known "in the midst" of a person. It affects the emotions and the will. There's an inner wisdom that can somehow know what is wise independently of thinking things through intellectually.

Wisdom thus affects the whole of life, not just its fringes. The opening line about building a house or tearing it down (v. 1) parallels the portrait of Ms. Wisdom and Ms. Stupidity in chapter 9, but it speaks rather of the woman who embodies wisdom, the wise mother to whose teaching Proverbs often refers. The "house" there denoted a place where you could come and learn wisdom; outside that context it could denote the household that the wise woman seeks to build up (that is, her family). Either way, she'll have to be aware of forces that can demolish what she wants to build. But Proverbs also promises that the house of the **faithless** will be destroyed, while the tent of the upright will flourish (v. 11); "tent" can denote a regular abode, though here setting tent over against house makes for a nice contrast between an abode that looks strong but isn't and one that looks vulnerable but isn't. Things will come out right in the end (vv. 19, 22). At the very end, the faithless may face death with fear, but the **faithful** can do so with a sense of security (v. 32). Proverbs knows that people cannot look forward to a very exciting life after death but only to a rather drab existence in **Sheol**, so it's quite a statement. So is the declaration that wisdom makes itself known in the midst of stupid people, though it actually rests in the mind of a discerning person (v. 33). Perhaps the idea is that even dense people will be compelled to recognize the nature of wisdom when it hits them in the face.

So the wise will end up doing well and stupidity will be its own reward for the stupid (v. 24). The wise will express their wisdom in being hard workers rather than people who sit around talking (v. 23), and they will recognize that you have to put up with some mess if you want to do well (v. 4).

You'll also have to accept the fact that everyone then wants to be your friend, whereas people prefer to avoid the poor who may make demands of them (v. 20). The chapter nicely juxtaposes that realistic observation with another indicating how the fact that human instincts work this way doesn't mean one accepts them (v. 21). There's a theological argument to undergird that point (v. 31). Thus **awe** for **Yahweh** is a key to living uprightly (v. 2). As a consequence, it's a key to security and life for oneself and for one's children (vv. 26, 27).

The opposite of awe and submission is mockery, the arrogance that thinks it has nothing to learn (v. 3). To describe the mocker as seeking wisdom (v. 6) is rather paradoxical; perhaps the idea is that mockers may know they need to make sensible decisions, but their arrogance prevents their acquiring the wisdom to do so. Their insight concerning the action that they should take turns out to be deception (v. 8). They are hotheaded and confident where trepidation would be wiser (vv. 16, 29). Their shortness of temper can get them into trouble, though their considered deceptiveness can have worse consequences (v. 17; also vv. 5, 25). Making themselves unpopular may then be an irreversible development; there's no way their attempts to make up for their stupidity can succeed and generate the friendly relationships that happen between the upright (v. 9).

Thus people who want to learn need to be discerning about where they look for wisdom (v. 7). What appears upright may turn out to be unwise, a fact that even the wise need to bear in mind (v. 12), though the naive are in more need of doing so (vv. 15, 18). Leaders may sometimes recognize the fact and value their insightful staff accordingly (v. 35)—though the parallelism in this saying suggests that as usual insight is assumed to go along with integrity. Absent such insight, the nation may deservedly decline (v. 34), as will then the honor of being its leader (v. 28).

PROVERBS 15:1–33

A Gentle Response Turns Back Wrath

1. A gentle response turns back wrath,
   but a hurtful word arouses anger.
2. The tongue of the wise enhances knowledge,
   but the mouth of dense people pours out stupidity.
3. Yahweh's eyes are in every place,
   observing evil people and good people.
4. A healing tongue is a tree of life,
   but deviousness in it is brokenness in spirit.

5   A stupid person spurns his father's discipline,
      but one who heeds reproof shows shrewdness.
6   [In] the house of the faithful person is much wealth,
      but in the revenue of the faithless person, trouble.
7   The lips of the wise spread knowledge,
      but the mind of stupid people—not so.
8   The sacrifice of the faithless is an abomination to Yahweh,
      but the plea of the upright is favorable to him.
9   The way of the faithless person is an abomination to
        Yahweh,
      but he gives himself to one who pursues faithfulness.
10 Discipline is evil to one who abandons the path,
      but one who repudiates reproof dies.
11 Sheol and Abaddon are before Yahweh;
      how much more the minds of human beings.
12 An arrogant person doesn't befriend one who reproves
        him;
      he doesn't come to the wise.
13 A joyful heart enhances the face,
      but by hurt in the heart the spirit is crushed.
14 The mind of a person of understanding seeks knowledge,
      but the mouth of dense people feeds on stupidity.
15 All the days of a lowly person are evil,
      but a good heart is a continual feast.
16 Better a little with awe for Yahweh,
      than much treasure and turmoil with it.
17 Better a helping of greens when love is there,
      than a fattened bull when hatred is with it.
18 A heated man stirs up arguments,
      but one who is long-tempered quiets contention.
19 The way of a lazy person is like a hedge of thorns,
      but the path of the upright is cleared.
20 A wise son rejoices his father,
      but a stupid person despises his mother.
21 Stupidity is a joy to one who lacks sense,
      but a person of understanding makes his going upright.
22 Plans are frustrated in the absence of counsel,
      but with many advisers they stand.
23 In the response of his mouth there is joy to a person,
      but a word at its time—how good!
24 The path of life is upward for a sensible person,

so as to turn away from Sheol below.
25 Yahweh tears down the house of the arrogant,
   but establishes the territory of the widow.
26 Evil plans are an abomination to Yahweh,
   but graceful words are pure.
27 One who gets dishonest gain will make trouble for his
       household,
   but one who repudiates a gift will live.
28 The mind of a faithful person talks in order to answer,
   but the mouth of faithless people pours out evil things.
29 Yahweh is far away from the faithless,
   but listens to the plea of the faithful.
30 The lamp of the eyes rejoices the heart;
   good news builds up the bones.
31 The ear that listens to life-giving reproof
   lodges among the wise.
32 One who lets go of discipline despises himself,
   but one who listens to reproof acquires sense.
33 Awe for Yahweh is wisdom's discipline;
   lowliness is before honor.

Shortly I must attempt a third draft of a reply to a message concerning our congregation's terminating the employment of our longtime gardener, who is getting elderly and was finding it harder to do the work that needed doing. His daughter was incensed at our action and at the way we had gone about it. I didn't want to answer her protest point by point, but I was concerned about her threat to write to the local newspapers about the matter, and I wanted to say something about statements in the message that simply seemed mistaken. Yet at the same time I needed to pay heed to her sense of outrage at the way we had treated her father.

"A gentle response turns back wrath, but a hurtful word arouses anger" (v. 1). It's not only the tongue of the wise that enhances knowledge, whereas the mouth of dense people pours out stupidity (v. 2); the pen also does so. Better to quiet an argument by being long-tempered than to make things worse by counter-accusation that stokes the conflict (v. 18). I needed to talk to myself and to other people before answering the message, rather than simply pouring out words, as I can easily do (v. 28). I know about the importance of wise counsel (v. 28).

But even then, while it may be satisfying to formulate the right reply to someone, the right time is also important (v. 23). If the matter should reach the press, I shall not take an initiative to reply there, because when I read people's letters to the press seeking to give their side of a story, usually either I'm not impressed or I had not seen the original story and it draws my attention to it. "A joyful heart enhances the face, but by hurt in the heart the spirit is crushed" (v. 13). A tongue that seeks to be a source of healing is better than one that brings more brokenness (v. 4). It will be neat if our expressions of thanks, and a friendly and appreciative look in our eyes if we meet, can help us all find some resolution (v. 30). All those considerations work within the family, too (v. 17).

Yet discipline and reproof, too, are life-giving, and it's wise to heed them rather than mock at them (vv. 5, 10, 12, 20, 31, 32). As usual, Proverbs emphasizes the need to pay heed to good sense, which is also life-giving (vv. 7, 14, 24), whereas stupidity's apparent joyfulness is deceptive (v. 24).

Indeed, **awe** for **Yahweh** is wisdom's discipline, and accepting one's humble position before Yahweh is a prerequisite to honor (v. 33). Awe for Yahweh will result in our doing well; after all, Yahweh knows what is going on (v. 3). The saying about **Sheol** and Abaddon—another title for the abode of dead people—notes that Yahweh even has access to the ways we are thinking (v. 11). Yahweh surely takes action accordingly, for instance demolishing the house of the arrogant but protecting the land of the widow (v. 25). The houses and income of **faithful** and **faithless** thus contrast (v. 6). What applies to the house also applies to the people who live there (v. 27)—the "gift" will be a bribe, which thus stands in parallelism with "dishonest gain."

Such sayings are one-sided and unrealistic if taken as invariable generalizations, like the observation that lazy people blame the obstacles they confront, whereas upright people somehow don't seem to confront these obstacles (v. 19). But Proverbs also notes that it's better to have a little but to live in awe of Yahweh than to have much treasure and turmoil with it (v. 16). It thus implies that life is more complicated than such promises might imply in isolation. Proverbs knows that its "rules" don't always work and, even in this case, that there's a positive side to their not working, since wealth may add to your problems rather than solving them.

Nevertheless, Yahweh does **give** himself to the faithful; in contrast, the faithless are an abomination to Yahweh (v. 9). There's a related contrast in Yahweh's attitude to their sacrifice and prayer (v. 8)—one of Proverbs' infrequent allusions to our religious life. Whereas there's a sense in which Yahweh is present everywhere, there's another sense in which he's far away from the faithless while near to the faithful to listen to their pleas (v. 29). Evil plans—that is, plans to do wrong to people—are also an abomination to Yahweh; whereas graceful, generous, openhanded, and openhearted words are pure in his sight (v. 26).

PROVERBS 16:1–33

Arrogance Goes before Shattering

¹ The ordering of his mind belongs to a human being,
   but the answer of the tongue comes from Yahweh.
² All a person's ways are pure in his eyes,
   but Yahweh weighs spirits.
³ Roll your actions onto Yahweh,
   and your plans will stand.
⁴ Every deed of Yahweh is for what it responds to,
   even the faithless person for an evil day.
⁵ Anyone arrogant of mind is an abomination to Yahweh;

hand-to-hand he won't go innocent.

6 By commitment and truthfulness waywardness is expiated,
   and with awe for Yahweh there's a turning away from evil
      things.

7 When Yahweh is pleased with someone's ways,
   he causes even his enemies to be at peace with him.

8 Better is a little with faithfulness
   than much revenue without [right] exercise of authority.

9 The mind of a person plans his course,
   but Yahweh establishes his step.

10 There is divination on a king's lips;
   his mouth doesn't trespass in the exercise of authority.

11 Balance and scales for decision belong to Yahweh;
   all the stones in the bag are his making.

12 Acting with faithlessness is an abomination to kings,
   because the throne stands on faithfulness.

13 Faithful lips are what kings favor;
   he gives himself to one who speaks upright things.

14 The king's wrath is death's aide,
   but the wise person will expiate it.

15 There is life in the light of the king's face,
   and his favor is like a cloud with spring rain.

16 Acquiring wisdom—how much better it is than gold,
   and acquiring understanding is to be chosen rather than
      silver.

17 The highway of the upright is turning away from evil
      things;
   one who guards his way preserves his life.

18 Arrogance goes before brokenness,
   majesty of spirit before collapsing.

19 Humbleness of spirit with the lowly
   is better than sharing plunder with the arrogant.

20 One who is sensible about a matter will attain good things,
   and one who trusts in Yahweh [will attain] his blessings.

21 One who is wise in thinking is called understanding,
   but sweetness of speech increases persuasiveness.

22 The good sense of people who possess it is a fountain of
      life,
   but stupidity is the discipline of stupid people.

23 The mind of a wise person makes his speech sensible,
   and on his lips adds persuasiveness.

71

24 Nice words are a honeycomb,
    sweet to the soul and healing for the body.
25 There is a road that is right in someone's eyes,
    but its end is roads that lead to death.
26 The appetite of a laborer labors for him,
    because his mouth is pressing on him.
27 A worthless person plots evil things,
    and on his lip is like a scorching fire.
28 A crooked person stirs up arguments,
    and a gossip separates a friend.
29 A violent person misleads his neighbor
    and makes him go in a way that isn't good.
30 A person winks his eyes in planning crooked things;
    he purses his lips when he has accomplished evil things.
31 Gray hair is a splendid crown;
    it's attained by way of faithfulness.
32 Better to be long-tempered than a warrior,
    and ruling over one's spirit than taking a city.
33 The lot is cast in the lap,
    but every decision it makes is from Yahweh.

So I wrote a third draft and I now have responses from some other members of our church council, and I must finalize and send the message later today. In a sense it's easy enough to think through the issues, but it may be harder to work out exactly what to say without giving the wrong impression and inflaming the situation. It now also reminds me of another comment by the friend I referred to when discussing Proverbs 14. When he and his wife were trying to sort out what had happened between them, he was aware that there was a difference between the way he saw the situation and what he thought it wise to say to his wife. He recognized that the way he saw the situation might not be quite right, but even if he was right, it might not help to say everything that he saw.

The opening saying in this chapter (v. 1) makes me reflect on such dynamics in our interactions with people. Admittedly the saying is elusive or oblique, but such sayings that make you think and could be understood in several ways can be just as useful as sayings that are quite clear. In connection with the message I have to finalize, the reflection it prompts is that I depend on God for the right words that will have a constructive rather than offensive affect (compare vv. 21, 23, 24). The person I have to write to isn't an enemy, but it will be nice if God is involved in our correspondence in such a way as to bring peace where at the moment there's tension (v. 7). Words are so powerful, often for bad ends (vv. 27, 28, 29, 30).

Another possible implication of the opening saying is that we have less control over what we say than over how we think. That idea fits with other aspects of the insights expressed in this section of Proverbs, where the focus has moved to a more explicit consideration of God's involvement in our lives. You can decide what you plan to do, but **Yahweh** establishes your step (v. 9). Again, the saying can have more than one implication. It reminds us of God's involvement in our lives that helps us fulfill our plans and reminds us to look to God, be dependent on God, and be confident in God (compare v. 3 with its neat image; also vv. 20, 25). It also reminds us that our plans are one thing but their implementation is another and that God may arrange things so that they work out differently from the way we planned. It reminds us to be humble before God. We are unwise to assume we have total insight into our own motives (v. 2) or to be arrogant (v. 5); "hand-to-hand" may again imply "you can shake hands on it," it's guaranteed (see further vv. 18, 19). On the other hand, Yahweh's **commitment** and **faithfulness** do open up the possibility of our waywardness being expiated, though this cleansing also requires our own turning to **awe** for Yahweh instead of arrogance, and our turning from wrong ways (v. 6). Further, we are unwise to make our awareness that "man proposes but God disposes" a reason for quietism or laziness; we may end up with nothing to eat (v. 26).

Such principles apply even to people acting in a **faithless** way (v. 4). They may be pursuing their own agenda, but God may utilize their action in order to deal with some situation that requires a response (Yahweh's raising up imperial powers such as Assyria and Babylon to trouble Judah is an example).

Alongside the theme of God's involvement in our lives, the chapter has much to say about government or leadership. The juxtaposition of these two is suggestive; the teaching we have already noted in this chapter applies especially to people in leadership. The opening saying about the king (v. 10) can again be read in more than one illuminating way. Divination on a king's lips may imply a recognition that what the king says goes and that he needs to acknowledge the responsibility resting on him to ensure that he's careful about what he says; the parallel comment about the way he exercises **authority** then supplements this implicit exhortation. Further, it's the power of the king that makes his wrath death-bringing to its victims—so appease it if necessary rather than keep insisting that you're right (v. 14). On the other hand, when the king is pleased with you, his power also has the capacity to be life-giving like the rains that come in spring and take the crops to their full growth (v. 15). So leaders have to be careful about the self-control with which they exercise their power (v. 32).

But divination on a king's lips may also be a kind of promise or offer (compare v. 33). The king has access to sources of divine guidance for the nation's affairs and has the possibility of governing in a faithful way. The comment about government significantly follows on the earlier declaration that a little with faithfulness is better than much income without right government (v. 8), which suggests a principle for the king's own life and his political and economic policies. Wisdom is more important than gross domestic product (v. 16). The foundation of his throne is faithfulness (v. 12; compare v. 13). Again it's a saying that can suggest several insights. The stability of his throne depends on his faithfulness to God and to his people and on their faithfulness to one another. In the context, again, the preceding comment about commercial honesty (v. 11) suggests a policy he needs to implement in encouraging faithfulness within the community.

If the king reads this chapter saying much about him, he'll discover that he'll be wise to pay attention to wisdom and the upright, faithful ordering of his life. It may enable him to survive threats to his throne and live long (vv. 17, 22, 31).

PROVERBS 17:1–28

Yahweh Tests Minds

1 Better a dry crust and quiet with it,
   than a house full of contentious sacrifices.
2 A sensible servant will rule over a disgraceful son,
   and share the property with the brothers.
3 The crucible for silver, the furnace for gold,
   and Yahweh tests minds.
4 A person who does what is evil pays attention to a wicked lip;
   a lie gives ear to a destructive tongue.
5 One who mocks the poor person insults his maker;
   one who rejoices at calamity will not go innocent.
6 Grandchildren are the crown of elders,
   but their parents are the glory of children.
7 An eloquent tongue isn't fitting for a mindless person,
   much less a lying tongue for a leader.
8 A bribe is a favorable stone in its possessor's eyes;
   wherever he turns, he'll succeed.
9 One who seeks a relationship covers over rebellion,
   but one who repeats a matter separates a friend.
10 A rebuke gets down into a person of understanding
   more than lashes into a stupid person—a hundred of them.
11 An evil person seeks only rebellion,
   but a cruel aide will be sent against him.
12 Let a bereaved bear meet with someone,
   but not a stupid person in his denseness.
13 Someone who returns evil for good—

evil will not depart from his household.

14 The beginning of an argument releases waters;
before contention breaks out, abandon it.

15 One who declares a faithless person faithful or declares a
faithful person faithless,
both of them are an abomination to Yahweh.

16 Why is the price in a stupid person's hand
for acquiring wisdom when he has no sense?

17 A neighbor is a friend at any time;
a brother is born for trouble.

18 A person lacking in sense pledges his hand,
standing surety before his neighbor.

19 One who likes rebellion likes strife;
one who builds a high gate seeks breaking down.

20 Someone crooked of mind doesn't attain good things,
and someone who twists with his tongue falls into evil
things.

21 One begets a stupid person to one's grief;
the father of a mindless person doesn't rejoice.

22 A joyful heart enhances healing,
but a crushed spirit dries up the bones.

23 A faithless person takes a bribe out of his pocket,
to divert the processes of decision making.

24 Wisdom is right before someone of understanding,
but the eyes of the stupid person are at the end of the
earth.

25 A stupid son is a vexation to his father,
and bitterness to the one who bore him.

26 Surely penalizing a faithful person isn't good—
flogging leaders for uprightness.

27 One who knows knowledge holds back his words;
a person of understanding is cool of spirit.

28 Even a stupid person, keeping silence, is thought wise;
one who keeps his lip closed [is thought] understanding.

A year after we came to California, one Sunday evening my
son called to tell us that they had just had their first child on
Monday morning in London. When Monday morning came
in California, I rushed to book an air ticket to go back to
London for the next weekend to greet our first grandchild.

Over the weekend, I was astonished to be allowed to take him out in his stroller, and I found myself looking down at him in a confused way. Was this baby really my son's son? Or was I my son, and was this my son? Two years later, his sister was born, and I concluded that my work as a human being was done. I had played my part in the continuing existence of the human race.

Grandchildren are the crown of elders (v. 6). The statement that parents are the glory of their children takes my thinking in a different direction. It doesn't so obviously fit with Western instincts, or at least with European instincts; there's a difference between attitudes in Europe and the United States that may derive from the way children gain economic independence in Europe earlier than they do in the United States, because of the way the state supports the cost of education—at least, it has been so in the past, though in Britain at least it's less so now. Maybe the Proverbs saying looks descriptive but is actually prescriptive and has one eye on the dynamics implicit in other sayings, that children may take insufficient notice of their parents' teaching and standards (vv. 2, 21, 25). Maybe one can also hear a parental lament in the saying about riotous parties (v. 1). The allusion to sacrifices will be a reference to the way joyful fellowship sacrifices are shared by God and the family, which will make them a cross between an act of worship and a family party. One can imagine middle-aged parents getting weary because the younger people are having too much of a good time and/or getting into arguments when they have eaten and drunk well. I'd settle for a sandwich and a nap, says father.

I have no complaint about my children in this connection. If anything, they complain about their father being too noisy. They then have a right to wonder whether he's wise, because wise people tend to talk less (v. 27). Perhaps they know they need time to think; perhaps (like Ecclesiastes) they know that things are complicated and most big problems don't have answers; perhaps (unlike Job's friends) they know that answers rarely do anyone any good. Thus even stupid people can give the impression of wisdom if they talk less (v. 28). Such a stance might even open them to wisdom; they might not have as far to look as they think or imply with the scattered nature of their attention span (v. 24). The trouble is that even though they have access to wisdom they lack the good sense to lay hold of it (v. 16). Meanwhile, it's better to be met by a bear bereaved of her cubs than to be met by a stupid person mouthing off as such a person does (v. 12).

If there's something worse than a dolt full of words it's such a person whose words are also crooked (v. 20). If there's something even worse, it's a leader whose talk is full of lies (v. 7). A lie gives ear to a destructive tongue (v. 4)—that is, a liar does so. There's then a kind of collusion between people who talk about doing wrong and people who listen to them and are willing to join them or use them or who simply decline to distance themselves from them, in the way Scripture describes when it speaks of **repudiating** or **hating** evil and evildoers. Related to these sayings are the chapter's comments about bribes, which are an effective way to pervert the exercise of **authority** (vv. 8, 23). A favorable stone is a magic stone, like a good-luck charm. The task of leadership is to ensure that when there's a dispute in the community, **faithful** people are treated as faithful and **faithless** as faithless; **Yahweh** hates it when the elders or a person such as the king operates in another way (v. 15). Neither would Yahweh be impressed if someone with power such as a king treats senior people in the community—maybe people who confront the king—in such a way (v. 26).

The chapter includes complementary observations about rebellion against authority. Rebels need to recognize that the authorities will get to know and will take action (v. 11). For society, the problem is the strife that rebellion brings (v. 19). The crash it causes might be that of the rebel or that of the society (we don't know what "building a high gate" refers to). Given the problem of such strife, in general it's better to abandon disputation before it gets out of hand and opens a sluice of crashing waters (v. 14).

As a rebel's best friend you have to balance responsibility as a citizen and your relationship with your friend (v. 9). Maybe this rebel is someone who doesn't quite fit into the category of an evil person and the action in question is less radical or is just a matter of talk. This might not mean you simply say nothing, as if the action didn't matter. Maybe you should talk to your friend rather than to the authorities, and maybe that is in the authorities' interests—a word from you may be more effective than their chastisement (v. 10). The chapter recognizes that friendship and neighborliness are important, along with the mutual commitment such relationships entail (v. 13). It also recognizes that blood is thicker than water (v. 17) and that there are limits to what someone will do for a friend or neighbor (v. 18), as maybe there are not for a brother. Mutual commitment within the family is key to society working well in the Old Testament, though the repeated saying about mocking a poor person (v. 5) presupposes that the family isn't one's only obligation. The saying here spells out how such mocking is an expression of schadenfreude, the pleasure that derives from noting someone else's misfortune.

In connection with all these matters, Yahweh tests people's minds or hearts (v. 3). To go back to the chapter's beginning, there can be enthusiastic worship reflecting enthusiasm for God, and enthusiastic worship reflecting—well, just enthusiasm, or a need to feel happy. In Israel, even if public worship was offered to Yahweh, private worship might be offered to a different god. There could be outwardly friendly attitudes to other people but inner resentment or plotting. Is God really interested in our hearts rather than our outward actions? Old Testament and New Testament assume God is interested in both. It's also appropriate for people to look at their own hearts, given that a joyful heart enhances healing, but a crushed spirit dries up the bones (v. 22).

PROVERBS 18:1–24

Yahweh's Name Is a Refuge

1. One who isolates himself seeks for what he desires;
   he breaks out against all [people of] good sense.
2. The stupid person doesn't delight in understanding,
   but rather in disclosing his thinking.
3. When a faithless man comes, contempt comes,
   and with humiliation comes reproach.
4. The words from a person's mouth are deep waters;
   a fountain of wisdom is a flowing wash.
5. Lifting the face of the faithless person isn't good,
   by pushing aside one who is faithful when making a
   decision.
6. The lips of a stupid person come to contention,
   and his mouth summons to blows.
7. The mouth of a stupid person is his ruin,
   and his lips are a trap for his life.
8. The words of a gossip are like bites of food,
   and they go down into the inner rooms of the stomach.
9. Really, one who is slack in his work—
   he is brother to someone destructive.
10. Yahweh's name is a strong tower,
    into which the faithful person runs and is safe.
11. A rich person's wealth is his strong city,
    and like a safe wall in his view.
12. Before being broken a person's mind is arrogant,
    but before honor comes lowliness.
13. One who returns word before he listens—
    it's his stupidity and shame.
14. A person's spirit sustains his sickness,
    but a crushed spirit—who can bear it?
15. An understanding mind acquires knowledge,
    and the ear of the wise seeks knowledge.
16. A person's gift widens the way for him,

and conducts him before the great.
17 The first person in a dispute seems right,
       then his neighbor comes and examines him.
18 The lot puts an end to arguments
       and separates powerful people.
19 A brother acting rebelliously [is stronger] than a strong
         city,
       and arguments are like the barrier of a fortress.
20 From the fruit of a person's mouth his stomach gets full;
       from the revenue of his lips he gets full.
21 Death and life are in the hand of the tongue;
       those who give themselves to it eat its fruit.
22 When someone finds a wife, he finds good things
       and obtains favor from Yahweh.
23 The poor person speaks prayers for grace,
       but the rich person answers fierce things.
24 There are neighbors to act like neighbors,
       and there's one who gives himself, who sticks firmer than
         a brother.

We recently went for nine days to a country we had not previously visited. For some time beforehand, my wife was apprehensive because she had a sense that demonic spirits were active in this country. Kathleen doesn't often talk in these terms, and neither am I sensitive to the demonic. When she talked about her apprehensions, I didn't have much to say beyond expressing the conviction that there could hardly be anywhere in the world where demonic spirits were more active than Los Angeles, where we live. The women's Bible study group was more helpful. They encouraged her to take a stand against such spirits, to claim this country in the name of Jesus, and to rely on Jesus' name as she did so. While we were there, on two occasions she felt she could see something that seemed demonic; she did as the women said, and the "things" disappeared.

Kathleen's experience presupposed the truth in what Proverbs describes in calling **Yahweh's** name a strong tower, into which the **faithful** person runs and is safe (v. 10). She also illustrates Proverbs' comment about marriage (v. 22). The Old Testament itself doesn't talk much about the demonic (which may be one reason why I don't think much in these terms), perhaps partly because the surrounding culture did so, and it wants to ignore the demonic as an aspect of making the radical Israelite affirmation that only Yahweh is Lord. But when Israelites came across those realities and this way of thinking, they could do as Proverbs says. They could also do so when threatened by powers that might be simply earthly, such as human enemies.

It's easier for Western people to affirm that a rich person's wealth is his strong city (v. 11). The gap between rich and poor in the country we were visiting was even more marked than the gap in the United States. But here, and I guess there, people's response is to hope that they can somehow get a part of the action, realize the American dream. The telling qualification "in his view" is harder to take into account.

The image of a strong city recurs in a different connection when Proverbs compares a rebellious brother to a strong city and compares the conflict that ensues to the defenses of a fortress (v. 19). In such passages "brother" likely means not an immediate member of the family but a member of the wider community; the Old Testament sees the other people in one's village or town as one's brothers and sisters. The turmoil in the twenty-first-century world reminds us that such conflict is a more powerful force in the world than is wealth. The situation is exacerbated by the tough stance of rich nations toward poorer ones (v. 23). We prefer to be neighbors who act like neighbors, with a minimum of generosity but keeping ourselves to ourselves to make sure we do not compromise our own position, than to be the kind of neighbor who **loves** and behaves more like a brother in the more literal sense (v. 24). Yet the great wealth of major powers doesn't provide them with a way of suppressing the assertiveness of peoples who don't share in that wealth. One might see the chapter's opening comment (v. 1) as another way of describing the rebelliousness that insists on having one's share and will not be put off or held back. On the other hand, there's wisdom (at least in person-to-person disputes) in letting matters be resolved by the toss of a coin (v. 18); you might even trust God to ensure that the drawing of lots comes out right.

The chapter incorporates more sayings about words. Stupid people are more interested in answering than in hearing out the person who addresses them; this also issues in shame (v. 13). A broader illustration of the principle about listening is that it's possible to be convinced by the first speaker in a debate or a court case, but things may look different when you hear the opposition's response (v. 17). It also links with having a greater interest in pontificating than in learning (v. 2). Such a priority isn't the way to wisdom, which relies on the activity of the ear (v. 15). If we ignore that principle, our words may be unfathomable and copious (v. 4), but not in a good way. In a meeting yesterday my boss recalled the observation of the philosopher Ludwig Wittgenstein that what can be said at all can be said clearly, though this may make someone laugh who has read the later Wittgenstein. People who don't understand things may well be unintelligible when they try to explain them, whereas if I understand, I'll be able to explain. When students ask me how they can explain some point to their congregation, I reply that they need to focus on understanding it for themselves; communication will then look after itself. While deep and profuse words can be wise, they can be simply murky. Wise words are more like clear water flowing through a wash or wadi sometime after rain, when the runoff has cleared.

Murkiness isn't the only problem about the words of stupid people. They may not care what they say and may thus engender conflict (v. 6), which can be disastrous for them personally as well as for society (v. 7). Gossip illustrates these dynamics, tasty though its revelations may be for gossiper and listener (v. 8). For both wise and stupid, their well-being can be determined by their words. Metaphorically speaking, the tongue decides what you eat. It decides your fate. More literally, it decides whether you enjoy life or get overtaken by death (vv. 20, 21). The association between wisdom and faithfulness means that, less dramatically, **faithlessness** issues in contempt, and humiliation issues in reproach (v. 3). Thus it's possible to be respected and confident of one's position in the community but to find that one loses everything, so it's better to be someone of lowly status who may come to a position of honor (v. 12). The loss may make life itself hard to bear and make one unable to cope with further reverses (v. 14). The association between wisdom, faithfulness, and hard work suggests another related insight (v. 9).

The tongue may decide the fate of other people as well as yourself, if you let it be the means of pushing aside one who is in the right when you're making a decision about a case, and instead "lift the face of the faithless"—that is, making lifting of the face possible for a person who is actually guilty and is looking down in shame or in simple submission and supplication before the court (v. 5). Such action may often reflect bribery, on which the chapter comments in another connection (v. 16).

PROVERBS 19:1–29

Does God Have a Wonderful Plan for Your Life?

1 Better one who is poor who walks with integrity
    than one who is crooked with his lips and stupid.
2 Indeed, without knowledge a person isn't good,
    and one who is hasty on his feet offends.
3 A person's stupidity overturns his way,
    but his mind rages against Yahweh.
4 Wealth makes many friends,
    but a poor person becomes separate from his friend.

5 A false witness will not go innocent,
    one who testifies lies will not escape.
6 Many seek the face of a ruler,
    and everyone befriends the person with a gift.
7 All the brothers of a poor person repudiate him—
    how much more do his neighbors keep their distance
      from him;
    the person who pursues words—he doesn't have them.
8 One who acquires sense befriends himself;
    one who guards understanding attains good things.
9 A false witness will not go innocent;
    one who testifies lies will perish.
10 Luxury isn't fitting for someone stupid,
    still less for a servant to rule over officials.
11 A person's good sense lengthens his anger,
    and his glory is to pass over an act of rebellion.
12 The king's rage is a growl like a lion's,
    but his favor is like dew on grass.
13 A stupid son is a disaster to his father,
    but a woman's arguments are a continuing drip.
14 House and wealth are the property of parents,
    but a woman with good sense comes from Yahweh.
15 Laziness makes deep sleep fall,
    and a slack person gets hungry.
16 One who guards a command guards his life;
    one who despises his ways will die.
17 One who is gracious to a poor person lends to Yahweh,
    and he'll pay him his recompense.
18 Discipline your son when there is hope;
    don't apply yourself to putting him to death.
19 One who is big in wrath carries a penalty;
    if you rescue [him], you'll do it again.
20 Listen to counsel and accept instruction,
    so that you may be wise when you come to the end.
21 Many plans are in a person's mind,
    but Yahweh's counsel is the one that stands.
22 Commitment is a person's desire;
    a poor person is better than a liar.
23 Awe for Yahweh leads to life;
    one eats one's fill, spends the night, doesn't fear evil.
24 The lazy person buries his hand in the bowl;

he can't even bring it back to his mouth.
25 Flog an arrogant person and the naive person will become
shrewd;
reprove someone of understanding—he'll understand
knowledge.
26 One who destroys a father or drives out a mother
is a son who brings shame and disgrace.
27 Son, stop listening to discipline,
and you'll stray from words of knowledge.
28 A worthless witness is arrogant toward the taking of
decisions,
and the mouth of the faithless swallows wickedness.
29 Decisions are prepared for the arrogant
and blows for the back of stupid people.

Students who would like to find their way into teaching sometimes ask how I came to be a professor, so as to make plans for their career trajectory. My answer is that I drifted into where I am now. They don't like this answer, because it doesn't help them make plans. But it's the true answer. My work life began with a time as a pastor. Then I drifted into a time as a seminary teacher because I was asked to teach. Then I drifted into a time as an administrator, because it was what the seminary needed. Then I drifted into a time as a teacher in California because I was asked to come, and into a time when I could do more writing because I was no longer involved in administration. Now I've drifted into also being a pastor because my church needs one.

Proverbs isn't exactly against planning your career trajectory, but it likes warning people about assuming they can be in control of their lives and implement their plan. You can make plans for your life, but "**Yahweh's** counsel is the one that stands" (v. 21). To judge from the way Scripture speaks about God's counsel, plan, or intention, the implication isn't that God has a plan for the details of our lives and that we should therefore focus on seeking God's advice for those details. Like any other good parent, God doesn't have a plan for the details of our lives—God wants us to run our lives. Rather, our lives are lived in the context of a big sovereign purpose of God in the world that embraces much more than the details of our lives, and we shouldn't be surprised that this big sovereign purpose sometimes involves things that clash with our plans. Sometimes some aspect of our lives may directly relate to an aspect of that big purpose, so neither should we neglect to seek to set our lives in its context and to be open to discovering that God has a specific plan for us. But when our seeking doesn't discover anything, the answer isn't more seeking and worrying. We are then wise to go with the flow.

So Proverbs doesn't tell people to seek God's counsel, but neither does it tell us simply to make up our minds on our own; it tells us to seek other people's counsel (v. 20). Linking that recommendation with an exhortation to accept instruction suggests that it has in mind not consulting one's peers but asking the advice of one's wise teachers, who are the regular vehicles of instruction in Proverbs. The "end" of this process might refer to a time when we graduate from our course of instruction in wisdom, though the wise teachers of Proverbs imply that this moment never comes; Proverbs believes in lifelong learning (cf. v. 25). The "end" may rather be the end of the process whereby we discover the answer to a particular question about our life. But it might be the end of our actual life. This idea would fit the observation that people who take notice of their teacher's commands guard their life, whereas people who despise their ways (their own ways or the teacher's ways) will die (v. 16). But perhaps the commands one is to heed are God's. Certainly **awe** for Yahweh leads to life and means (for instance) that when you're on a journey, you can eat well and then go to sleep without worrying about who may attack you during the night (v. 23).

In practice it's easy to make decisions on the basis of our own wisdom, which turns out to be stupidity not wisdom, and when things go wrong, to blame God rather than ourselves (v. 3). Stopping to take advice is wiser than rushing into something (v. 2). Thus acquiring good sense means we are doing ourselves a favor. We attain good things (v. 8). The point isn't merely that there's pragmatic wisdom in such reflectiveness. It brings forth a character that is good rather than one that offends or sins. But ignoring wisdom does bring trouble. People who mock wisdom end up with the elders making decisions to punish them (v. 29). Whether or not such punishment brings the mockers to their senses, it may have a beneficial effect on the naive (v. 25).

The reference to such decisions and to mockers suggests a segue to three other sayings about community decision making. Proverbs emphasizes the critical importance of honesty on the part of witnesses to that process. Potential dishonest witnesses must recognize the depravity of such dishonesty, which mocks at this decision making with its need for honesty (v. 28). That attitude constitutes "worthlessness." It's the Hebrew word "Belial," which eventually becomes a name for Satan. The word also looks as if it has something to do with the Hebrew word for "swallow," which here appears in the same saying—**faithless** and dishonest people swallow wickedness as if it were good food, as they hope other people may swallow their dishonest testimony. Proverbs undergirds its concern by warning potential dishonest witnesses that they will pay for their dishonesty (vv. 5, 9).

The opening saying (v. 1) makes related assumptions. It's better to be a poor person who lives an upright life than someone who is crooked in speech, and thereby gets rich, yet is morally stupid. Everyone is looking for **commitment** or **faithfulness** from others, so that a poor person isn't only morally better than a liar but someone more appreciated (v. 22). Admittedly, a wealthy person always has friends—of a kind; whereas if you fall into poverty you may lose the only friend you had (v. 4)—who thus also turns out to be only a certain kind of friend. Indeed, both your family and your friends and neighbors may turn away from you. One can imagine them quoting the sayings about laziness and arguing that the poor have only themselves to blame (vv. 15, 24).

If they do so, they ignore the **Torah's** expectations, but realistically one can imagine them believing that they must not imperil their own immediate family's position by bailing you out (v. 7)—the last clause perhaps suggests that you can't find the words to persuade them. With another dose of realism, Proverbs notes how money buys status, opportunity, and influence (v. 6), but it frets over such facts. It's inappropriate for stupid people to do well in life (v. 10), as inappropriate as the turning of things upside down that is involved when a servant comes to rule over officials (because of their incompetence or the king's arbitrariness?). Proverbs is realistic about wealth, but it also lays before us a challenge to look at things in a different way and see that God identifies with poor people, though as we do so we don't have to reconcile ourselves simply to being selfless (v. 17).

The chapter considers a number of aspects of strife in the community. There's the trouble caused by people who are inclined to fly off the handle and who are unlikely ever to change (v. 19). Their lives contrast with those of people who are prepared or able to be long-suffering (v. 11). Passing over rebellion suggests someone in authority, and thus this saying leads into one about the king's rage (v. 12). It can have disastrous consequences like those of meeting with a lion, though the power of the king means that on another day his action can be more like that of the dew that plays a vital role in bringing crops to fruition during the summer drought.

Family life knows the conflict of parents and children, whose lives may ignore the wisdom their parents seek to inculcate (vv. 13, 27). Eventually they become the people in the family with energy and authority as their parents become old and useless, and they gain control of the family assets from their parents (v. 14) but then have the power to ignore the command about honoring them and may do the opposite (v. 26). Family life also knows the conflict of husbands and wives (v. 13) that make the man who finds the right wife eternally grateful to God (v. 14).

PROVERBS 20:1–30

Drink Is a Brawler

1 Wine is arrogant, drink is a brawler,
   and anyone who goes astray through them isn't wise.
2 The king's dreadfulness is a growl like a lion's;
   one who infuriates him loses his life.
3 Ceasing from contention is an honor for a person,
   but every stupid person breaks out.
4 After fall the lazy person doesn't plow,
   but he asks at harvest and there is nothing.
5 The counsel in a person's mind is deep waters,
   but a person of understanding can draw it up.
6 A multitude of people may declare, "a person of
      commitment,"
   but a person of truthfulness who can find?
7 A faithful person walks about with integrity—
   the blessings of his children after him!
8 A king sitting on a throne of authority
   winnows all evil things with his eyes.
9 Who can say, "I've kept my mind pure,
   I'm clean from my offense"?
10 Stone and stone, measure and measure,
   both of them are an abomination to Yahweh.
11 It is indeed by his deeds that a youth reveals himself,
   if his action is pure and upright.
12 The ear listens, the eye sees;
   Yahweh made both of them.
13 Don't give yourself to sleep lest you become poor;
   open your eyes—be full of food.
14 "Bad, bad," says the buyer,
   goes off, then boasts.

15 There is gold and abundance of jewels,
   but lips with knowledge are a valuable object.
16 Take his coat, because he made a pledge to a strange man;
   bind him, on account of a foreign woman.
17 Dishonest bread is tasty to a person,
   but afterward his mouth will fill with gravel.
18 Plans stand through counsel;
   make war with steering.
19 One who reveals a confidence goes about as a slanderer;
   don't share with someone who has his lips open.
20 One who humiliates his father and his mother,
   his lamp will go out at the approach of darkness.
21 Property hastened at the beginning,
   at the end of it will not be blessed.
22 Don't say, "I'll pay back an evil deed";
   be expectant of Yahweh and he'll deliver you.
23 Stone and stone is an abomination to Yahweh;
   lying scales are not good.
24 A man's steps come from Yahweh;
   how can someone understand his way?
25 It's a snare when someone is wild about holiness,
   and after [making] vows asks questions.
26 A wise king winnows faithless people,
   rolls the wheel over them.
27 The breath of a person is Yahweh's lamp,
   revealing the heart's inner rooms.
28 Commitment and truthfulness protect a king;
   he maintains his throne by commitment.
29 The glory of youths is their strength;
   the majesty of elders is their gray hair.
30 Blows that wound scour evil things,
   and beatings [scour] the inner rooms of the heart.

A friend who is a recovering alcoholic sometimes comments with dark humor on the process whereby drinking ruins people's lives. It all but ruined his life, and it has ruined the lives of people he knows. At first, drinking can seem like a great adventure that's going to lead you to brilliant ideas. You're free to have meaningful, unencumbered relationships and to realize your full potential as the hero of your own story. Then one day you find yourself in a dark, piss-filled alley wondering how you got there and unable to find your way back through the maze in order to escape. In other words, drink is a big lie that wants to destroy you, darkness seeking to consume you.

Proverbs 20 opens with a beautiful understatement: someone who goes astray as a result of drink is "not wise" (v. 1). It would not be surprising if an expression of un-wisdom such as drinking went along with another such expression, the un-wisdom of neglecting your work. It would be tempting to relax after harvest time in the fall (v. 4). The story of Eli and Hannah in 1 Samuel 1 reflects how harvest celebration was incidentally an occasion for serious imbibing. After a good harvest, you have enough to eat for now and for the coming months, and you've worked hard to ensure that it's so, so why not take a few weeks holiday …? But if you don't start the new year's work now, you'll imperil the entire agricultural cycle and end up with nothing to eat in a few months' time—end up like a drunk, in fact. If you want to eat tomorrow, you can't afford to surrender to the instinct to sleep all day today (v. 13).

Another expression of un-wisdom that could bring family disaster to which Proverbs has already referred is risking your family's financial position by standing surety for someone. Doing so to foreigners is especially risky as they may disappear overnight just as they perhaps did from their home country (v. 16). The exhortation to take the person's coat and bind him is addressed to the lender, encouraging him to insist that the unwise person accept responsibility for the loan, but it functions as a vivid way to discourage people not to stand such surety. Something similar is true about vows (v. 25). It's unwise to promise with wild enthusiasm to give something to **Yahweh** when you haven't thought about the consequences and counted the cost. Conversely, buying something in a hurry, maybe because it looks like a bargain, may turn out to be unwise (v. 21).

A further example of stupid action within the community is getting into arguments; it only earns you a bad reputation (v. 3). Another is trusting your confidences to the kind of person who likes talking to everyone about everything (v. 19). Another is starting to believe your own publicity (v. 9). You may be wise and you may be a model of right living, as Proverbs expects of wise people and knows to be a realizable ideal. But don't fool yourself into thinking that you're invulnerable to moral and religious failure. Don't be naive about other people, either: lots of people may say that they are **committed** to you or may say that someone else is a committed friend (either understanding of v. 6 is possible), but it's unwise to take such claims or testimonies at face value. People who are really truthful and steadfast are hard to find. Similarly, one implication of the saying about the counsel in someone's mind (v. 5) is that one shouldn't assume one knows what people are thinking, even if they tell you. They may not even know their own mind. It takes insight to reach into that mind. The inherent limitations of one's insight have another aspect. We can decide what to do, and make the best decisions possible, but we are always subject to God's making things work out in a way we could not have expected (v. 24).

The saying about God being the maker of eye and ear (v. 12) does act as an encouragement to anyone who seeks such insight. God made us with these capacities. The same implication emerges from the saying about our breath being a kind of lamp that God has put into us (v. 27). It's a slightly cryptic image, but its implication is clear enough, that God has made us able to look inside ourselves and see what is there. Alongside that conviction is the less comfortable fact that chastisement can have the effect of not only revealing what is in our hearts but of cleansing them (v. 30). The wisdom we can thus acquire is more valuable than jewels (v. 15).

Proverbs makes a point about young people that it has already made more generally, emphasizing that the index of real commitment is outward action and not merely attitude of heart or the words a person speaks; the question is how does a person behave (v. 11). Its other point about youth is the contrast between the glory and majesty of youths and older people (v. 29). Young people have energy; older people the gray hair that symbolizes wisdom. So let the two play to their strengths and respect the strengths of the other.

Then there's the need to take into account the power and the foibles of the king, especially if you work in the administration. The king has the power of life and instant death (v. 2). The king's **authority** therefore has the potential to be a formidable force for exercising that power to support **faithfulness** and purge wrongdoing (v. 8). He can winnow **faithless** people, separating the chaff from the wheat by tossing it into the air and letting it blow away after threshing it (v. 26). It's a chilling image that can both frighten the faithless and encourage their victims. The king has a personal interest in faithfulness and commitment being characteristics of the administration and of the community; his throne depends on it (v. 28). The saying will just as easily suggest a challenge to the king himself; his throne depends on his commitment and truthfulness toward his people. His policies' success does also depend on his thinking things out and planning well, which applies especially to his role as commander in chief (v. 19) with his responsibility for steering things.

The chapter twice refers to God's abhorrence for the idea of people swindling one another in their trading (vv. 10, 23): expressions such as "measure and measure" signify using different measures so as to give less than a pound when you're selling and to take more than a pound when you're buying. In the end, dishonesty will not work (v. 17). The point is made with dark humor. There's more humor about another scene from the process whereby people trade with one another (v.

14). Bartering means haggling shrewdly and often means claiming that the other person is being tough when actually you're getting a good deal (one needs to remember that there's no such thing as money through most of Old Testament times, so barter is the regular way to dispose of surplus assets and to acquire things one needs that one has not grown or made for oneself). As the victim of a swindler, it will be tempting to take matters into one's own hands, but Proverbs typically advocates against implementing that instinct, on the basis of one's knowledge that God is involved in working things out (v. 22).

Faithfulness pays not only in one's own life, but in the life of one's children (v. 7). While the sins of parents can affect the immediate family, the commitment of parents can affect a thousand generations. As parents can derive joy from the way their children can benefit from their faithfulness, so children can derive joy from the faithfulness of their parents and not give in to the temptation to put them down, maybe as they get older and become a burden (v. 20). They may look forward to their parents' lamp going out but find that their own lamp does so, too.

PROVERBS 21:1–31

The Way of a Man Can Be Strange

¹ The king's mind is a water channel in Yahweh's hand,
   which he directs wherever he wishes.
² All a person's way is upright in his own eyes,
   but Yahweh weighs minds.
³ Exercising authority in a faithful way
   is preferable to Yahweh over a sacrifice.
⁴ Exaltedness of eyes and wide of mind:
   the yoke of the faithless is an offense.
⁵ The plans of the determined person do end up in gain,
   but everyone who is hasty does end up in want.

6 Working for treasures by means of a lying tongue
   is a breath driven off, people seeking death.

7 The violence of the faithless sweeps them away,
   because they refuse to exercise authority [aright].

8 The way of a man [may be] twisting and strange,
   but his action innocent and upright.

9 Living on a corner of the roof
   is better than an argumentative woman and a shared
     house.

10 The appetite of the faithless person desires evil things;
   his neighbor isn't favored in his eyes.

11 Through the punishing of someone arrogant a naive
     person gets wise,
   and through paying attention to someone wise he gets
     knowledge.

12 One who is faithful pays attention to the house of the
     faithless person,
   overturning the faithless to their misfortune.

13 One who stops his ears to the cry of the poor person—
   he too will call and not be answered.

14 A gift in secret calms anger,
   a present in the pocket [calms] fierce wrath.

15 Exercising authority [aright] is joy to the faithful
   but ruin to the wrongdoer.

16 Someone who wanders from the way of good sense
   will rest in the congregation of ghosts.

17 One who gives himself to enjoyment is a person in want;
   one who gives himself to wine and oil will not get
     wealthy.

18 The faithless person is the ransom for someone faithful,
   and the treacherous person in place of the upright.

19 Living in wilderness land
   is better than an argumentative and vexatious woman.

20 Valuable treasure and oil are in the dwelling of someone
     wise,
   but a stupid person will consume them.

21 One who pursues faithfulness and commitment
   finds life, faithfulness, and honor.

22 A wise person went up to a city of warriors
   and brought down the stronghold in which it was
     confident.

23 One who guards his mouth and his tongue

> guards his life from troubles.
> 24 The haughty, presumptuous person—arrogant his name—
> acts in a frenzy of haughtiness.
> 25 The desire of the lazy person kills him,
> because his hands have refused to act.
> 26 All day someone may feel desire,
> but the faithful gives and doesn't spare
> 27 The sacrifice of the faithless is an abomination,
> yes, because he brings it with scheming.
> 28 A lying witness will perish,
> but one who listens to the end will speak.
> 29 A faithless person looks firm in his face,
> but one who is upright—he understands his way.
> 30 There is no wisdom, there is no understanding,
> there is no counsel against Yahweh.
> 31 The horse is prepared for the day of battle,
> but the deliverance belongs to Yahweh.

A newly married couple came to talk to us about a tension within their marriage (as if we were experts, being married for only a year ourselves). The husband is a lively, young man whom his wife regards as handsome. He can be effusive in his casual relationships with other young women, whom he doesn't see as a threat to their marriage. He says he isn't interested in them, but his apparent encouragement of their interest in him upsets her and causes ill-feeling between them. She doesn't exactly fear that he'll go off with one of them; she just feels hurt or threatened by the way he relates to them.

The way of a man can be twisting and strange, though his action may be innocent and upright (v. 8). Proverbs has several Hebrew words that have traditionally been translated "man" but that refer to a human being rather than a male, and I translate these by words such as person, but it here uses a word that more specifically suggests a male; *Brown-Driver-Briggs Hebrew and English Lexicon* defines it as "man as strong, distinguished from women, children, and non-combatants" (a related word means a warrior). But the actions of both men and women can seem enigmatic and be open to misinterpretation (Proverbs implies), so don't assume you're reading them aright. Of course the man or woman may be self-deceived: maybe that young husband is deceiving himself about the innocence of his relationships with other women. While our actions can be odd but "upright," they can also be "upright" in our own eyes but something else in the eyes of God, who has more insight into our thinking than we do (v. 2). That fact isn't merely threatening but potentially encouraging; God can grant us insight into ourselves. It's fortunate, because there are other ways in which our mind can get us into trouble (v. 4). In Western metaphor, being broad-minded is a positive image, but in the Old Testament it's a negative one; it suggests being too big for your boots or for your hat. It goes along with having high eyes, which make it possible to look down on people. Thus the yoke or dominion of such **faithless** people is offensive to God.

There's also both pause for thought and encouragement in the fact that God is in a position to direct the king's mind as much as anyone else's (v. 1). The implication isn't that God forces the king to act against his better judgment, anymore than was the case with the Pharaoh whose hardening of his own attitude went alongside God's hardening. It does mean God can prod the king as God can prod anyone else into the right direction. The king has particular responsibility for exercising **authority** in a **faithful** way, which God views as more important than showing up in the temple for worship (v. 3). A similar principle applies to anyone who might be inclined to combine scheming with faithfulness in worship (v. 27). The proper exercise of judgment is an encouragement to the faithful, not least because it means their security or deliverance, and it means ruin for the wrongdoer (v. 15). The saying about the faithful person doing something to put down the faithless (v. 12) will likewise apply in particular to the king; at least, Proverbs doesn't elsewhere speak of the ordinary member of the community in these terms.

If instead the king becomes the faithless person who **gives** himself to violence in oppressing his people, he'll find himself swept away (v. 7). It's one of the passages where Proverbs doesn't speak of divine intervention to produce the result; there's a built-in logic about such a consequence. The chapter does close with sayings that assert God's direct involvement. No matter how carefully leaders make plans, they need to recognize that God has the last word. The principle applies in particular when it comes to the king's key role as commander in chief, in making plans for war (vv. 30, 31). Conversely, he needs to recognize that wisdom on the part of an attacker can count for more than the mere strength of his fighting force and the defenses of his city.

The king or anyone else who is set on plans that will issue in gain needs to be wary of acting too fast because such haste can issue in loss (v. 5). A related insight is that giving oneself to self-indulgence means ending up in poverty (v. 17). Stupid people simply consume resources; wise people conserve them (v. 20). The desire involved in such consumption can be our downfall in more than one way. It may make us concerned only for ourselves and unwilling to be generous to others (v. 26). Combined with laziness it may be the death of a person (v. 25), whether that desire is to do nothing or to have things that will never materialize because of this lethargy. Further, pursuing plans for gain in a dishonest fashion is like driving off a breath of wind that you were trying to capture—indeed, it involves imperiling your very life (v. 6).

In turn, to put that point even more vividly, people who wander from the way of good sense will rest in the congregation of ghosts (v. 16), a neat description of life in **Sheol**. The faithless have no way of ransoming themselves from the deathly consequences that will follow from their actions, whereas the faithful need no such ransom (v. 18 puts this point rather obliquely). They may make a point of looking strong, but it's not they who establish their ways (v.

99

29). They may act in a frenzy of arrogance and mockery, but their downfall will come, and they will provide an object lesson for other people (vv. 24, 11). In contrast, people who are careful about what they say avoid getting into trouble (v. 23). The promise applies particularly to the business of giving testimony, where it's wise to listen well before speaking (v. 28).

It's people who pursue faithfulness and **commitment** who find life, faithfulness, and honor (v. 21). The attitude of the faithless is so dominated by desire for gain that they don't care about relationships with other people (v. 10). The saying involves a neat use of similar words, as the word for "evil things" and "neighbor" are almost the same. One of the ways the faithless may pay the price for their attitude is that people who decline to listen to the cry of the poor can find themselves crying out for help and not being answered (v. 13). There's again a natural process here; listening to others builds up community, declining to listen destroys it. Conversely, but possibly more cynically, when someone gets angry, it may pay you to buy them off, even secretly (v. 14).

Neatly, the saying about the man who behaves strangely is paired with one about tension within a marriage of the kind that such a man may provoke but that backfires on him. He can't really blame his wife for being quarrelsome, and he may wish he had a quiet corner on the roof (where people in the Old Testament world often took refuge to find quiet) than sharing the house with her (v. 9), or even that he had a quiet corner in the wilderness away from where anyone lives (v. 19).

PROVERBS 22:1–16

Rich and Poor Meet

1   A name is preferable to much wealth;
       favor is better than silver and gold.
2   Rich and poor meet;

Yahweh makes each of them.

3 The shrewd person sees misfortune and hides;
    naive people pass on and pay the penalty.

4 The effect of lowliness is awe for Yahweh,
    wealth, honor, and life.

5 Thorns [snares] are in the way of the crook;
    one who guards his life keeps away from them.

6 Initiate a youth with regard to his way;
    even when he gets old, he won't turn from it.

7 The rich person rules over the poor,
    and the borrower is a servant to the one who lends.

8 One who sews wrongdoing will reap wickedness;
    their furious club will fail.

9 One who is good of eye will be blessed,
    because he gives of his bread to the poor person.

10 Drive out the arrogant person and arguments will depart;
    lawsuit and humiliating will cease.

11 One who gives himself to being pure in mind,
    with grace on his lips—the king is his friend.

12 Yahweh's eyes guard knowledge,
    but he overturns the words of the treacherous person.

13 Someone lazy says, "A lion in the street,
    in the middle of the square I shall be slain!"

14 The mouth of alien women is a deep pit;
    one with whom Yahweh is indignant falls there.

15 Stupidity is bound up in a youth's mind;
    the club of discipline will take it far away from him.

16 One who oppresses the poor person—it's to make much for
    him;
    one who gives to the rich person—it's only to come to
    want.

Getting dressed this morning, I noticed there was no change in my pocket. I remembered giving my change to someone in the street and wondering whether I was helping him get a meal or just get another drink. I thought about the fact that I shall cycle through intersections today where people stand asking for change from motorists waiting at the lights, and I shall wonder what is going through the minds of the people and through the minds of the motorists. In the news I then read an item about a marketing agency getting homeless people to wander around a technology conference carrying mobile Wi-Fi devices and offering delegates Internet access in exchange for donations; the experiment caused some discomfort among delegates. Tomorrow I shall join with people from our church in cooking and serving dinner for people living in a homeless shelter near where we live.

In Western culture, the meeting of rich and poor may be largely confined to such contexts. At our church, we may meet homeless people outside, but we don't have much success in inviting them in. In Israel it would likely be different. Poor and rich had the temple in common; both went to worship there. The worship itself would remind them that God creates both (v. 2). Typically, Proverbs leaves its readers to work out the implications (though it has pointed out that oppressing or mocking the poor is an insult to their maker: see 14:31; 17:5). People who are doing OK in life might take that fact as an affirmation from God and take the predicament of the poor as indicating God's judgment on their lives. Sometimes the inference is correct, but it easily becomes an unjustified knee-jerk reaction that has forgotten who is the poor person's creator.

The one explicit implication of God's being the creator of both rich and poor comes in the closing verse (v. 16). It doesn't talk about God's judgment but does make a declaration that works within Proverbs' other framework for thinking about life, that life itself works out our actions' consequences in our lives. There's a kind of moral structuring to the way life works, which operates often enough for it to be worthwhile and wise to take it into account. You don't have to appeal to God in order to commend it as a piece of wisdom to people who don't take God into account in their thinking. Paradoxically, the poorer people are, the more there may be an inclination to oppress them. The Hebrew word for "oppress" often means "extort," and that is the form oppression often takes; they are poor already, but they may pay a larger amount of their income in taxes.

That possibility is open because the wealthy people are also the people who determine the tax system. The rich rule over the poor, and the borrowers serve the lenders (v. 7). Conversely, the richer people are, the more they may be inclined to augment their wealth by the way the law works and by bribery, again because they have power as well as wealth. Ultimately their expectation is inclined to be disappointed, says Proverbs. Mysteriously but appropriately, people who extort from the poor can end up building up the resources of the poor themselves; people who give to the wealthy are inclined to end up in want. To put it more metaphorically and concretely, people who sow wrongdoing reap wickedness (that is, become the object of **faithlessness** on the part of others) as well as finding they can no longer wield the club they wield on the poor (v. 8). On the other hand, blessing will come to people who share their resources (presumably honestly obtained) with the needy. They thus show that they are "good in eye" or have good eyes—that is, eyes that look with goodness on such people (v. 9). They must be realistic about the dynamics that sometimes take people into poverty, as one of Proverb's most vivid lines notes (v. 13). But they can't make that consideration the excuse for hardness of heart or evilness of eye.

The saying about the king (v. 11) makes a further comment about power. A wise leader needs and befriends people who are pure in mind (for instance, they think in ways that are not spoiled by personal ambition) and gracious in speech (that is, they speak honestly out of those pure minds and thus say what needs to be said, but do so with delicacy). To put it the other way (as Proverbs may intend), if you're the king's friend or confidante, make sure you're a person with both those characteristics, otherwise you may be no use to him and ineffective as an adviser, and you may risk your life. The following comment about treacherous people (v. 12) will have special significance for people who are thus involved in the administration. Behave in a knowledgeable, wise way, and God will see that your counsel is effective. Join in plotting against the administration, and expect to fail. Let your speech be gracious rather than mocking if you want to encourage unity in the administration and in the community, and also safeguard your own position (v. 17).

It may be hard to believe, but a good name and the favor of one's community are more worth having than wealth (v. 1). On the other hand, wealth along with honor and life does issue forth from lowliness or ordinariness or weakness and from its correlate, **awe** for **Yahweh** and submission to Yahweh (v. 4). Conversely, the life of the crook turns out to be obstructed by thorns and snares, whereas people who pay attention to the proper shaping of their lives thereby avoid such threats and dangers (v. 5). So such paying of attention is an expression of shrewdness, the kind of wisdom that contrasts with the unthinking ingenuousness that fails to see potential pitfalls and evade them, and instead blunders on and pays the penalty (v. 3). Such naiveté is to be expected of the person who is too young to have learned otherwise: hence the need to initiate the young in the wise shaping of their ways, which will have long-standing effectiveness if done properly (v. 6). Admittedly the word "properly" may need nuancing (v. 15); some young people are not merely pardonably naive but already stupid. If so, tough treatment may be needed. A teacher once told us he could have made a good mathematician out of my son, but he's not allowed to use a cane on pupils nowadays. The warning about the foreign woman whose independence of the community enables her to sit loose to its moral expectations (v. 14) is one Proverbs often connects with young men, who may be especially susceptible to her charms and may pay a terrible price.

PROVERBS 22:17–23:21
Don't Let Your Nap Go On Too Long

17 Bend your ear and listen to the words of the wise,
   apply your mind to my knowledge.
18 Because it will be gratifying when you keep them inside you;
   they will be ready all at once on your lips.
19 So that your trust may be in Yahweh, I let you know today
   —yes, you:
20 have I not written down for you thirty, with counsels and knowledge,
21 to enable you to know the truth (reliable words)
   so as to respond in words reliably to the ones who send you?
22 (a) Don't rob the poor person because he is poor,
   don't crush the lowly person at the gate.
23 Because Yahweh will contend for their cause
   and will despoil the people who despoil them of life.
24 (b) Don't befriend a person characterized by anger,
   don't go about with someone hot-tempered,
25 lest you learn his ways
   and get a snare for your life.
26 (c) Don't be among the people who shake hands,
   among the people who stand surety for debts.
27 If you have nothing to pay,
   why should someone take your bed from under you?
28 (d) Don't remove an age-old boundary mark,
   one that your ancestors made.
29 (e) You've seen a person quick at his work?—he'll stand before kings,
   he won't stand before people who are in the dark.
23:1 (f) When you sit to eat with a ruler,
   understand well what is before you,
2 but put a knife to your throat
   if you're someone with an appetite.
3 Don't long for his tidbits,
   given that it's deceptive food.
4 (g) Don't get weary in order to become wealthy;
   out of your understanding, desist.
5 Should your eyes flit upon it, it's gone,
   because it definitely makes itself wings;

105

like an eagle, it flies to the heavens.

6   (h) Don't eat the food of someone who is evil of eye,
don't be desirous of his tidbits.

7   Because like a hair in the throat, so is he;
he says to you, "Eat and drink,"
but his heart isn't with you.

8   The crust you have eaten you'll throw up,
and spoil your pleasing words.

9   (i) In the ears of a stupid person don't speak,
because he'll despise the good sense of your words.

10   (j) Don't remove an age-old boundary mark,
and don't go into the fields of orphans.

11   Because their restorer is strong;
he will contend their cause with you.

12   (k) Bring your mind to discipline,
and your ear to words of knowledge.

13   (l) Don't withhold discipline from a youth;
if you flog him with a club, he won't die.

14   You may flog him with a club,
and save his life from Sheol.

15   (m) Son, if your mind is wise,
my mind will also be glad.

16   My heart will exult,
when your lips speak with uprightness.

17   (n) Your mind must not be envious of people who offend,
but rather of [people who live in] awe for Yahweh all day.

18   Indeed there will be a future,
and your hope will not fail.

19   (o) You, my son, listen, and be wise,
and direct your mind on the way.

20   Don't be among the people who toss down wine,
among those who gorge themselves on meat.

21   Because one who tosses down and gorges will lose his
property,
and slumbering will clothe him in rags.

When I was a student and we were working in the library in
the afternoon, my friend Jim would wrap his scarf around his
head, put up the hood of his coat over his head, lean forward
onto his desk, and nap. I lacked that ability and instead would

sit with the lines on the pages of a book wavering before me as I read the same sentence several times without understanding it. Over subsequent decades I developed Jim's ability, and when I'm done with this chapter, I shall have a nap and then work better at grading student papers. In between these two stages in my sleep history over my lifetime, I did sometimes go to sleep in the afternoon, but it would tend to be for an hour or two, and after a sleep of that length I would usually be unable to do anything for the rest of the day. Now that I can nap, things are much better.

Maybe the slumbering of which Proverbs speaks at the close of this section is that kind of disabling slumber, or maybe the slumberer is someone who simply doesn't want to get out of bed in the morning. That difficulty might link with the reference to guzzling and stuffing oneself in the closing three lines. The Old Testament is enthusiastic about feasting, but it associates such indulgence with special occasions such as the harvest festival at the end of the agricultural year when people also celebrate what God did in bringing them out of Egypt. But once you unwind it may be hard to wind up again, as Proverbs has suggested earlier in describing the danger of failing to plow after harvest, if you are to have anything to harvest next year. This saying is more solemn. While the exhortation from father to son pictures it as addressed to young men, it applies at least as solemnly to heads of households. If you cannot give due attention to making the family farm work, you'll lose it. Even having something to wear depends on growing crops such as flax or having a surplus of other crops in order to barter. You can't afford to sleep off your indulgence for too long or too often.

Whereas for many chapters the sayings have been one-liners, this section and the next comprise many units of two or three lines, and the introduction apparently describes the two sections as a collection of thirty such units. I have given them the letters (a), (b), and so on. There's an Egyptian document also organized into thirty numbered units, expressed as a father's teaching for his son; this teacher, Amenemope, lived maybe a century after the time of Moses. A number of the sayings are too similar to units in Proverbs for it to be a coincidence, though Amenemope and Proverbs may be independent versions of common Middle Eastern wisdom rather than one being directly dependent on the other. The link does reflect the way Proverbs in general makes the assumption that we can learn from other people's experience of life and their reflections on it, as well as on our own within the chosen people. God set life up to make sense if people used their God-given good sense, even before they knew the fullness of who God is. But like the very opening to Proverbs, the introduction to these thirty sayings sets their teaching in the context of people's relationship with **Yahweh**, and specifically of trust in Yahweh. Its reference to "the ones who send you" will also imply that this section of Proverbs is especially concerned to offer teaching to people involved in the administration. It indicates that this administration needs to operate in the context of that trust.

The thirty sayings interweave ones where one can see a special significance for people involved in the administration and ones that are quite general in their application. Proverbs' characteristic concern for the poor is applied to the public arena (unit a), where it's possible for the people who make decisions about legal questions at the city gate to make such decisions in a way that ignores the rights and needs of poor people. Proverbs immediately brings in Yahweh's involvement in such matters. In earlier chapters its characteristic concern about anger (unit b) indicated the importance of this area for people serving the king; anger can get you in big trouble. The father's pragmatic career advice to his son is that he show himself keen and quick (unit e); the people in the dark are perhaps people who live and work in obscurity rather than with prominence in public life. He also needs to watch his table manners (unit f). The food before you is deceptive in the sense that it can tempt you into overindulgence and into giving a bad impression.

In life in general, it's wise to be careful about taking on financial commitments on behalf of other people; shaking hands refers to the formalizing of such commitments. You don't want to find the bailiffs taking away everything you possess, even the bed you lie on (unit c). It's incumbent on you to respect people's land ownership, because it's their livelihood and their life (unit d)—that commitment would have implications for the obligations of people involved in the administration. The topic recurs later (unit j) with a further reminder that Yahweh, the great restorer, will take the side of people you cheat out of their land—such as orphans after the death of their father. Within the extended family, someone with power and resources was under moral obligation to come to the help of a member of the family who was in trouble, in order to put things right and "restore" the situation to what it was supposed to be (the word is often translated "redeem"). The Old Testament takes that as an image for the way God acts on behalf of his people, and here on behalf of the individual who has been cheated of the land that is vital for the family's life.

Don't let getting wealthy become your preoccupation in life (unit g). Wealth is another deception, because it can disappear much more easily than it is gained. Parallel to the warning about eating at court is the warning about going out to dinner in ordinary life (unit h), where your host may be someone secretly looking at you with ill-feeling. He's grudging in hospitality and has perhaps invited you only because he thinks he can get something out of it. His tidbits will therefore be nothing to enjoy; they may even make you throw up, and you'll be wasting your conversation. Refuse the invitation if you can. More generally, don't waste words on someone stupid (unit i).

The listener is urged to keep accepting correction (unit k) and thus to rejoice his father (unit m) and also to be prepared to give correction because of its capacity to deliver people from a worse fate (unit l). He is to be jealous (unit n), but jealous or ambitious to emulate people who live in **awe** of Yahweh, not people who offend Yahweh. The exhortation doesn't invite listeners to a disinterested stance. They don't need to be jealous, because living in awe of Yahweh does give a person a future and a basis for hope that life will turn out OK, whereas living as an offender doesn't do so.

I'm going to have my nap now.

PROVERBS 23:22–24:22

Acquire Truth, Don't Sell It

²² (p) Listen to your father who begot you,
    and don't despise your mother when she is old.
²³ Acquire truth, don't sell it—
    wisdom, discipline, and understanding.
²⁴ The father of someone faithful will truly rejoice,
    the one who begets someone wise will rejoice in him.
²⁵ May your father and your mother rejoice,
    the one who bore you exult.
²⁶ (q) Give your mind to me, son,
    may your eyes observe my ways.
²⁷ Because an immoral woman is a deep pit,
    a foreign woman is a narrow well.
²⁸ Indeed, she lies in wait as if for prey,
    and multiplies the treacherous people among humanity.
²⁹ (r) Who says "Oh," who says "Aagh,"
    who has arguments, who has complaints,
who has wounds without reason,
    who has bleary eyes?—
³⁰ people who linger over wine,
    who come to investigate mixed wine.
³¹ Don't look at wine because it's red,
    because it gives its eye in the chalice, goes down
        smoothly.

³² At its finish it bites like a snake,
  poisons like a viper.
³³ Your eyes will see strange things,
  your mind will speak twisted things.
³⁴ You'll become like someone lying down in the midst of the
    sea,
  like someone lying down on the top of the rigging.
³⁵ "Though they hit me, I did not hurt,
  though they beat me, I did not know.
When will I wake up?—
  I'll look for it again!"
^{24:1} (s) Don't envy evil people,
  don't desire to be with them.
² Because their mind mutters violence,
  and their lips speak of oppression.
³ (t) By wisdom a house gets built,
  and by understanding it gets established.
⁴ By knowledge its rooms get filled
  with all valuable and pleasing wealth.
⁵ (u) A wise man is might itself,
  a knowledgeable person increases strength.
⁶ Because by steering you make war to your advantage,
  and deliverance comes through a multitude of advisers.
⁷ (v) Wisdom is too high for a stupid person;
  at the gate he doesn't open his mouth.
⁸ (w) While they may call one who plans to do something
    evil
    "a master of scheming,"
⁹ a stupid scheme is an offense,
  and an arrogant person is an abomination to people.
¹⁰ (x) If you show yourself weak on a day of trouble,
  your strength is in trouble.
¹¹ (y) Rescue people who are being taken off to death,
  who are tottering toward slaughter; if you hold back,
¹² when you say, "Really, we didn't know this,"
  won't the one who weighs minds perceive?
Won't the one who guards your life know,
  and render to someone in accordance with his deed?
¹³ (z) Eat honey, son, because it's good,
  liquid honey will be sweet to your palate.
¹⁴ In this way acknowledge wisdom for your spirit;

111

if you find it, there is a future—your hope will not be cut off.

15 (aa) Don't lie in wait, faithless one, at the house of a faithful person,
   don't do violence to his dwelling.

16 Because seven times a faithful person may fall, and rise,
   but the faithless will collapse through one misfortune.

17 (bb) When your enemy falls, don't rejoice,
   and when he collapses, your heart should not be glad,

18 lest Yahweh sees and it is evil in his eyes
   and he turns his anger from him.

19 (cc) Don't get heated at people who do evil things,
   don't get mad at the faithless,

20 because there is no future for the evil person;
   the lamp of the faithless goes out.

21 (dd) Be in awe of Yahweh, son, and of the king,
   and don't share with dissidents,

22 because suddenly calamity may come from them,
   ruin from them both: who can know?

As we were walking toward our car after a concert, we passed a store front where a man was working a Heidelberg letterpress printing machine. It was odd because it was 10 p.m. and because I didn't think anyone printed that way nowadays and because the man was neatly dressed (printing is a messy business). For me it also was strangely moving because my father operated a rather large version of such a machine. In fact it made me cry, and it made me cry again this morning as my wife and I discussed returning to the venue. My reaction is something to do with the fact that my father was just an ordinary working man who spent most of his work life with one of those machines, yet who had reason to be proud of his work, and I have reason to honor him as someone who (with my mother) was worth listening to as a source of wisdom, discipline, and understanding—someone not to be belittled or despised and someone who I trust had reason to rejoice in me.

So my parents fit the opening of the second half of these thirty sayings (unit p), and I don't want to grow beyond their wisdom. I don't remember their being fearful of my getting into a mess with women (unit q). Maybe that fact says something about differences in social context, which have changed since my youth. Nowadays parents would more likely worry about their daughters than about their sons and about porn and social networking sites. We noted in connection with Proverbs 5 some possible background for Proverbs' concern about "foreign" women. Here, too, the sequence whereby a general exhortation to pay heed to the wisdom that comes from one's parents leads into a warning about sex signifies the conviction that there's nothing as stupid as sexual unfaithfulness.

As I write, tomorrow is also Saint Patrick's Day, and in the United States I'm amazed as well as sad that people are clueless about Patrick's significance; he preached the gospel in Ireland after being initially captured in England or Wales and taken as a slave there. Tomorrow my favorite Irish pub will open at 6 a.m.; Saint Patrick's Day is simply an occasion for drinking large quantities of green beer. People will be proving the truth of Proverbs' warnings about how alcohol generates fights, quarrels, bleariness, an insensible inability to remember how one got into the mess one got into, and then a simple desire to start drinking again the next day (unit r). Wine or beer sparkles in the glass and looks up at you invitingly; resist its gaze, Proverbs urges. There could be a link with the exhortation not to envy evil people (unit s). They can look as if they are having a good time, but they will finally get you into trouble: maybe they will be planning some act of violence (perhaps in connection with robbing someone), or maybe the drink will take them that way. If you want to have a nice house filled with nice things, go about it the wise way, that is, the honest way (unit t). Proverbs sees nothing wrong with such a desire (as it rejoices in alcohol in moderation); the question is how you seek to fulfill it.

Likewise Proverbs sees nothing wrong with exercising power, and it sees wisdom as the key if you want to do so (unit u). This declaration leads into a comment about a particular form of the exercise of power, the power involved in winning a battle, which reminds us again of the significance of these thirty sayings for people involved in the administration. It restates Proverbs' reminder that one aspect of wisdom lies in not relying only on one's own wisdom. The second line in the unit also underlines an implication of the first. The point isn't merely that wisdom helps you attain power but that wisdom is itself a form of strength. In weight lifting, the key isn't brute strength but a knowledgeable way of using one's strength; that insight applies in life more broadly. A wise person has a strength not possessed by a physically strong but stupid person. Another indication of that fact is the way a stupid person cannot exercise influence in debates that lead to the making of decisions (unit v). Or a stupid person can present plausible-looking suggestions for doing something that is wrong and offensive to God, and eventually the community as a whole will be outraged (unit w).

The saying about showing yourself weak (unit x) involves another skillful use of related words. If leaders look weak on a day of trouble or pressure, they raise questions about themselves and may weaken their position. There could be a link with the saying about taking action when people are imperiled (unit y). On an occasion when people in danger need you to take decisive action, it's no use claiming you didn't really know what is going on. It's your job to know, and God will know you failed to exercise your responsibility. In Proverbs, one of the contexts where people's lives are in danger is where they are yielding themselves to folly and wickedness in one form or another; the exhortation would then apply to the responsibility to them that belongs to people with wisdom. We cannot simply say it's not our business. God will see that we pay for such negligence.

The saying about honey (unit z) works like a parable. At first it seems to be encouraging self-indulgence, or at least to make one ask why it's talking about something like honey. The answer comes in the second line. We need to take the same attitude to wisdom as we take to something sweet like honey. The promise attached to wisdom suggests a contrast with the preceding unit. Wisdom is an expression of the attitude that rescues you from belonging either to the company of the people on their way to death or to the company of those who fail to warn them and risk joining them. The subsequent exhortation to the **faithless** (unit aa) is perhaps really intended for overhearing by the **faithful** and wise. They don't have to fear that the faithless may be the death of them. They may fall multiple times, but they will get up again, whereas the faithless will not (cf. unit cc). But when that happens, don't celebrate (unit bb), because that reaction may cause God to become even more displeased with you than with your attacker.

The last of the thirty sayings (unit dd) returns to the specificity of life in the administration. Respect and submission are advisable both to God and to the king. Loyalty to the king is part of one's responsibility to God as well as to the king, and failure in this area can put you in trouble with both of them. Don't take the risk.

PROVERBS 24:23–25:22

On Heaping Coals

23 These also belong to the sages.

Having regard for the person in making a decision
  isn't good.

²⁴ Someone who says to the faithless person "You're in the
      right":
   peoples curse him, nations are indignant at him.
²⁵ But for people who issue reproof, it will go well,
   and upon them will come the blessing of prosperity.
²⁶ He kisses with the lips,
   the one who replies with straight words.
²⁷ Establish your work outside,
   get it ready in the fields for yourself;
   afterward build your house.
²⁸ Don't become a witness against your neighbor without
      reason;
   will you mislead with your lips?
²⁹ Don't say, "As he did to me, so I'll do him,
   I'll return to the man in accordance with his deed."
³⁰ I passed by the field of someone who was lazy,
   and by the vineyard of one lacking sense.
³¹ There: it all had come up in weeds,
   chickpeas covered its surface, its stone wall lay in ruins.
³² When I myself looked, I applied my mind;
   when I saw, I grasped a lesson.
³³ A little sleep, a little slumber,
   a little folding of the hands to lie down,
³⁴ and your poverty will come walking about,
   your want like someone with a shield.

^{25:1} These, too, are sayings of Solomon that the men of
      Hezekiah king of Judah compiled.

² It's God's honor to conceal a thing,
   and the king's honor to explore a thing;
³ the heavens regarding height, the earth regarding depth,
   and the mind of kings—there's no exploring.
⁴ Remove the dross from silver,
   and a vessel emerges for the smith;
⁵ remove the faithless person before the king,
   and his throne stands firm in faithfulness.
⁶ Don't exalt yourself before the king,
   and don't stand in the place of important people,
⁷ because it's better for someone to say to you "Come up
      here,"
   than put you down before a leader.

What your eyes have seen
⁸ should not come out into contention quickly,
   lest—what will you do at the end of it,
      when your neighbor puts you to shame?
⁹ Contend for your cause with your neighbor,
      but don't reveal the secret of another person,
¹⁰ lest someone who hears it reproach you
      and the charge against you doesn't turn away.
¹¹ Golden apricots in silver settings
      is a word appropriately spoken.
¹² A gold earring or an ornament of fine gold
      is a wise person reproving into a listening ear.
¹³ Like the cold of snow at harvest time
      is a trustworthy envoy
      to the people who sent him;
      he restores his master's spirit.
¹⁴ Clouds and wind but no rain
      is someone who boasts of a false gift.
¹⁵ Through being long-tempered a commander can be
         enticed;
      a gentle tongue can break a bone.
¹⁶ When you find honey, eat [just] enough for yourself,
      lest you get your full of it and throw up.
¹⁷ Let your foot hold back from your neighbor's house,
      lest he gets his fill of you and repudiate you.
¹⁸ A hammer, a sword, a sharpened arrow,
      is a person who testifies against his neighbor as a false
         witness.
¹⁹ A bad tooth and a wobbly foot,
      is confidence in a treacherous person on a day of trouble.
²⁰ One who takes away a coat on a cold day,
      vinegar on a wound,
      and a singer of songs to a troubled heart.
²¹ If your enemy's hungry, give him bread to eat;
      if he's thirsty, give him water to drink,
²² because you're heaping coals on his head,
      and Yahweh will reward you.

Like many Libyans involved in the rebellion against Colonel
Mu'ammar al-Gadhafi's government, Abdul Ghani
Aboughreis, a worship leader in a Tripoli mosque, could

reasonably have felt bitter against Gadhafi's supporters. He had supported the rebellion with a sermon at Friday prayers in his mosque, which became a center of resistance. Many of his people were killed; he was put in prison. Five days after the rebels gained control of the area where the prison was and released him, he was again preaching in the mosque. According to a news report, the message he was now preaching was that Libyans now needed to forgive each other, to leave the implementation of justice to the law, and not to take revenge on each other.

Both paragraphs in this section warn against the taking of revenge. The first paragraph is a kind of supplement to the thirty sayings; the second is the beginning of another collection of sayings that extends for five chapters and mixes one-liners with two-liners and some slightly longer units. The first warning (v. 29) simply says "Don't do it," without giving any reasons, in the manner of several of the Ten Commandments. Sensing no compulsion to do so, it implies that no one really needs to be given reasons for such an exhortation. People know in their heart of hearts that revenge is wrong, as they know that adultery, murder, and theft are wrong, unless perhaps they have so stifled their conscience that they have quite overlaid this awareness—in other words (in Proverbs' framework), unless they have become fools. We are created with an awareness of such obligations as aspects of being human. It fits with the fact that Amenemope (to which we referred in connection with the Thirty Sayings) and other Middle Eastern peoples had sayings similar to these. Yet our being human does include our sinfulness (our folly, in Proverbs' framework), so elsewhere the Bible indeed provides us with arguments for acting as we really know we should, and the second paragraph (vv. 21–22) does so. It goes beyond the earlier saying in suggesting that you not only refrain from taking revenge but also do something positive for the person who wrongs you. It suggests two motivations. The second is clear enough—God will reward you. Jesus' teaching thus fits with Proverbs both in urging people to **love** their enemies and in promising that they will be rewarded for shaping their lives by his teaching (e.g., Matthew 5–6). The first of the motivations is more enigmatic, though one of Amenemope's sayings refers to the other person getting full and weeping, which supports the idea that coals suggests a sense of burning shame and regret for the hostile action. In taking up the sayings, Paul notes that we thus overcome evil with good rather than being overcome by evil and driven to behave in the same way as the enemy (Romans 12).

The paragraphs include a number of other sayings about relating to your neighbors, other people in your village or your city. They begin with treating everyone the same when making decisions about some dispute (v. 23), rather than taking account of who the people are and favoring the rich over the poor or powerful people over ordinary people or Israelites over foreigners (literally, one must not take account of the face). Thus people such as the elders gathered at the gate must not make decisions in favor of the person in the wrong instead of the one in the right; everyone knows such action is wrong (v. 24). In contrast, blessing comes to people who issue reproof when reproof is warranted (v. 25). The saying about kisses (v. 26) makes a related point. When you speak straight to someone, you use your lips in a way that is similar in significance to their use in giving the kiss that indicates commitment and friendship. Conversely, don't mislead with your lips by giving testimony that has no basis (v. 28).

The other topic in the first paragraph is the need to pay proper attention to work. The results of laziness and a liking for a snooze are easy to see (vv. 30–34): a field covered in weeds, a vineyard whose wall has lost its protection from wild animals, which in turn mean poverty walking through your front door, so well-defended you'll never overcome it. But you need not only the commitment to work hard but also the insight to observe the right work priorities. It's no good giving your energy to building a nice house (maybe the saying has in mind a man building a house for him and his bride where they can live separately from his parents) at the expense of doing the work on the farm that means you'll have something to eat (v. 27).

The sayings compiled by Hezekiah's staff begin with material appropriate to people in that position. The first two (vv. 2–3) compare and contrast God and king. God is above everyone, including the king, and if God doesn't want to reveal something, it stays secret; that declaration applies to some big questions about topics such as creation and suffering. Subject to that qualification, the king has vast capacity to investigate things and sponsor research; the Old Testament pictures kings such as Solomon and Hezekiah doing so. As a one-man Supreme Court, he also has vast capacity and obligation to investigate and resolve tricky issues in the community. Further, he has the freedom to keep his thinking to himself; if he does so, his staff can do nothing about it. Their task is to ensure they eliminate from his court people who would confuse his decision making or imperil his position by the **faithlessness** of their attitude to truth or to him (vv. 4-5). They had better also make sure that they are not such people. Regarding their own position on his staff, they are wise not to push themselves forward and risk embarrassment (vv. 6-7). It's another piece of advice that Jesus takes up (see Luke 14) that contrasts with the assumption in some Western cultures that it's important to promote yourself.

When the second paragraph turns to relationships in the community, it, too, warns about unjustified accusations against one's neighbor, by urging avoidance of hasty accusation; one might end up looking stupid (vv. 7–8). If you make an accusation on the basis of confidential information from someone else, not of what you have seen, be wary of revealing your source and simply relying on what amounts to gossip, or you make things worse for yourself (vv. 9–10). Operate with wisdom in such contexts (vv. 11–12). The listening ear may be that of the elders or may be that of the neighbor; either way, a word appropriately spoken is more likely to get heard than one spoken at the wrong moment or in the wrong way. Indeed, a gentle tongue may be able to melt a tough person in the same way that you may be able to prevail over your commanding officer if you keep cool and stick with rational argument (v. 15).

The saying about honey (v. 16) leads into the one about not outstaying your welcome with your neighbor (v. 17). Then Proverbs notes the devastating implications that can attach to the giving of false testimony before the elders (v. 18). If your trouble is less serious than that of a person falsely accused and in dire danger, the unfaithfulness of a neighbor is still damaging (v. 19). Similarly, it's disappointing to be made a promise that doesn't get kept, like a time when the weather promises rain but fails to deliver (v. 14). Being unable to rely on aides you send to act on your behalf is a depressing burden, but if you can get someone to act for you **faithfully**, it's a profound and spirit-raising relief (v. 13). The saying about taking away a garment, putting vinegar on a wound, and singing to someone with a sad heart (v. 20) puts the three actions alongside each other without a verb and without any links between them except the "and" before the last phrase. It also relates to the neighbor, if it's the kind of saying that reaches its real point with its punch line.

PROVERBS 25:23–26:28

Things Complicated and Back to Front

23 A north wind may stir up rain,
    and a secretive tongue an indignant face.

²⁴ Living on a corner of the roof
    is better than an argumentative woman and a shared
      house.

²⁵ Cold water to a dry throat
    is good news from a distant land.

²⁶ A muddied spring, a ruined fountain,
    is a faithful person collapsing before a faithless person.

²⁷ Eating much honey isn't good,
    nor is it honorable to investigate people's honor.

²⁸ An open city where there's no wall
    is someone for whose spirit there's no restraint.

²⁶:¹ Like snow in summer and like rain at harvest,
    so honor is not fitting for someone stupid.

² Like a sparrow flitting and like a swallow flying,
    so humiliation without reason will not come about.

³ A whip for a horse, a bridle for a donkey,
    and a club for the back of stupid people.

⁴ Don't answer someone stupid in accordance with his
      denseness,
    lest you become like him, you too.

⁵ Answer someone stupid in accordance with his denseness,
    lest he become wise in his own eyes.

⁶ Someone cuts off his feet, drinks violence,
    sends words by someone stupid.

⁷ Legs hang down from a disabled person,
    and an aphorism in the mouth of stupid people.

⁸ Like binding a stone in a sling,
    so is one who gives honor to a stupid person.

⁹ A thorn grows in the hand of a drunk
    and an aphorism in the mouth of stupid people.

¹⁰ An archer wounding everyone
    and one who hires a stupid person or hires people
      passing through.

¹¹ As a dog returns to its vomit,
    a dense person repeats his stupidity.

¹² I've seen a person wise in his own eyes;
    there's more hope for a stupid person than for him.

¹³ A lazy person says, "There's a cougar on the road,
    a lion among the squares."

¹⁴ The door turns on its hinge,
    the lazy person on his bed.

15 The lazy person buries his hand in the bowl;
   he's too weary to bring it back to his mouth.
16 The lazy person is wiser in his own eyes
   than seven people responding with discernment.
17 One who seizes the ears of a passing dog
   is one who gets furious at a dispute that isn't his.
18 Like a madman who is shooting
   fiery arrows of death,
19 so is someone who deceives his neighbor
   and says, "I was joking, wasn't I?"
20 In the absence of wood a fire goes out,
   and when there's no gossip, arguments go quiet.
21 Charcoal for embers and wood for a fire,
   and an argumentative person for heating up contention.
22 The words of a gossip are like bites of food,
   and they go down into the inner rooms of the stomach.
23 Silver dross laid over pot,
   smooth lips but an evil mind.
24 With his lips an enemy disguises himself;
   in his heart he keeps deceit.
25 When he makes his voice gracious, don't rely on him;
   because seven abominations are in his mind.
26 His enmity conceals itself in deception;
   his evil things will reveal themselves in the congregation.
27 One who digs a pit will fall into it,
   one who rolls a stone, it will come back onto him.
28 A lying tongue repudiates the people crushed by it;
   a smooth mouth works ruin.

The time of our move to the United States in 1997 happened to be the moment when my disabled first wife, Ann, became totally wheelchair-bound. When I had been offered a job here a few months previously, she could still get about a little with a walker, but by the time of the move, that ability had gone. It was scary that the first restaurant we visited had a restroom into which you couldn't get a wheelchair (it has since closed) and that taxis didn't take wheelchairs as London taxis do, but it was encouraging that the Americans with Disabilities Act had led to improvements in accessibility in other areas of life in the United States. It was also a time when anything that looked like prejudice against disabled people was under pressure. That pressure includes a questioning of the way the Bible talks about disability and uses blindness and deafness as negative images. Ann used to laugh at this attitude, which she saw as a kind of political correctness that had lost sight of the real issues.

I don't know that we ever discussed the saying that compares legs hanging down from a disabled person (as hers did) with an aphorism in the mouth of stupid people (26:7), but I'm pretty sure she would have been amused, as she would have been by the earlier suggestion that a club is as necessary and as effective for a stupid person as a whip for a horse and a bridle for a donkey (v. 3) and by the conflicting advice about how to answer questions from stupid people (vv. 4–5). Answering such questions implies accepting that they are good questions. Perhaps the implication is that we should point out the faults in the way the question is framed or in what it takes for granted. Perhaps it's that we should simply ignore the question. Yet if we do so, we may leave the person preoccupied by it and inclined to go off and ask someone else. So it might be better to treat it as a sensible question and provide an answer that takes the person forward in some way and not simply trusting his or her own wisdom—because that wisdom is actually stupidity. And if there's anything worse than regular stupidity, it's self-delusion about how wise one is (v. 12). A related saying declares in a telling image that if we don't recognize we have made mistakes, we can't learn from them but only repeat them (v. 11). The section relates its concern with such self-delusion to another of its favorite topics, laziness, in a series of amusing but sharp vignettes (vv. 13–16). It supplements these with another vignette about someone with the opposite weakness, an inclination to interfere in other people's conflicts (v. 17), a saying with political application in the Western world where some nations are fond of getting involved in the conflicts of others.

There's a broader significance to the collocation of the sayings about answering questions from stupid people. By taking individual sayings in isolation, it's easy to provide evidence that Proverbs has a vastly oversimplified view of life. Actually, a club isn't always effective on stupid people (v. 3). It's not always the case that when there's no gossip, contention goes quiet (v. 20). And people who dig pits don't always fall into them (v. 27). The people who formulate and collect sayings are not stupid themselves; they know life is more complicated than their generalizations imply. They are capable of saying that wealth is the strong city of rich people (10:15), that wealth doesn't avail on the day of wrath (11:4), and that someone who trusts in his wealth falls (11:28). They know there's some truth in both sorts of statement. Juxtaposing the sayings about answering a stupid question makes explicit their awareness that truth is more complicated than a simpleminded quotation of one insight implies. Proverbs' teaching provides people with resources for approaching life, but they need wisdom in order to apply it wisely and to see which insight applies in a given context. It's in the absence of such wisdom that wise sayings are about as useful as legs are to a disabled person. Worse, they are about as dangerous as a thorn bush to a drunk—it may hurt the drunk or the person against whom the drunk wields it (26:7, 9).

The need for that kind of wisdom also finds expression in the way the meaning of an individual saying may require some thought. In this section, half the sayings work backward. First they make a statement about something that isn't the real subject—the north wind, a muddied spring, eating honey, an unwalled city, snow in summer, and so on. You can't make sense of the line by just reading the first half. English translations often help us along by turning the sentence around so that it becomes easier to understand, but the order is deliberate. In effect the sayings begin by raising a question you have to answer, like a riddle. What is like the north wind, a muddied spring, or eating honey? The sayings get you to involve yourself with the question rather than sitting there writing down the answer without being involved. They also get you to agree that the north wind, a muddied spring, and the consumption of too much honey are bad things, without your yet knowing what insight you're in danger of accepting. Then they tell you what the insight is; and it's too late to withdraw. You have accepted that a secretive tongue, the defeat of a **faithful** person, and seeking honor are bad things.

The sayings about legs that don't work and about responding to a stupid question relate to a recurrent theme, the significance of words. The section begins with the negative effect of a secretive tongue (25:23), which implies an unwillingness to keep confidences, and then with argumentativeness (v. 24). Later sayings implicitly recognize that contentiousness isn't just a woman's problem, that gossip and a contentious inclination encourage contentiousness but that gossip is hard for either giver or receiver to resist (26:20–22). On the other hand, unjustified denigration will get no further than the aimless flight of little birds (v. 2). While receiving good news is like a drink of cold water on a hot day (25:25), sending words by means of someone stupid (26:6) is likely to cause so much trouble (it will never get there, or it will get garbled, or it will be delivered in undiplomatic fashion) that it's like cutting off your own feet or willfully stirring up violence. More generally, hiring someone stupid or someone passing through who has no obligation to you is likely to end in trouble (v. 10). The same is true of deceptiveness that one claims not to have been serious (vv. 18–19), whether one is being honest or dishonest. Nice words can conceal treacherous intent and may crush people, but this intent will eventually be exposed and the deception will backfire (vv. 23–28).

That promise envisages a proper reversal of things. Other reversals are to be bemoaned. There's the faithful person overcome by the **faithless** person (25:26), perhaps before the elders at the city gate when someone who is in the right has a decision go the wrong way. There's the honoring of someone stupid (26:1); the comparison with a stone in a sling (v. 8) perhaps suggests that it fails to achieve the point. But the fact that honor is to be welcomed doesn't mean that preoccupation with prestige is appropriate (25:27).

PROVERBS 27:1–27

Faithful Are the Wounds of a Friend

1 Don't boast about tomorrow,
      because you don't know what the day will give birth to.
2 A stranger should boast about you and not your mouth,
      a foreigner and not your lips.
3 A stone is weighty and sand is heavy,
      but a stupid person's vexation is heavier than both of
         them.
4 There is the cruelty of fury and the flooding of anger,
      but who can stand before passion?
5 Open reproof
      is better than concealed friendship.
6 The wounds of a friend are trustworthy;
      the kisses of an enemy are importunate.
7 A full person despises honey,
      but as for a hungry person: anything bitter is sweet.
8 Like a sparrow flitting from its nest,
      so is a person flitting from his home.
9 Oil and incense gladden the heart,
      and the sweetness of one's friend more than one's own
         counsel.
10 Don't abandon your friend or your father's friend,
      or go to your brother's house on your day of calamity.
    Better one who dwells near

than a brother far away.

11 Be wise, son, and gladden my heart,
  so that I may respond to someone who insults me with a
    word.

12 When a shrewd person sees something evil, he hides;
  naive people pass on and pay the penalty.

13 Take his coat, because he made a pledge to a strange man;
  bind him, on account of a foreign woman.

14 One who blesses his neighbor in a loud voice in the
    morning early:
  it will be counted for him as humiliating [his neighbor].

15 A continuing drip on a rainy day
  and an argumentative woman are alike.

16 One who hides her hides the wind,
  and oil on his right hand announces her.

17 Iron sharpens iron,
  and a person sharpens the edge of his friend.

18 One who guards a fig tree will eat its fruit,
  and one who watches his master will be honored.

19 Like water, face-to-face,
  so the heart of a person to a person.

20 Sheol and Abaddon don't get full,
  and the eyes of a human being don't get full.

21 The crucible for silver, the furnace for gold,
  and an individual with regard to his praise.

22 If you grind a stupid person in a mortar,
  in the midst of the grain in a pestle,
  his stupidity will not depart from him.

23 You should really know the faces of your flock,
  apply your attention to your herds,

24 because wealth isn't forever
  or a crown for generation after generation.

25 The hay goes away and the new grass appears
  and the growth of the mountains is gathered.

26 The lambs are for your clothing,
  the goats for the price of a field,

27 enough goats' milk for your food,
  for food for your household and life for your young girls.

Austin Farrer, the warden (that is, president) of my
undergraduate college, was one of the great preachers of the

day, though more for the wisdom and insight of his content than for the singsong style of his delivery. My friends and I didn't necessarily make a point of going to chapel on evenings when we had already been there on Sunday mornings, but if he was preaching we would be there. On one occasion he preached on Christian joy and told the congregation that Christian joy didn't consist in greeting your neighbor in a loud voice early in the morning; whereupon my friends in several parts of the chapel looked around at me.

His quotation came from this section (v. 14), and I suppose it's no use my denying its applicability, especially as my wife also protests at my enthusiasm for getting up and getting on with things in the morning (though she wishes to point out that she is also cheerful and says "I love you" on waking). How otherwise would I get The Old Testament for Everyone done? I've already noted in this volume that I have to apply to this project the warning about not boasting about tomorrow (v. 1). Who knows whether I shall be able to fulfill the schedule that raised the editor's eyebrows in agreeing that I would take on the project? I must also make sure I don't get too pleased with myself as I enter the homestretch, with just four more volumes to go (v. 2). Let others decide whether it was a good idea. I must continue not taking myself too seriously. I don't have too much problem with anger, either; I wouldn't want to weigh other people down with a stupid person's vexation (v. 3), nor with the wrong kind of passion (v. 4)—in this context, the Hebrew word for "passion" will have its more specific connotation of jealousy or envy. I can occasionally envy other scholars because of their books that I wish were mine or the repute or influence that they have that I might wish were mine.

If I seem to take myself too seriously, get angry too often, or get consumed by envy, it will be my friends' job to tell me. A friend tells you things straight (vv. 5–6). You can assume that you should trust a friend's hurtful statements, as well-meant and likely reliable. That principle even applies if the rebuke is uttered in public, which is better than support that a person keeps secret and certainly better than the effusive friendliness of someone who may actually be against you. As an iron whetstone sharpens the edge of an iron weapon or tool, a person sharpens the "edge" of a friend (v. 17). Only stupid people are incorrigibly dull (v. 22), behave in a way that fails to give their parents something to boast about (v. 11), fail to notice dangers they are walking into (v. 12), or make pledges to people who may disappear and leave them with their obligation (v. 13).

The principle of wariness about effusive displays of purported support also provides one context in which to apply the saying about honey (v. 7). If you have good friends, you'll not be itching for affirmation; if you lack such friends, you may be gullible and may mistake enmity for friendship. In turn, maybe the saying about leaving home (v. 8) complements the one about friends. Proverbs would then compare with two attitudes that surface in Western culture. We have some sympathy with the Greek and Roman view that a man's friends are likely to be men and that a woman's friends are likely to be women. Yet we are often inclined to assume that our spouse should be our best friend and to yearn for it to be so, and I can be sure that my wife will not let me down when I need a friendly, straight rebuke. Perhaps the further saying about the contentious wife (v. 15) indicates that Proverbs shares the assumption of the Romans and the Greeks, and perhaps it reminds a man of the danger of receiving loving rebuke as contentiousness or of ignoring such rebukes and having them turn into contentiousness. The companion saying (v. 16) may also be double-edged. A wife might take it as a compliment that trying to control your wife is like trying to control the wind; the point about the oil on your hand may be that you can't avoid taking her and her perfume with you even when you think you have escaped her.

The inadvisability of leaving home may also underlie the double saying about abandoning your friend or your father's friend (v. 10), if the idea is that a friend near home is a wiser resource in a crisis than a brother who lives far away.

Our friends' rebuke and counsel are important as safeguards against trusting our own instincts (v. 9); they are even sweeter than expensive luxuries. It might not be surprising if some Israelites (like some Westerners) found incense got into their eyes and up their nose, and thus they didn't find it sweet. Similarly, a friend's counsel may not seem sweet. But if the only counsel you get is sweet, do you have any real friends? Or are you just choosing to hang out with flatterers or people whose nice words counteract your poor image of yourself?

The chapter has further insights on the individual and on our self-knowledge. Proverbs 17 noted that **Yahweh** needs to test our hearts or inner beings; we can be self-deceived. At the same time, the inner person is the core of the being, so the inner being indicates the real person. An individual needs to look inside to find the real person, not be taken in by the image one wants to project. The saying about seeing one's reflection in water (v. 19) makes the point; it may imply that another person also needs to look into the inner being to find the real person, not simply to take for granted the outward projection. The succeeding sayings nuance the point. Consider your desires and their all-consuming nature (v. 20). Consider the way you respond to praise or consider the objects of your praise or consider what kind of people praise you (v. 21).

A positive counterpart to Proverbs' recurrent warnings about laziness comes in the description of the kind of work in which most Israelites would be involved. Positively, keep a close eye on your herd and flock. Good shepherds know their sheep, and the faces in one's flock and herd will indicate something of how well they are—as is so with human beings.

Wealth and a crown are all very well, but they don't last. A farmer sees that he and his family can have a future. There's an annual cycle about the growth of the fodder that the animals need, and if you look after them, they will provide you what you need by way of clothing and food (the young girls are maybe mentioned because of their key role in looking after flocks).

The straightforward meaning of the lines thus makes entire sense, though if the man who literally wore the crown and acted as the nation's shepherd read it as an allegory of the way he needed to conduct his care for his flock, the authors of Proverbs would hardly object. It would be the other side of the coin in relation to the saying about caring for a fig tree (v. 18).

PROVERBS 28:1–28

For Lenten Thought

¹ The faithless flee when there's no one pursuing,
    but faithful people are as confident as a lion.
² When there's rebellion in the country,
    its rulers are many,
  but when there's someone who understands,
    someone who knows, stability will last long.
³ A man who is poor and who oppresses the destitute:
    rain that is beating down and there's no bread.
⁴ People who abandon instruction praise the faithless
      person;
    people who keep instruction fight against them.
⁵ Evil people don't understand the exercise of authority,
    but people who seek guidance from Yahweh understand
      everything.
⁶ Better a poor person walking in integrity,
    than someone crooked in his ways, but rich.
⁷ An understanding son guards instruction,
    but one who befriends gluttons disgraces his father.

8 Someone who increases his wealth by means of interest
    and profiteering,
      amasses it for someone who will be gracious to the poor.
9 One who turns his ear from listening to instruction:
    even his prayer is an abomination.
10 The person who misleads the upright into an evil way—
    he'll fall into his own pit,
      but people of integrity come to possess good things.
11 A rich person is wise in his own eyes,
    but a poor person of understanding sees through him.
12 At the exulting of the faithful there is much glorying,
    but at the rise of the faithless, people have to be searched
      for.
13 One who covers his rebellions will not succeed,
    but one who confesses and forsakes will be shown
      compassion.
14 The blessings of the person who is continually in awe!—
    but the person who stiffens his resolve falls to
      misfortune.
15 A roaring lion or a prowling bear:
    a faithless ruler over a poor people.
16 A leader lacking understanding and big in acts of
      oppression...;
    one who repudiates dishonest gain will extend his days.
17 One oppressed by the murder of someone will flee to the
      Pit;
    people should not hold him back.
18 A person who walks in integrity will find deliverance,
    but one who is crooked in his ways will fall at one of
      them.
19 One who serves his land will be full of food,
    but one who pursues empty things will be full of poverty.
20 A person of trustworthy deeds will be rich in blessings,
    but one hasty to get rich will not go innocent.
21 Having regard for the person isn't good,
    but a man will rebel for a piece of bread.
22 One who is evil in eye hurries for wealth
    and doesn't acknowledge that lack will come to him.
23 One who reproves a person in the end
    will find more grace than one who makes his tongue
      smooth.
24 One who robs his father and his mother

and says "It's not an act of rebellion"—
he is a companion of one who destroys.
25 One broad of appetite provokes argument,
but one who trusts in Yahweh will be refreshed.
26 One who trusts in his own mind—he is stupid,
but one who walks in wisdom—he will escape.
27 One who gives to a poor person—there is no lack,
but one who shuts his eyes—many are the curses.
28 When the faithless rise up, a people hide,
and when they perish, the faithful become many.

It's the third week in Lent, and we have the third of our Lent Study Groups this evening. The group is studying the Psalms, and I've been excited at the way people have been finding this a means of discovering new resources for their praying, as they have been doing their "homework" each week (I didn't call it homework). At the same time, I'm aware that the book of Psalms begins by reminding people that a relationship with God works only if you're studying **Torah** and putting it into practice.

These themes come together in Proverbs 28. Lent is a time for us to confess and forsake our rebellions rather than trying unsuccessfully to conceal them, and a time when we can find compassion, and a time to be in **awe** rather than stiffening our resolve (vv. 13–14). Proverbs' talk about rebellion and awe could apply in relation to human authorities and to God, though we might think that the first involves more risk than the second. It would take some courage to come clean with the king that you'd been plotting a coup d'état, believing he will have mercy on you. Maybe one point of the saying is to encourage the king himself to take that attitude. The chapter adds the comment that such rebellion makes for ongoing disorder (v. 2), as the story of the northern kingdom in Israel indicates. That story relates coup after coup and also provides evidence for Proverbs' contention that a country's lack of stability derives from its rulers' lack of wisdom (in Proverbs' sense of awe for **Yahweh**). The slightly incoherent saying about the stupid, oppressive ruler (v. 16) makes a related point. In the context, one might apply to the king the following saying about someone oppressed by a murder (v. 17), given that kings were in particular danger of causing people's undeserved death; it declares that murderers are on the way to **Sheol**, and so they should be. The next saying (v. 18) generalizes the point about crooked people finding no deliverance, and it might again apply in particular to a ruler. Related to these insights are other devastating effects of a people's ruler being **faithless** (v. 15) and the way society collapses and people make themselves scarce when **faithlessness** comes to rule the country (vv. 12, 28).

Is it easier to have that expectation of God than of the human king? Many people are afraid of God and his wrath, but the Bible likens God to a (good) father or mother. Come clean, and you'll find compassion (no doubt, like many parents, God knows about things before we come clean, but the health of the relationship involves our taking the action). Lent is a good time to come clean and forsake the things we need to forsake, in that confidence. But then so is any time. The same applies to being in awe of God. That previous line makes clear that awe is different from fear (the word that comes in some English translations). You don't have to be afraid of the king or of God. You do need to be in awe and to be submissive. It's the opposite of stiffening your resolve. In other contexts that toughness can be an asset, but this expression is the one used of Pharaoh in Exodus when he is resisting God. His story shows it's a bad idea. Proverbs associates awe and trust, rather than seeing them as in tension: God is someone solid whom we can lean on because of his great strength and also someone of great compassion into whose arms we can fall. This chapter begins with the confidence that a faithful life makes possible, a confidence that contrasts with the fear that overwhelms faithless people, or should overwhelm them (v. 1).

One could reconceptualize awe before God as seeking guidance from God (v. 5). This saying is the only one where Proverbs speaks of seeking guidance or help from God; it more often speaks of seeking wisdom, which in its framework would have similar meaning. It's another Lenten motif. It makes the extraordinary promise that seeking from God issues in an understanding of everything. The nature of "everything" is nuanced by the warning that evil people don't understand the proper exercise of **authority**, the way to make the right kind of decisions in the community. Actually they don't want to understand it; that disinclination is the nature of their evil. But people who look to God will know how to make all the decisions that need to be made in a fair and proper way. They will have real wisdom rather than fooling themselves and will also escape calamity (v. 26).

The chapter emphasizes "instruction"; it uses this term four times. It's the word *torah*, which in a context such as Psalm 1 refers to "Yahweh's Instruction" whose supreme embodiment of is "the Torah of Moses," to which we usually refer as the Law of Moses. In Proverbs the word *torah* is used in its broader sense to refer to the instruction of parents or the instruction of the wise, but much of the content of this instruction will be the same. So here, following torah means fighting faithless people rather than praising them (v. 4). It means not associating with gluttons—in other words, not following their lifestyle (v. 7); moderation in food and drink is a virtue in Proverbs, and the common motif of Lenten discipline fits this emphasis. And it means God may listen to your prayers; at least, failing to heed torah means your prayer becomes an abomination to God (v. 9), like arrogance or dishonesty. That shocking declaration corresponds to Psalm 1 and to the warnings of the Prophets and also provides food for Lenten thought for people who are learning new lessons about prayer.

At least as telling is the sad observation that even poor people may oppress poor people (v. 3); they then become like the driving rain that can destroy crops. While it's nice to think that hardship brings people together, it can make every family concerned only for itself: Imagine that you're the head of a family whose own children are crying out for something to eat. You could be tempted to get involved in falsifying justice for the sake of something to eat (v. 21). Better to be a poor person walking in integrity, even if you have little, than someone crooked in his ways but rich or eating well (v. 6). You may well have more understanding about life than rich people (v. 11). It's better to be someone who is doing just OK than someone who makes his pile by lending to the poor and charging them interest, which the Torah forbids (lending is to be a way of supporting the needy rather than a way of making money). The warning is that you won't retain your profit but will lose it to someone who is gracious to the poor (v. 8; compare v. 20). It's people of integrity who will come to possess good things (v. 10).

It's much worse to be someone who robs his own parents of the means to live when he has taken over the family farm as they grow older and who is without conscience about it (v. 24). More generally, having an eye to the main chance and paying no attention to needy people will mean you end up needy yourself (v. 22; compare v. 27). Such greed also produces division and conflict in the community (v. 25). Conversely, you may even find that reproving someone for greed (among other things) builds up relationships in the community (v. 23). As usual, Proverbs combines its concern for the poor with the awareness that they need to be able to avoid the charge of having brought their poverty on themselves through their laziness or their having given their energy to projects other than tending their land (v. 19).

PROVERBS 29:1–27
You Could Suddenly Break, and There Could Be No Healing

1 A person of many reproofs who stiffens his neck
   will suddenly break, and there will be no healing.
2 When the faithful increase, the people rejoice,
   but when a faithless person rules, the people groan.
3 Someone who gives himself to wisdom rejoices his father,
   but someone who keeps company with immoral women
      destroys wealth.
4 A king gives a country stability by his exercise of authority,
   but a man inclined to taxes tears it down.
5 A man who flatters his neighbor
   spreads a net for his feet.
6 In an evil person's rebellion there is a snare,
   but a faithful person resounds and rejoices.
7 A faithful person acknowledges the cause of the poor;
   a faithless person doesn't understand acknowledgment.
8 People who mock stir up a town,
   but the wise turn away anger.
9 A wise person may dispute with a stupid person,
   but he'll rage and joke and there will be no peace.
10 Murderous people may repudiate someone of integrity,
    but the upright will have recourse to the person.
11 A stupid person expresses all his feelings;
    a wise person holds them back.
12 A ruler who pays attention to words that are false:
    all his ministers will be faithless.
13 A poor man and a man given to acts of violence meet:
    Yahweh enlightens the eyes of them both.
14 A king who decides for the poor in truth:
    his throne will stand firm forever.
15 Club and reproof give wisdom,
    but a youth let loose shames his mother.
16 When the faithless increase, rebellion increases,
    but the faithful will see their downfall.
17 Discipline your son and he'll let you have peace,
    and give much delight to your spirit.
18 When there is no vision, the people throw off restraint,
    but the person who guards instruction—his blessings!
19 By words a servant will not be disciplined,

because he understands but there's no response.
20 If you see someone hasty with his words,
 there's more hope for a stupid person than for him.
21 Someone who indulges his servant from youth:
 at the end he'll become his offspring.
22 An angry person provokes arguments,
 and a hot-tempered person rebels much.
23 An individual's majesty will make him fall,
 but one lowly of spirit will attain honor.
24 Someone who divides [the proceeds] with a thief
 repudiates himself;
 he hears the oath and doesn't tell.
25 A person's anxiety sets a snare,
 but one who trusts in Yahweh will be kept safe.
26 Many seek audience with a ruler,
 but a person's decision comes from Yahweh.
27 A wrongdoer is an abomination to the faithful,
 and someone upright in his way is an abomination to the
 faithless person.

The news is full of the story of a soldier in the U.S. army who ran amok and killed sixteen people in Afghanistan. When we discussed it at our Lent group last night as we prayed a psalm for him and for his victims, one of the participants talked about his own experience as a soldier in Afghanistan and Iraq. He could quite understand how a man in his fourth tour of duty in a context of that kind could snap. He desperately wants to get home and resents the fact that the people in the country where he's posted are the cause of his being there. An action of the kind this man undertook expresses his resentment, and it means he gets home. For the participant in our group, a relationship he developed with the chaplain's driver, with whom he often shared watch duty, not only kept him going but changed his life; the driver was always telling him about things in the Bible, and it led him to become someone who read the Bible.

His story resonates with Proverbs. People in the military are people who receive many reproofs (v. 1). An army's functioning depends on an interiorized discipline that says "Yes sir," without thinking about it. Yet the discipline may go against the grain. There may be an inner locus of resistance within a person. Indeed, there needs to be such a locus, otherwise the person may be open to undertaking actions that should be resisted. It also means that the person may become resistant and suddenly break, and there may be no healing; it's hard to see how there could be healing in that story about Afghanistan. The story we were told at the group also illustrates how anxiety acts as a snare for the anxious person, but trust in God can make all the difference (v. 25). It's tempting to think that your commanding officer is the person whose authority ultimately counts, but it's not so (v. 26).

In an evil person's rebellion there's thus a snare—that is, the rebellion is a trap that the rebel falls into; in contrast, **faithful** people will have reason for loud rejoicing over the way their lives turn out (v. 6). Wrongdoers and **faithless** people on one side, upright people and faithful people stand inexorably over against each other (v. 27). Yet in what sense is that soldier an evil person? One of yesterday's commentators observed that it's dangerous for the rest of us to assume that he's inherently much worse a person than the rest of us. He was a man under terrible pressure. Who is to say that we would have survived the pressure better than he did? Even the man in our group who offered a clue about such survival was still saying, "there but for the grace of God go I." In effect he was taking account of something a poor man and someone given to acts of violence have in common, the fact that **Yahweh** enlightens the eyes of both of them (v. 13). Someone who acts violently to the poor needs to take that fact into account; the poor person can also find encouragement in it. The saying about people dividing up the proceeds of theft, and withholding evidence when the elders consider the crime, makes the point in another vivid way (v. 24); such people are doing themselves a disservice.

It's a related insight that mockery stirs up a town, but the wise turn back anger (v. 8). I sometimes discuss with a friend the temptation to fall into naiveté (my temptation) or into cynicism (his temptation). Mockery is related to cynicism; it suspects motivation and has a hard time believing in good news. Naiveté is gullible and believes when it should question. Wisdom knows when to question and when to believe. When cynics dismiss the plans of the town's leaders that are designed to deal with some issue arousing strong feeling in the town, wise people in the community have to decide whether the anger the cynics encourage will simply make things worse. They also have to take into account the likelihood that they will not get far with the mockers themselves (v. 9). The mockers are a variant on the stupid who hold back none of their feelings (literally, none of their spirit), whereas the wise are more restrained (v. 11). The mockers are not only stupid but dangerous, in the way they both provoke conflict and show how anger leads to rebellion (v. 22). The mocker is closely related to the person who has no mechanism for censoring his own words, who is a hopeless case (v. 20); I also recognize that criticism of myself.

The wise will recognize that the cynics may well be right to suspect the motivation of the community's leadership. Murderous instincts are not confined to people under terrible pressure. They can be felt by people who get into leadership, want to do well for themselves, and are willing to trample on people of integrity in order to do so (v. 10). The chapter contains a number of other observations on leadership. It notes how the community grieves when its ruler is a faithless person (they know they will suffer) but rejoices when faithful people increase in number in its midst (v. 2). A ruler can be someone willing to pay attention to "information" that he knows to be false; if he is, then he encourages faithlessness in his entire government (v. 12). That willingness will have implications for ordinary people, because faithless people won't be interested in policies that take account of the poor (v. 7). That facts links with the way a king can give his country stability by the way he exercises his governmental **authority** but can be inclined to multiple taxes to finance his lifestyle, his war-making plans, and his building projects. He can thus tear down that stability by undermining people's economic viability (v. 4), as Samuel warned Israel when they dreamed up the idea of having a king. The real measure of government is how the poorest and the least important people are doing, not how much success *some* of the people are experiencing. Whether or not he sees that his decisions work out well for the poor makes a difference to the stability of his own throne, too (v. 14). Encouraging faithlessness in the government and in the country is likely to rebound on him (v. 16). Similar implications likely attach to the saying about vision and instruction (v. 18), if it suggests the importance of a leader's paying attention to the instruction of the wise and being open to a message from God, which are key to his blessing and to maintaining social order.

The chapter incorporates a number of sayings relating to the family. It offers some variants on the recurrent emphasis that children need to heed parents and parents to discipline children (vv. 3, 15, 16). Disciplining one's teenage or young adult children may involve violence; letting them do what they like may mean they bring shame on you (v. 15). Disciplining them promises peace and delight to your spirit (v. 17). Offspring giving themselves to wisdom means joy for their parents, but one way in which their going astray sexually is stupid is the loss it brings (v. 3). As Proverbs assumes elsewhere, sexual looseness is the embodiment of stupidity. The other side of the coin within the family is that if a father treats a servant as a son, he may end up as his heir (v. 21). Such treatment means disciplining the servant forcefully, just as much as a son, because mere words may get you nowhere, any more than they do with a son (v. 19). The implication isn't that people can regard their servants as their property, which they can treat as they like; Exodus 21 is explicit on that point. Elsewhere Proverbs implies that a servant taking the place of a son is an inversion of proper order, so perhaps the point about the saying is to act as a warning to a recalcitrant son. He needs to watch it lest he changes places with a servant.

The recipients of wisdom teaching, and everyone else, need to be wary of flattery and of taking themselves too seriously (vv. 5, 23).

PROVERBS 30:1–14

I'm Just a Weary Sojourner, but I Have Some Words from God

1 The words of Agur son of Jaqeh. The oracle. The utterance
    of the man to Ithiel, to Ithiel and Ukal.
2 Because I am more a brute than a person,
    and I don't have human understanding.
3 I have not learned wisdom
    and I don't possess knowledge of the holy ones.
4 Who has gone up to the heavens and come down,
    who has collected the wind in his open hands?
  Who has confined the waters in a cloak,
    who has established all the boundaries of the earth?
  What is his name and what is his son's name,
    if you know?

5 Every word of God is tested;
    he is a shield to those who rely on him.
6 Don't add to his words,
    lest he reprove you and you prove a liar.
7 Two things I ask of you;
    don't hold back from me before I die.
8 Emptiness and a lying word keep far from me,
    poverty and riches do not give me,
    let me grab the food that is my due.
9 Lest I get full and renounce and say, "Who is Yahweh?"
    or lest I get poor and rob, and take the name of my God.

10 Don't mention a servant to his master,
     lest he humiliate you and you pay the penalty.

11 A company that humiliates its father
     and doesn't bless its mother!
12 A company that is pure in its own eyes,
     but its filth isn't washed off!
13 A company—how their eyes are high,
     and their eyelids rise!
14 A company whose teeth are swords and their jaws knives,
     to consume the lowly from the earth, the needy from
       humanity!

My wife sits at the desk next to mine working harder than me
at a course that is part of her degree program. There's some
kind of incompatibility between the subject and/or the
teacher's method of teaching that is driving Kathleen mad.
She spent three times as many hours on the work over the
first three weeks of the term and still got a B so far instead of
her usual A. Nor does she think she's really learning, though I
expect that conviction will turn out to be mistaken. It often
seems so with her as with other students, and it will in due
time probably emerge that she's learning a lot. But the
experience is frustrating, and all she can do apart from send
the professor emails and mutter to me is make herself sit
down and work at the material, day in and day out.

It looks as if Agur had the same feeling on a broader front
than Kathleen does. We don't know who Agur, Jaqeh, Ithiel, or
Ukal were, and it wouldn't be surprising if they were
foreigners, like Lemuel in the next chapter and like the
characters in the book of Job. They thus reflect the
international links of Proverbs that emerged in the Thirty
Sayings in chapters 22–24, and they testify to the awareness
that people outside Israel have their wisdom to share, even to
share with Israel. **Yahweh** isn't merely a God who makes
himself known to the chosen people. Other people can
discover truth about God and about life, even if they can't

discover the key truths about what God has done to set about the deliverance and restoration of the entire world by getting involved with Israel.

Agur also reminds us of the Mesopotamian seer Balaam in Numbers 22–24, to whom God appears and whom God uses to bless Israel. "Oracle" is a word you would use to describe a prophecy; so is "utterance," which is in fact a word used to describe Balaam's prophecy. So Balaam's story and Agur's story also testify to God's freedom to speak to and through people outside Israel, not just Israelites.

Yet what God has to say though Agur is then rather paradoxical. It's basically, I don't understand anything. The book of Proverbs is working its way toward an intriguing ending. We have noted that it often gives the impression that it has the answers to life's big questions and the rules for how life works all sown up. Its awareness that things are really more complicated than any one saying implies now becomes more explicit. Its last chapters form a mirror image of its opening chapters. Chapters 1–9 spoke of wisdom as conveying an understanding of revelation and creation; Agur denies having such an understanding. Proverbs as a whole is thus a mirror image of Job and Ecclesiastes. Proverbs focuses on confident assertions but forbids us to take them as tying everything into a neat package. Job and Ecclesiastes focus on raising questions but forbid us to take their questions as indicating that they have no answers.

Another feature of Agur's opening words underscores his emphasis. Alongside the fact that we don't know anything about the four named people is the fact that the names ring bells in another sense, particularly the last two. The phrase "to Ithiel" is virtually the same as the Hebrew for "I'm weary, God," while "and Ukal" is virtually the same as the Hebrew for "and I am exhausted." So Agur is more or less saying "I'm weary, God; I'm weary, God, and I'm exhausted." Such words lead well into what follows. Agur has given himself to seeking to understand the big questions about life and has failed. Paradoxically, his oracle from God, his utterance from God, is that you have to acknowledge that we don't know the answers to those questions—at least we don't know them "under the sun," as Ecclesiastes puts it; we cannot know them on the basis of ordinary, everyday human experience. I am no better off than an animal in this respect, Agur acknowledges. I don't have the kind of understanding that angels have. Nobody else does either. He follows up his declaration concerning his ignorance with some questions that invite us to acknowledge that he isn't alone; no human being has the knowledge he's talking about. Nobody has been able to go up to the heavens and master the cosmos in order to understand it. Maybe these questions point to a significance in Agur's own name, which is related to the Hebrew word for a resident alien and could be understood to mean "I abide as an alien, I sojourn." I'm just a temporary resident in this world. What would I know?

So we are dependent on God's reaching down to us. We can have the understanding we yearn for only if God gives it. And we do have such a revelation, the second paragraph assumes. The description of Agur as someone with an oracle, an utterance, isn't merely ironic, as if his prophetic utterance had only the gloomy implications of his opening lines. It has the positive connotations it should have. We have words from God that are tested, that we can rely on, and that we would be unwise to attempt to expand on. The phrases Agur uses come from other parts of the Old Testament, such as Deuteronomy and Psalm 18, which support the assumption that the revelation Agur refers to is that contained in the **Torah** and elsewhere in the Old Testament, which speaks of God coming down to act and to speak.

Adding to God's words would make one a liar. Agur isn't merely referring to a specific untruth but to being turned into someone who has more comprehensively been exposed as someone who doesn't serve God's words but betrays them—

virtually an apostate. Agur therefore prays that he may not become a liar and that neither poverty nor wealth may have the effect of making him turn from God, as both can for different reasons.

The line about not talking about a servant to his master (not complaining or informing), lest he insult you for interfering, seems to stand on its own. In the subsequent four sayings we might see Agur declaiming the kind of word of God to which he has referred, like a prophet, denouncing what he sees as besetting temptations of the community in which he lives.

PROVERBS 30:15–33

Creation and Numbers

15 The leech has two daughters, "Give, give!"—
    three things don't get full, four don't say "Plenty!"—
16 Sheol, a barren womb, a country that isn't full of water,
    and fire that doesn't say "Plenty!"

17 The eye that mocks a father
    and despises a mother's teaching:
    the ravens in the wash will gouge it out,
    and young eagles will eat it.

18 Three things are too extraordinary for me,
    four I don't know:
19 an eagle's way in the heavens, a snake's way on a crag,
    a ship's way in the heart of the sea, and a man's way with
      a girl.
20 Such is the way of an adulterous woman:
    she eats and wipes her mouth and says, "I haven't done
      wrong."

21 Under three things the earth shudders,
    and under four that it cannot bear:
22 under a servant when he becomes king,
    under a mindless person when he's full of food,

147

23   under a woman who has been repudiated when she
          marries,
      and under a servant when she replaces her mistress.

24   There are four smallest things on earth,
          but they are the wisest of the wise.
25   Ants are a people that are not strong,
          but they provide their food in summer.
26   Hyraxes are a people that are not mighty,
          but they make their home in a crag.
27   Locusts have no king,
          but they go out organized, all of them.
28   You can take hold of a lizard in your hands,
          but it's in the palaces of a king.

29   Three things are good in their stride,
          four that are good in moving.
30   The lion is the warrior among beasts;
          it doesn't turn back from before anyone.
31   One belted around the thighs, or a goat, and a king—
          no rising against him.

32   If you've been mindless in exalting yourself,
          and if you've schemed—hand on your mouth!
33   Because pressing milk produces butter,
          pressing the nose produces blood,
          and pressing anger produces contention.

A skunk shuffled along the grass walkway beyond our patio in broad daylight the other day, which was odd because skunks are nocturnal creatures. They are beautiful but anxiety-making because of the extraordinary stink they can produce when they are threatened. A few minutes later the skunk shuffled past again, and again. We watched and realized it was a mother (we inferred) carrying her newborn babies one by one from the nest where she had given birth to some other location. At first we thought the reason she was taking them somewhere was that they were all dead, but a little skunk research suggested there was no need for that gloomy inference; she was simply taking them from her winter semi-hibernal, birthing home to the new place where she would look after them as they grew. She seemed an embodiment of motherly care.

Proverbs assumes there are lots of things to learn from animals. It's not so surprising; elsewhere the Bible describes how the same God created human beings and animals, and science assumes we're related to them. Proverbs here starts with leeches, which are virtually insatiable in their bloodsucking. The paragraph noting this fact is also one of several using numbers in a way that propounds a kind of riddle. What are the two or three or four things that are insatiable? They are death; an infertile woman's longing for a child; a country like Canaan that doesn't get enough rain; and a fire that can consume a whole forest or city.

The next paragraph speaks of animals to observe in a more frightening connection. They not only teach but also are the means whereby a fate we deserve comes on us. The saying about the raven and the eagle thus again assumes the oneness of the animate and human creation but also sees the animate creation as part of the interconnected reality whereby wrong or stupid deeds have their "natural" consequences. It thus allies the animate world with wisdom. Ignore wisdom and the animate world sees you pay the price for your stupidity. Proverbs constantly contradicts the old saying that "ignorance is bliss."

There follows a further paragraph combining numbers and creatures. What are the three or four things that seem quite extraordinary? They are the flight of an eagle, the darting of a snake, the tossing and adventurousness of a ship, and the nature of human lovemaking. Here Proverbs invites us to put together realities we would not think belong together and to see what they have in common. The saying about the adulterous woman forms a painful coda to the paragraph; it might even be its point. You can rejoice with wonder at the love of a man and a woman, but you have to grieve with disbelief when marriages that start with such bliss go so wrong. Last night we watched a movie called *Young Adult* about a sad divorced woman who returns to her hometown to try to win back her onetime sweetheart, now married with a baby. In effect she wipes her mouth and says, "I haven't done anything wrong." He really belongs with me— he's not happy with her. The sadness in a man's or a woman's life can make them look at situations solely from their individual angle.

The third numerical saying makes no reference to the animate world but starts from the earth itself and exposes another aspect of the unity of creation. Indeed, it deconstructs the distinction between the animate and inanimate creation by portraying the earth itself as unable to bear what it sees. An earthquake involves earth shuddering at what it witnesses. Proverbs is socially conservative in the sense that it's aware of the danger when the social order gets turned upside down. Yet it hardly implies that the three or four things that make the earth anxious are a list of things that are all inherently wrong. At least, that is true of the nice circumstance that a woman who has been turned down or divorced may end up able to marry. More likely the section concerns the way people doing very well against all the odds *can* lead to trouble. For instance, what if the servant doesn't have what it takes to be king or mistress? What if the mindless person behaves in the way the closing saying in the chapter describes? So such developments are reason for the earth to feel some anxiety.

The fourth numerical saying notes how clever are ants, hyraxes (creatures like a large guinea pig), locusts, and lizards. They are the very embodiment of wisdom, quite a complement in a book like Proverbs. The fifth describes four beings that embody confidence as they stand before the world: a lion, something belted around the thighs (maybe a war horse), a goat, and then a king. The closing verses draw attention to a couple more ways in which nature and human experience show themselves part of one reality. In terms of theme, they constitute comments on preceding sections, offering a piece of advice to the mindless person and to those self-assured creatures (such as the king).

PROVERBS 31:1–9

The Demon Drink

1 The words of King Lemuel. An oracle with which his
     mother disciplined him.

2 What, my son, what, son of my womb,
     what, son of my vows?
3 Don't give your strength to women,
     your ways to women who wipe out kings.
4 It's not for kings, Lemuel, not for kings to drink wine,
     and for rulers, or liquor;
5 lest they drink and forget what has been decreed,
     and repudiate the cause of all lowly people.
6 Give the liquor to someone who is perishing,
     the wine to one who is bitter in spirit.
7 He can drink and forget his poverty,
     and his oppression he won't remember anymore.
8 Open your mouth for the dumb,
     for the cause of all the people who are passing away.
9 Open your mouth, exercise authority faithfully,
     decide for the lowly and needy person.

A student came to talk to me this week because he was puzzled about his church's negative, all-or-nothing attitude to alcohol. Should pastors drink, or are they like Nazirites in the Old Testament who abstained from alcohol, or like the priests who were told not to drink in case they made the offerings in the wrong way? Doesn't the Bible rather commend moderation, while recognizing that drink can be someone's downfall? What about the drinking that God expected at religious festivals? What about the fact that Jesus apparently drank? On the other hand, the student thought there were many pastors in his circle who spoke against drink from the pulpit but drank in private, and perhaps to excess. Eventually the student himself suggested that we tend to formulate the question around the antithesis of right and wrong when really it needs formulating around the antithesis of smart and dumb.

Lemuel's mother would agree. We don't know who Lemuel was or where he was king, though like Agur he was presumably a non-Israelite (the Old Testament doesn't mention him among the kings of Israel). The Queen Mother was often a powerful figure in the Middle East, and it's not surprising to see her laying down the law to her son, like any mother. She speaks of him as not only the son of her womb but specifically the son of her vows or promises: that is, like Hannah in 1 Samuel 1, she had prayed for a son and promised to dedicate him to God, so that her exhortation to him issues out of her commitment to God.

Opening the last chapter in Proverbs, it begins a conclusion that balances the opening nine chapters; the beginning and end of the book constitute a framework affirming the importance of feminine teaching and activity. The framework encloses the intervening chapters that have a more dominantly male focus. You could compare the way the exodus story in Exodus 1–15 sets Moses and Pharaoh in the context of the work and words of a series of women without whom the events would not be possible or complete.

Lemuel's mother starts with the standard warning about getting entangled with a number of women, which can destroy kings; ironically in the context of Proverbs, it's what happened to Solomon according to 1 Kings. But her focus is on drink. It destroys kings in another sense. It takes their attention away from "what has been decreed," which is spelled out in the parallel second part of the line. As usual, the Old Testament assumes that a leader's first obligation is to protect the ordinary, lowly, weak people. Drink will take a ruler's attention away from his primary vocation. The lines about leaving drink to people who need something to numb their pain and don't have to worry about important tasks they must remember are ironic, another way of trying to get through to the leader. His mother then restates his task in the last two lines. His job is to be a voice for people who cannot speak for themselves, people who are passing away, the lowly, the needy. A king such as Ahab in 1 Kings 21 collaborated with voices speaking against someone belonging to that group. The king's job is to stand up to them and use his **authority** in relation to the community's leadership to make sure its priority lies here.

PROVERBS 31:10–31

The Strong Woman

¹⁰ Who can find a strong woman?—
　her value is far above rubies;
¹¹ her husband's mind trusts her,
　and he lacks no plunder.
¹² She does him good not evil,
　all the days of her life.
¹³ She looks for wool and flax,
　and works with enthusiasm with her hands.
¹⁴ She becomes like a trader's ships,
　when she brings her food from far away.
¹⁵ She rises while it's still night, and gives a bite to her
　　household,
　and an allocation to her servant girls.
¹⁶ She schemes about a field and gets it;
　from the fruit of her hands she plants a vineyard.
¹⁷ She wraps her hips in vigor,
　and braces her arms.
¹⁸ She checks that her trading is good;
　her lamp doesn't go out at night.
¹⁹ She extends her hands to the spindle,
　and her palms grasp the wheel.

20 She opens her palm to the lowly person,
   extends her hands to the needy person.
21 She doesn't fear for her household because of snow,
   because her entire household is dressed in crimson.
22 She makes coverlets for herself;
   her clothing is linen and purple.
23 Her husband is known at the gates,
   as he sits with the country's elders.
24 She makes fabric and sells it,
   and gives a sash to the merchant.
25 Strength and splendor are her clothing;
   she can smile about the future.
26 She opens her mouth in wisdom;
   committed teaching is on her tongue.
27 She watches over the goings of her household;
   she doesn't eat the food of laziness.
28 Her children rise up and declare her blessed;
   her husband praises her:
29 "Many women show strength,
   but you surpass all of them."
30 Grace is deceptive, beauty is empty,
   but a woman who is in awe of Yahweh—she is to be
      praised.
31 Give to her from the fruit of her hand;
   her deeds should praise her at the gates.

My wife is about to complete her graduate program in theology, and people ask her from time to time what she plans to do with her degree. She then expresses her irritation to me. "I've had two careers [she has been an architect and a project manager]; I don't need another. I want to cook. I want to be the pastor's wife. I want to sew. I want to write. I want to spend time with my granddaughter." Yet the question is a natural one, because women in the West have been given the impression that they don't really count unless they make it in some specific way in their own right outside the home.

In that context, Proverbs' depiction of the strong woman arouses varying reactions, because it's a picture of a woman who exercises a lot of responsibility, yet it portrays the home as her base. One consideration we have to bear in mind is that women (and men) in the West are the victims of a cultural assumption linked with urbanization and industrialization that not only divided the world of home and family from the world of paid employment and the public world but also implied that the latter was the world that counted. So if you simply stayed home and worked there (as women mostly did) you were doing something much less significant than if you worked in the world (as men mostly did). Thus for women to count as productive human beings, they needed to be working in the world.

Proverbs presupposes a different sort of society—not necessarily wholly better or wholly worse, but different. Imagine an Israelite village of a couple hundred people belonging to three extended families which then comprise a number of households. Each extended family has its senior male figure, and the households also have one. The males of the family spend the daylight hours out in the fields, while the females spend their days in the village baking, cooking, sewing, and looking after the children who are too young to go out into the fields. There's no implication that the skilled work the women do in the village is less important than the skilled work the men do in the fields. Presumably the senior figures among the men and among the women exercise the leadership as people go about their tasks. It will then be vital to a woman that her husband knows what he's doing and vital to a man that his wife knows what she's doing.

The section is the only one in the book that is an alphabetical poem—that is, the first line begins with the Hebrew equivalent of A, the second with B, and so on (there are twenty-two letters in the Hebrew alphabet). An alphabetical poem covers its entire subject, from A to Z. It's the sequence of the alphabet that provides the "logic" for the sequence of the lines. There's no other structure or development. The poet begins by thinking up an A-line, then

155

a B-line, and so on, without worrying about any other connection with the preceding line. But several themes recur in the poem as a whole.

First is the importance the wife has for her husband. The question with which the poem starts (v. 10) need not imply that the quest is a difficult one; Proverbs often asks rhetorical questions. The question's point is that the issue it raises is important, not least for the young men Proverbs often has in mind. When you're looking for a wife, don't just focus on her looks. In some Arab countries, I understand, it's an insult to say the bride looks beautiful, because it implies she isn't valuable in other ways; it's at least as important to be smart and to belong to a well-connected family. Proverbs says to look at the size of her muscles (v. 17) and at her capacity to burn the midnight oil (v. 18). You want to be proud of her (vv. 23, 27–28, 31).

If the man and the woman are lucky, there are other, more romantic aspects to their relationship than the ones this poem highlights (the kind that feature in the Song of Songs), but the focus here lies on practical considerations. The man whom the poem imagines knows about the capability of the woman it imagines, and he doesn't have to worry about her half of the partnership. Although she operates from the home base, in her conduct of the family's affairs she's like a warrior going out to battle and coming home with the spoils for its benefit (v. 11). Talk in terms of imagining also invites us not to be too literalistic about the picture. While a woman could be encouraged by the range of responsibility expected by it, she could also be daunted. Remember it's a poem.

The role of women in making clothes features in the lines about wool and flax (v. 13) and weaving (v. 19). It also means people don't have to worry about the cold winters in the mountain settlements (v. 21), by night or by day (v. 22). There's nothing lazy about this woman, unlike some of the men we've met in Proverbs (v. 27). It means she doesn't have to worry about her own appearance or about everybody's provision next year (v. 25). Her role in cooking and baking features in the lines about food (v. 14) and about getting up early to put it on the table (v. 15).

Both these comments may presuppose an urban setting, with the man perhaps working in the administration. But even in the village the acquisition of fabric and foodstuffs, and their manufacture, will involve bartering (cf. vv. 18, 24). A family will not necessarily be self-sufficient but will use its surplus to obtain things it needs but doesn't produce. The woman is in charge of this process and of the process whereby the family spots a way of extending its land and plants an extra vineyard (v. 16).

Her family isn't one that just looks after itself (v. 20). She makes sure it looks after other people in the village, in keeping with biblical principles. Nor does her provision limit itself to her family's material needs (v. 26). If we were in any doubt about the question whether a mother shares in the teaching of the family, this poem removes it. It's related to the fact that she isn't merely a hard worker and a dedicated teacher but someone in **awe** of Yahweh (v. 30).

PROVERBS BY TOPICS

We have noted that many topics recur in different places in Proverbs. Presumably the compilers intended it that way, to encourage people to reflect on one saying at a time. Proverbs mirrors the Bible as a whole in not being ordered systematically. But there's also value in putting together its sayings on different topics. The following pages collect the sayings on a topic.

Anger

6:34 Jealousy [arouses] a man's fury;

he won't pity on the day of redress.

11:23 The longing of the faithful is only good;
the expectation of the faithless is wrath.

12:16 A stupid person—his vexation makes itself known at the
time,
but a shrewd person conceals a humiliation.

14:16 A wise person fears and turns from what is evil,
but a stupid person rages and is confident.

14:17 One who is short-tempered will do stupid things;
a person of schemes will be repudiated.

14:29 Long-temperedness is abundant in understanding,
but shortness of spirit exalts stupidity.

14:35 The favor of a king [will be] toward a servant of good sense,
but his rage will be [toward] a shameful one.

15:1 A gentle response turns back wrath,
but a hurtful word arouses anger.

15:18 A heated man stirs up arguments,
but one who is long-tempered quiets contention.

16:14 The king's wrath is death's aide,
but the wise person will expiate it.

16:32 Better to be long-tempered than a warrior,
and ruling over one's spirit than taking a city.

19:11 A person's good sense lengthens his anger,
and his glory is to pass over an act of rebellion.

19:12 The king's rage is a growl like a lion's,
but his favor is like dew on grass.

19:19 One who is big in wrath carries a penalty;
if you rescue [him], you'll do it again.

20:2 The king's dreadfulness is a growl like a lion's;
one who infuriates him loses his life.

21:14 A gift in secret calms anger,
a present in the pocket [calms] fierce wrath.

21:19 Living in wilderness land
is better than an argumentative and vexatious woman.

21:24 The haughty, presumptuous person—arrogant his name—
acts in a frenzy of haughtiness.

22:8 One who sews wrongdoing will reap wickedness;
their furious club will fail.

22:24 Don't befriend a person characterized by anger,
don't go about with someone hot-tempered,

22:25 lest you learn his ways

and get a snare for your life.

25:23 A north wind may stir up rain,
and a secretive tongue an indignant face.

27:3 A stone is weighty and sand is heavy,
but a stupid person's vexation is heavier than both of
them.

27:4 There is the cruelty of fury and the flooding of anger,
but who can stand before passion?

29:8 People who mock stir up a town,
but the wise turn away anger.

29:22 An angry person provokes arguments,
and a hot-tempered person rebels much.

30:33 Because pressing milk produces butter, pressing the nose
produces blood,
and pressing anger produces contention.

Arguments

3:30 Don't contend with someone for no reason,
when he hasn't done you any wrong.

10:12 Animosity stirs up strife,
but giving oneself conceals all acts of rebellion.

13:10 Only by means of arrogance does someone produce strife;
wisdom is with people who take advice.

15:16 Better a little with awe for Yahweh,
than much treasure and turmoil with it.

15:18 A heated man stirs up arguments,
but one who is long-tempered quietens contention.

16:28 A crooked person stirs up arguments,
and a gossip separates a friend.

17:1 Better a dry crust and quiet with it,
than a house full of contentious sacrifices.

17:14 The beginning of an argument releases waters;
before contention breaks out, abandon it.

17:19 One who likes rebellion likes strife;
one who builds a high gate seeks breaking down.

18:6 The lips of a stupid person come to contention,
and his mouth summons to blows.

18:18 The lot puts an end to arguments
and separates powerful people.

18:19 A brother acting rebelliously [is stronger] than a strong city,
and arguments are like the barrier of a fortress.

159

20:3 Ceasing from contention is an honor for a person,
    but every stupid person breaks out.

21:9 Living on a corner of the roof
    is better than an argumentative woman and a shared
        house.

21:19 Living in wilderness land
    is better than an argumentative and vexatious woman.

22:10 Drive out the arrogant person and arguments will depart;
    lawsuit and humiliating will cease.

23:29 Who says "Oh," who says "Aagh,"
    who has arguments, who has complaints,
who has wounds without reason,
    who has bleary eyes?—

23:30 people who linger over wine,
    who come to investigate mixed wine.

25:7 What your eyes have seen
    should not come out into contention quickly,

25:8 lest—what will you do at the end of it,
    when your neighbor puts you to shame?.

26:17 One who seizes the ears of a passing dog
    is one who gets furious at a dispute that isn't his.

26:20 In the absence of wood a fire goes out,
    and when there's no gossip, arguments go quiet.

26:21 Charcoal for embers and wood for a fire,
    and an argumentative person for heating up contention.

27:15 A continuing drip on a rainy day
    and an argumentative woman are alike.

27:16 One who hides her hides the wind,
    and oil on his right hand announces her.

28:25 One broad of appetite provokes argument,
    but one who trusts in Yahweh will be refreshed.

29:9 A wise person may dispute with a stupid person,
    but he'll rage and joke and there will be no peace.

29:22 An angry person provokes arguments,
    and a hot-tempered person rebels much.

30:33 Because pressing milk produces butter, pressing the nose
    produces blood,
    and pressing anger produces contention.

Friends and Neighbors

3:28 Don't say to your neighbor, "Go, and come back,

and tomorrow I'll give [it to you]," when it's with you.

3:29 Don't devise evil against your neighbor,
when he's living trustingly with you.

13:20 One who walks with the wise gets wise,
but the friend of stupid people experiences evil things.

14:7 Get away from the presence of the stupid person;
you won't have known knowledgeable lips.

14:20 Even by his neighbor a poor person is repudiated,
but the friends of a wealthy person are many.

14:21 One who despises his neighbor is an offender,
but one who is gracious to the lowly: his blessings!

16:28 A crooked person stirs up arguments,
and a gossip separates a friend.

16:29 A violent person misleads his neighbor
and makes him go in a way that isn't good.

17:9 One who seeks a relationship covers over rebellion,
but one who repeats a matter separates a friend.

17:17 A neighbor is a friend at any time;
a brother is born for trouble.

17:18 A person lacking in sense pledges his hand,
standing surety before his neighbor.

18:24 There are neighbors to act like neighbors,
and there's one who gives himself, who sticks firmer than
a brother.

19:4 Wealth makes many friends,
but a poor person becomes separate from his friend.

19:6 Many seek the face of a ruler,
and everyone befriends the person with a gift.

19:7 All the brothers of a poor person repudiate him—
how much more do his neighbors keep their distance
from him.

22:24 Don't befriend a person characterized by anger,
don't go about with someone hot-tempered,

22:25 lest you learn his ways
and get a snare for your life.

24:28 Don't become a witness against your neighbor without
reason;
will you mislead with your lips?

25:9 Contend for your cause with your neighbor,
but don't reveal the secret of another person,

25:10 lest someone who hears it reproach you

161

and the charge against you doesn't turn away.

25:17 Let your foot hold back from your neighbor's house,
lest he gets his fill of you and repudiate you.

26:18 Like a madman who is shooting
fiery arrows of death,

26:19 so is someone who deceives his neighbor
and says, "I was joking, wasn't I?"

27:6 The wounds of a friend are trustworthy;
the kisses of an enemy are importunate.

27:9 Oil and incense gladden the heart,
and the sweetness of one's friend more than one's own
counsel.

27:10 Don't abandon your friend or your father's friend,
or go to your brother's house on your day of calamity.
Better one who dwells near
than a brother far away.

27:14 One who blesses his neighbor in a loud voice in the
morning early:
it will be counted for him as humiliating [his neighbor].

27:17 Iron sharpens iron,
and a person sharpens the edge of his friend.

28:7 An understanding son guards instruction,
but one who befriends gluttons disgraces his father.

29:5 A man who flatters his neighbor
spreads a net for his feet.

Husbands and Wives, Men and Women

5:15 Drink water from your own cistern,
running water from within your own well.

5:16 Should your fountains gush outside,
your streams of water in the squares?

5:17 They should be for you alone,
so that there is none for strangers with you.

5:18 May your spring be blessed,
may you rejoice in the wife of your youth.

5:19 She is a doe to love,
a graceful deer.
Her breasts should satisfy you all the time;
be crazy on her love always.

5:20 So why be crazy on a stranger, son,
and embrace the bosom of a foreigner?

6:28 If a person walks on coals,
    will his feet not burn?

6:29 So it is with someone who has sex with his neighbor's wife;
    no one who touches her will go free.

6:30 People don't despise a thief when he steals
    for the sake of his appetite, when he's hungry.

6:31 But if he's found out, he'll pay back sevenfold;
    he'll give all the wealth of his household.

6:32 The person who commits adultery with a woman is lacking
    in sense;
    one who so acts is destroying himself.

6:33 He'll meet with injury and disgrace;
    his reproach will not be wiped away.

6:34 Because jealousy [arouses] a man's fury;
    he won't pity on the day of redress.

6:35 He won't have regard for any compensation;
    he won't agree, even if the inducement is great.

11:16 A woman of grace attains honor;
    violent men attain wealth.

11:22 A gold ring in a pig's nose
    is a beautiful woman turning away from discernment.

12:4 A strong woman is her husband's crown,
    but a shameful one is like decay in his bones.

14:1 The wisest of women builds her house,
    but stupidity tears it down with her own hands.

15:17 Better a helping of greens when love is there,
    than a fattened bull when hatred is with it.

17:1 Better a dry crust and quiet with it,
    than a house full of contentious sacrifices.

18:22 When someone finds a wife, he finds good things
    and obtains favor from Yahweh.

19:13 A stupid son is a disaster to his father,
    but a woman's arguments are a continuing drip.

19:14 House and wealth are the property of parents,
    but a woman with good sense comes from Yahweh.

21:9 Living on a corner of the roof
    is better than an argumentative woman and a shared
    house.

30:21 Under three things the earth shudders,

and under four that it cannot bear:

30:22 under a servant when he becomes king,
   under a mindless person when he's full of food,

30:23 under a woman who has been repudiated when she
      marries,
   and under a servant when she replaces her mistress.

See also the description of "the strong woman" in 31:10–31

Honor, Humility, and Arrogance

3:34 [Yahweh] himself behaves arrogantly to the arrogant,
   to the lowly he gives grace.

6:16 These six Yahweh repudiates,
   seven are abhorrent to him:

6:17 haughty eyes, a lying tongue,
   and hands that shed innocent blood ....

8:13 Superiority and self-importance and the way of evil,
   and a crooked mouth, I repudiate.

11:2 Arrogance comes, then humiliation comes;
   with modest people there is wisdom.

13:10 Only by means of arrogance does someone produce strife;
   wisdom is with people who take advice.

13:18 Poverty and humiliation—one who rejects discipline,
   but one who heeds correction is honored.

14:3 In the mouth of the stupid person is a shoot of arrogance,
   but the lips of wise people guard them.

15:25 Yahweh tears down the house of the arrogant,
   but establishes the territory of the widow.

15:33 Awe for Yahweh is wisdom's discipline;
   lowliness is before honor.

16:5 Anyone arrogant of mind is an abomination to Yahweh;
   hand-to-hand he won't go innocent.

16:18 Arrogance goes before brokenness,
   majesty of spirit before collapsing.

16:19 Humbleness of spirit with the lowly
   is better than sharing plunder with the arrogant.

16:31 Gray hair is a splendid crown;
   it's attained by way of faithfulness.

17:6 Grandchildren are the crown of elders,
   but their parents are the glory of children.

18:12 Before being broken a person's mind is arrogant,

164

but before honor comes lowliness.

20:3 Ceasing from contention is an honor for a person,
but every stupid person breaks out.

21:4 Exaltedness of eyes and wide of mind:
the yoke of the faithless is an offense.

21:21 One who pursues faithfulness and commitment
finds life, faithfulness, and honor.

22:1 A name is preferable to much wealth;
favor is better than silver and gold.

22:4 The effect of lowliness is awe for Yahweh,
wealth, honor, and life.

25:27 Eating much honey isn't good,
nor is it honorable to investigate people's honor.

26:12 I've seen a person wise in his own eyes;
there's more hope for a stupid person than for him.

27:2 A stranger should boast about you and not your mouth,
a foreigner and not your lips.

28:11 A rich person is wise in his own eyes,
but a poor person of understanding sees through him.

29:23 An individual's majesty will make him fall,
but one lowly of spirit will attain honor.

30:32 If you've been mindless in exalting yourself,
and if you've schemed—hand on your mouth!

The Inner Person (Mind and Heart)

3:1 Don't disregard my teaching, son;
your mind is to safeguard my commands.

3:3 Commitment and truthfulness must not abandon you;
bind them on your neck, write them on the tablet of your
mind.

3:5 Trust in Yahweh with all your mind,
don't lean on your own understanding.

4:23 Above everything that you guard,
protect your mind.

5:11 You'll groan at your end,
when your flesh and body are spent.

5:12 You'll say, "How I repudiated discipline,
and my mind spurned rebuke."

10:8 One who is wise of mind accepts commands,
but one stupid of lips comes to ruin.

11:20 The crooked in mind are an abomination to Yahweh;

people of integrity in their way are the ones he favors.

12:25 Anxiety in a person's mind weighs it down,
    but a good word makes it rejoice.

13:12 Hope deferred sickens the heart,
    but desire that comes about is a tree of life.

14:10 The heart knows its inner bitterness,
    and in its joy a stranger doesn't share.

14:13 Even in laughter a heart may hurt,
    and celebration—its end may be grief.

14:14 Someone who turns back in heart will be full from his ways,
    and the good person from his deeds.

14:30 A healthy heart is life for the flesh,
    but passion is rot for the bones.

15:11 Sheol and Abaddon are before Yahweh;
    how much more the minds of human beings.

15:13 A joyful heart enhances the face,
    but by hurt in the heart the spirit is crushed.

15:14 The mind of a person of understanding seeks knowledge,
    but the mouth of dense people feeds on stupidity.

15:15 All the days of a lowly person are evil,
    but a good heart is a continual feast.

16:1 The ordering of his mind belongs to a human being,
    but the answer of the tongue comes from Yahweh.

16:5 Anyone arrogant of mind is an abomination to Yahweh;
    hand-to-hand he won't go innocent.

16:9 The mind of a person plans his course,
    but Yahweh establishes his step.

16:21 One who is wise in thinking is called understanding,
    but sweetness of speech increases persuasiveness.

17:3 The crucible for silver, the furnace for gold,
    and Yahweh tests minds.

17:22 A joyful heart enhances healing,
    but a crushed spirit dries up the bones.

19:21 Many plans are in a person's mind,
    but Yahweh's counsel is the one that stands.

20:9 Who can say, "I've kept my mind pure,
    I'm clean from my offense"?

20:27 The breath of a person is Yahweh's lamp,
    revealing the heart's inner rooms.

21:2 All a person's way is upright in his own eyes,
    but Yahweh weighs minds.

166

21:4   Exaltedness of eyes and wide of mind:
     the yoke of the faithless is an offense.

23:7   He says to you, "Eat and drink,"
     but his heart isn't with you.

23:17   Your mind must not be envious of people who offend,
     but rather of [people who live in] awe for Yahweh all day.

28:26   One who trusts in his own mind—he is stupid,
     but one who walks in wisdom—he will escape.

Justice and Judgment

11:1   False scales are an abomination to Yahweh:
     a true weight is what he favors.

11:9   With the mouth the impious person destroys his neighbor,
     but through the knowledge of the faithful, people escape.

12:17   The person who testifies truthfully speaks with faithfulness,
     but a false witness with deceit.

13:23   The fallow ground of the poor—abundance of food,
     but it's swept away for want of the [right] exercise of
       authority.

16:11   Balance and scales for decision belong to Yahweh;
     all the stones in the bag are his making.

17:23   A faithless person takes a bribe out of his pocket,
     to divert the processes of decision making.

18:5   Lifting the face of the faithless person isn't good,
     by pushing aside one who is faithful when making a
       decision.

18:17   The first person in a dispute seems right,
     then his neighbor comes and examines him.

19:28   A worthless witness is arrogant toward the taking of
       decisions,
     and the mouth of the faithless swallows wickedness.

20:7   A faithful person walks about with integrity—
     the blessings of his children after him!

20:10   Stone and stone, measure and measure,
     both of them are an abomination to Yahweh.

21:3   Exercising authority in a faithful way
     is preferable to Yahweh over a sacrifice.

21:7   The violence of the faithless sweeps them away,
     because they refuse to exercise authority [aright].

21:13   One who stops his ears to the cry of the poor person—
     he too will call and not be answered.

21:15 Exercising authority [aright] is joy to the faithful
     but ruin to the wrongdoer.

21:28 A lying witness will perish,
     but one who listens to the end will speak.

22:28 Don't remove an age-old boundary mark,
     one that your ancestors made.

23:10 Don't remove an age-old boundary mark,
     and don't go into the fields of orphans.

23:11 Because their restorer is strong;
     he will contend their cause with you.

24:23 Having regard for the person in making a decision isn't
     good.

24:24 Someone who says to the faithless person "You're in the
     right":
     peoples curse him, nations are indignant at him.

24:28 Don't become a witness against your neighbor without
     reason;
     will you mislead with your lips?

28:21 Having regard for the person isn't good,
     but a man will rebel for a piece of bread.

29:14 A king who decides for the poor in truth:
     his throne will stand firm forever.

31:8 Open your mouth for the dumb,
     for the cause of all the people who are passing away.

31:9 Open your mouth, exercise authority faithfully,
     decide for the lowly and needy person.

The Mouth

4:24 Keep away from you crookedness of mouth;
     put deviousness of lips far away.

10:11 The mouth of a faithful person is a fountain of life,
     but the mouth of faithless people conceals violence.

10:18 The person who conceals repudiation [with] lying lips
     and the one who issues charges, he is stupid.

10:19 Where there is a multitude of words, rebellion isn't lacking,
     but one who restrains his lips is sensible.

10:21 The lips of a faithful person pasture many,
     but stupid people die for lack of sense.

10:31 The mouth of the faithful person is fruitful with wisdom,
     but the crooked tongue will be cut off.

11:11 A town rises up by the blessing of the upright,

168

but by the mouth of the faithless it breaks down.

12:6   The words of the faithless are a deadly ambush,
     but the mouth of the upright rescues them.

12:18   There is one who rants like sword-thrusts,
     but the tongue of the wise person is a healing.

12:19   A truthful lip stands firm forever,
     but a lying tongue lasts for the blink of an eye.

12:22   Lying lips are an abomination to Yahweh,
     but people who act truthfully are his favor.

12:25   Anxiety in a person's mind weighs it down,
     but a good word makes it rejoice.

13:2   From the fruit of his mouth a person eats what is good,
     but the appetite of the treacherous is for violence.

13:3   One who guards his mouth preserves his life,
     but one who opens his lips wide—ruin is his.

15:1   A gentle response turns back wrath,
     but a hurtful word arouses anger.

15:4   A healing tongue is a tree of life,
     but deviousness in it is brokenness in spirit.

15:23   In the response of his mouth there is joy to a person,
     but a word at its time—how good!

15:28   The mind of a faithful person talks in order to answer,
     but the mouth of faithless people pours out evil things.

16:24   Nice words are a honeycomb,
     sweet to the soul and healing for the body.

17:9   One who seeks a relationship covers over rebellion,
     but one who repeats a matter separates a friend.

17:27   One who knows knowledge holds back his words;
     a person of understanding is cool of spirit.

17:28   Even a stupid person, keeping silence, is thought wise;
     one who keeps his lip closed [is thought] understanding.

18:4   The words from a person's mouth are deep waters;
     a fountain of wisdom is a flowing wash.

18:7   The mouth of a stupid person is his ruin,
     and his lips are a trap for his life.

18:13   One who returns word before he listens—
     it's his stupidity and shame.

18:21   Death and life are in the hand of the tongue;
     those who give themselves to it eat its fruit.

20:15   There is gold and abundance of jewels,
     but lips with knowledge are a valuable object.

20:19 One who reveals a confidence goes about as a slanderer;
    don't share with someone who has his lips open.

21:23 One who guards his mouth and his tongue
    guards his life from troubles.

24:26 He kisses with the lips,
    the one who replies with straight words.

25:11 Golden apricots in silver settings
    is a word appropriately spoken.

26:4 Don't answer someone stupid in accordance with his
      denseness,
    lest you become like him, you too.

26:5 Answer someone stupid in accordance with his denseness,
    lest he become wise in his own eyes.

29:11 A stupid person expresses all his feelings;
    a wise person holds them back.

29:20 If you see someone hasty with his words,
    there's more hope for a stupid person than for him.

Family Life and Discipline

3:11 Don't reject Yahweh's discipline, son,
    don't despise his correction.

3:12 Because the one Yahweh gives himself to, he corrects,
    just like a father the son he favors.

6:20 Son, guard your father's command
    and don't turn your back on your mother's teaching.

6:21 Fasten them into your mind always,
    bind them onto your neck.

6:22 When you're going about, it will lead you,
    when you lie down, it will keep watch over you,
    when you wake up, it will talk to you.

6:23 Because the command is a lamp and the teaching is a light,
    and the rebuke that disciplines is the way to life ....

10:1 A wise son brings joy to a father,
    but a stupid son brings grief to a mother.

13:1 A wise son [listens to] a father's discipline,
    but an arrogant person doesn't listen to a rebuke.

13:22 A good man endows grandchildren;
    the strength of the offender is stored up for the faithful
      person.

13:24 The person who is sparing with his club repudiates his son,
    but one who loves him gets him up early with discipline.

15:5 A stupid person spurns his father's discipline,
  but one who heeds reproof shows shrewdness.

15:10 Discipline is evil to one who abandons the path,
  but one who repudiates reproof dies.

15:20 A wise son rejoices his father,
  but a stupid person despises his mother.

15:31 The ear that listens to life-giving reproof
  lodges among the wise.

19:26 One who destroys a father or drives out a mother
  is a son who brings shame and disgrace.

20:20 One who humiliates his father and his mother,
  his lamp will go out at the approach of darkness.

22:15 Stupidity is bound up in a youth's mind;
  the club of discipline will take it far away from him.

23:22 Listen to your father who begot you,
  and don't despise your mother when she is old.

25:12 A gold earring or an ornament of fine gold
  is a wise person reproving into a listening ear.

27:5 Open reproof
  is better than concealed friendship.

27:6 The wounds of a friend are trustworthy;
  the kisses of an enemy are importunate.

28:7 An understanding son guards instruction,
  but one who befriends gluttons disgraces his father.

28:23 One who reproves a person in the end
  will find more grace than one who makes his tongue
    smooth.

28:24 One who robs his father and his mother
  and says "It's not an act of rebellion"—
  he is a companion of one who destroys.

29:1 A person of many reproofs who stiffens his neck
  will suddenly break, and there will be no healing.

29:3 Someone who gives himself to wisdom rejoices his father,
  but someone who keeps company with immoral women
    destroys wealth.

29:15 Club and reproof give wisdom,
  but a youth let loose shames his mother.

29:17 Discipline your son and he'll let you have peace,
  and give much delight to your spirit.

30:11 A company that humiliates its father
  and doesn't bless its mother!

30:17 The eye that mocks a father
    and despises a mother's teaching:
  the ravens in the wash will gouge it out,
    and young eagles will eat it.

Wealth and Poverty

3:9 Honor Yahweh with all your wealth,
    with the first of all your revenue.

3:14 [Wisdom's] profit is better than the profit of silver,
    her revenue than gold.

10:15 The wealth of the rich person is his strong city;
    the poverty of the poor is their ruin.

10:22 Yahweh's blessing—it enriches,
    and toil doesn't add to it.

11:4 Wealth doesn't avail on the day of wrath,
    but faithfulness rescues from death.

11:24 There is one who scatters and gets still more;
    one who holds back beyond what is upright, only to be in
      want.

11:25 A person of blessing will be made fat;
    someone who refreshes—he'll also be refreshed.

11:26 One who withholds grain—the community will curse him;
    but blessing will be on the head of one who sells it.

11:28 One who trusts in his wealth—he falls,
    but the faithful flourish like foliage.

14:20 Even by his neighbor a poor person is repudiated,
    but the friends of a wealthy person are many.

14:31 One who oppresses a poor person insults his maker,
    but one who is gracious to a needy person honors him.

15:16 Better a little with awe for Yahweh
    than much treasure and turmoil with it.

19:1 Better one who is poor who walks with integrity
    than one who is crooked with his lips and stupid.

19:17 One who is gracious to a poor person lends to Yahweh,
    and he'll pay him his recompense.

21:6 Working for treasures by means of a lying tongue
    is a breath driven off, people seeking death.

21:13 One who stops his ears to the cry of the poor person—
    he too will call and not be answered.

21:20 Valuable treasure and oil are in the dwelling of someone
    wise,

but a stupid person will consume them.

22:2 Rich and poor meet;
    Yahweh makes each of them.

22:9 One who is good of eye will be blessed,
    because he gives of his bread to the poor person.

22:16 One who oppresses the poor person—it's to make much for
    him;
    one who gives to the rich person—it's only to come to
    want.

23:4 Don't get weary in order to become wealthy;
    out of your understanding, desist.

23:5 Should your eyes flit upon it, it's gone,
    because it definitely makes itself wings;
    like an eagle, it flies to the heavens.

27:20 Sheol and Abaddon don't get full,
    and the eyes of a human being don't get full.

28:8 Someone who increases his wealth by means of interest and
    profiteering,
    amasses it for someone who will be gracious to the poor.

28:11 A rich person is wise in his own eyes,
    but a poor person of understanding sees through him.

28:22 One who is evil in eye hurries for wealth
    and doesn't acknowledge that lack will come to him.

30:8 Emptiness and a lying word keep far from me,
    poverty and riches do not give me,
    let me grab the food that is my due.

30:9 Lest I get full and renounce and say, "Who is Yahweh?"
    or lest I get poor and rob, and take the name of my God.

Work and Laziness

6:6 Go to the ant, lazybones,
    look at its ways and get wise.

6:7 One that has no commander,
    officer, or ruler

6:8 produces its food in summer,
    gathers its provisions at harvest.

6:9 How long will you lie down, lazybones,
    when will you get up from your sleep?

6:10 A little sleep, a little slumber,
    a little folding of the hands to lie down,

6:11 and your poverty will come walking in,

your want like someone with a shield.

10:4 A slack hand causes poverty;
    the hand of determined people enriches.

10:5 One who gathers during summer is a sensible son;
    one who sleeps during harvest is a disgraceful son.

10:26 Like vinegar to the teeth, like smoke to the eyes,
    so is the lazy person to the people who sent him.

12:11 One who serves his land will have his fill of food,
    but one who follows empty pursuits lacks sense.

12:24 The hand of determined people rules,
    but slackness leads to subjection.

12:27 Slackness will not roast game,
    but the wealth of a person is valuable—determined.

14:23 In all toil there will be profit,
    but [in] the [mere] word of lips [there will be] only being
      in want.

15:19 The way of a lazy person is like a hedge of thorns,
    but the path of the upright is cleared.

16:26 The appetite of a laborer labors for him,
    because his mouth is pressing on him.

18:9 Really, one who is slack in his work—
    he is brother to someone destructive.

19:15 Laziness makes deep sleep fall,
    and a slack person gets hungry.

19:24 The lazy person buries his hand in the bowl;
    he can't even bring it back to his mouth.

20:4 After fall the lazy person doesn't plow,
    but he asks at harvest and there is nothing.

20:13 Don't give yourself to sleep lest you become poor;
    open your eyes—be full of food.

22:13 Someone lazy says, "A lion in the street,
    in the middle of the square I shall be slain!"

24:27 Establish your work outside,
    get it ready in the fields for yourself;
    afterward build your house.

24:30 I passed by the field of someone who was lazy,
    and by the vineyard of one lacking sense.

24:31 There: it all had come up in weeds,
    chickpeas covered its surface, its stone wall lay in ruins.

24:32 When I myself looked, I applied my mind;
    when I saw, I grasped a lesson.

24:33 A little sleep, a little slumber,
    a little folding of the hands to lie down,
24:34 and your poverty will come walking about,
    your want like someone with a shield.
26:13 A lazy person says, "There's a cougar on the road,
    a lion among the squares."
26:14 The door turns on its hinge,
    the lazy person on his bed.
27:23 You should really know the faces of your flock,
    apply your attention to your herds,
27:24 because wealth isn't forever
    or a crown for generation after generation.
27:25 The hay goes away and the new grass appears
    and the growth of the mountains is gathered.
27:26 The lambs are for your clothing,
    the goats for the price of a field,
27:27 enough goats' milk for your food,
    for food for your household and life for your young girls.
28:19 One who serves his land will be full of food,
    but one who pursues empty things will be full of poverty.

ECCLESIASTES 1:1-11

Under the Sun, Where Randomness Rules

1   The words of Churchman, son of David, king in Jerusalem.

2   "Utter emptiness," said Churchman, "utter emptiness,
    everything is empty.
3   What value is there for a person in all the toil that he
    undertakes under the sun?"

4   A generation goes, a generation comes,
    but the earth remains forever.
5   The sun rises and the sun sets,
    and rushes to the place where it rises.
6   The wind goes south and turns north, it turns,
    turns as it goes, and on its turnings the wind returns.
7   All streams go to the sea, but the sea isn't full;
    to the place where the streams go, there they go again.

8   All the things are laborious;
        no one could speak [of them].
    The eye isn't replete as regards looking,
        the ear isn't full as regards listening.
9   What has happened is what will happen;
        what has occurred is what will occur;
        there's nothing new under the sun.
10 Where there is something that someone says, "Look, this is
        new,"
    already it has happened in ages that were before us.
11 There is no remembering on the part of earlier people,
        and also on the part of the people who are to come.
    There will be no remembering on their part,
        among the people who will be after them.

I noted in connection with Proverbs 11 that I am inclined to
think that nothing I do has any effect, though from time to
time God sends me someone to tell me they have been
affected by something I've said or written, which reminds me
to be less gloomy. But if I doubt whether spending so much of
my time writing books has any effect on people, why do I do
it? Partly because it's like an artist painting a picture; it's a way
I do something a bit creative. Partly because I learn a lot; I've
never read through Ecclesiastes in Hebrew before. I am paid
to be a teacher, but I doubt if my teaching has any effect on
people. I can tell that it is so from many student papers I read;
and if some of my students "get it," I suspect they will soon
lose it after they finish at seminary. I celebrate the Eucharist
and preach every Sunday, and people appreciate my doing so,
but I've buried a couple of them in the past month, and there's
little sign of their being replaced by others. What's the point?

   I   therefore   identify   with   "Churchman's   opening
observation, that everything is totally empty." It's a striking
observation from a churchman. The Hebrew word for
"churchman" is *qohelet*, which is thus the name of the book in
Hebrew. It comes from the Hebrew word for a "congregation,"
which can denote any form of assembly but more often refers
to a religious or worshiping assembly. So "Ecclesiastes" is a

good Greek equivalent, as it comes from the equivalent Greek word *ekklēsia*, which means "church" and "churchman" would be an English equivalent. A key characteristic of Ecclesiastes is that it keeps saying things that you wouldn't have thought a churchman would say, and it's thus significant that it begins this way. The questions in Ecclesiastes are not the questions of an atheist or an agnostic. They are the questions of a believer who wants to keep faith honest.

"Son of David" has the same implications. A son of David could suggest any of the kings who were descended from David and could refer to Solomon, but the verse doesn't use his name, which suggests there's something else going on. More likely its point is that the author associates himself with David as "churchman," as the patron of Israel's worship, the person who arranged for the building of the temple and set up its worship arrangements. It's such a person's questioning that we'll be made to think about. It would be evident to readers that the book isn't written in the kind of Hebrew that Solomon would have used. It's as if someone wrote a play by "a son of Shakespeare" but used modern English.

The radical nature of the book's questions is immediately announced in the declaration about everything being "empty." The word more literally means a breath, so it suggests things that are evanescent, that pass away, that have no substance. The Old Testament applies the words to images of a god who has no real power, to plans that lead nowhere, and to promises that don't get fulfilled. But half the occurrences of the word come in Ecclesiastes, where it describes pleasure, achievement, work, wealth, politics, and the general randomness of the way life works. The expression "utter emptiness, everything is empty" recurs near the end of the book and thus forms a bracket around it and declares a basic conviction.

The next line, about the uselessness of all the effort that people put into their lives, in turn constitutes a summary of the reason for viewing everything as empty and helps us see in what sense things are utterly empty. There's no point putting effort into trying to achieve things, because life's randomness means you can never know whether you achieve anything in the long run. It's chance that determines things. This explanatory line introduces another of Churchman's key expressions, "under the sun," which occurs twenty-seven times. Although it never occurs in Proverbs or Song of Songs (or anywhere else in the Bible), it could have done so, because all these books look at life resolutely from this angle, from the perspective of what you can see. It doesn't mean leaving out God or leaving out right and wrong. It does mean focusing on what we can experience as human beings in the now, on the earthly plane. These books don't talk about the exodus or the covenant, about heaven or hell, or about a coming messiah. They talk about what we can see now. They ask, What can you learn by simply focusing on what you can see now? Here, randomness often rules. That fact is one aspect of how things are "under the sun."

The main paragraph that follows offers another comment on how things are "under the sun." There's nothing new there, it says. Things just go around and around. The nature of these observations introduces another feature of the book. You could take its point that nothing new ever happens as bad news or as good news. In Western culture we are inclined to put a positive estimate on new things. Advertisers seek to get us to buy things because they are new. But the reliable cycle of sun and moon and the unchanging circulation of water (evaporation, rain, rivers, sea; you could say that Churchman is talking about ecology) provides important undergirding for human life. Everything depends on how you look at the phenomena.

ECCLESIASTES 1:12–2:11
The Secret of Life Is …

[12] I, Churchman, became king over Israel in Jerusalem. [13] I gave my mind to studying and exploring with insight everything that occurs under the sun. It's an evil undertaking that God gave human beings to be busy with. [14] I looked at all the actions that occur under the sun. There: everything is emptiness, a chasing after wind. [15] "Something crooked cannot become straight; something lacking cannot be counted." [16] I spoke within myself: Here, I've grown great and increased in insight above everyone who was over Jerusalem before me. [17] I've given my mind to a knowledge of insight and a knowledge of madness and stupidity. I've come to acknowledge that this, too, was a chasing after wind. [18] Because "with much insight there's much vexation; the one who increases knowledge increases pain."

[2:1] I said within myself, "Come on, I'll test you with enjoyment. Look into what is good." There: that is also emptiness. [2] Of having fun, I said, "It's mad," and of enjoyment, "What does it achieve?" [3] I explored within myself stimulating my flesh with wine (while directing my mind with insight) and taking hold of stupidity, until I could see which one was good for human beings, which they should practice under the heavens for the number of the days of their life. [4] I multiplied my achievements. I built houses for myself, I planted vineyards for myself, [5] I made gardens and parks for myself and planted in them trees with every fruit. [6] I made pools of water for myself, to irrigate from them a forest flourishing with trees. [7] I acquired male and female servants and ones born in my household. I also had animals, cattle and sheep; I had more than all who had been before me in Jerusalem. [8] I also amassed for myself silver and gold and the treasure of kings and provinces. I got for myself male and female singers, and the pleasures of human beings, many women. [9] I multiplied and increased more than anyone who had been before me in Jerusalem; also my insight stayed with me. [10] Nothing that my eyes asked for did I keep from them. I didn't hold myself back from any enjoyment; rather, I myself gained enjoyment from all my labor. This was my share through all my labor. [11] But I turned to all the achievements that my hands had brought about and at the labor that I had put in to do it. There: everything was emptiness, a chasing after wind. There was no value under the sun.

We were in a bar last night to listen to a band playing blues. Behind and alongside us were people who at 8:30 were already rather the worse for wear. My wife commented that you could find some of these same people here every night. In front of and around us were dancers so expert as to intimidate me from asking Kathleen to dance; they had clearly spent a lot of time learning, and we recognized one or two from other places where we listen to music. The singer and the bass player were very fine, and it made me wonder (as it often does) what such players do all day and all week when they are not playing in a dive bar. It reminded me of an onstage remark by a famous blues singer, that she only feels really alive when she's playing in front of an audience. When the band, and the drinkers, and the dancers, and the bartenders get home, do they wonder whether it's all emptiness? Do architects (what Kathleen used to be) and scholars (what I try to be) ask the same question when they get home?

Churchman has done so. Here he speaks as king in Jerusalem, and both invites us to think of Solomon yet invites us not to take that idea too literally; he refrains from saying he is Solomon, yet gives a testimony that could come only from the lips of someone like him. Solomon is the man who had everything. His story in 1 Kings describes how he gained stupendous wealth, built up Jerusalem, had a thousand women in his harem, constructed the temple and initiated its worship, governed Israel when it became the most extensive realm it ever was, organized its administration with skill, built an ocean-going fleet, found recognition among the peoples around, and combined all these achievements with being the very embodiment of insight. If anyone was in a position to reflect on the significance of human achievement, it was Solomon.

Churchman thus imagines him doing so, and concluding that it was all empty. He doesn't imply that the things he investigates were totally pointless; neither will later sections of the book have this implication. He means he didn't find ultimate meaning in any of those pursuits. He didn't discover the secret of life. A Gretchen Peters song starts from two guys sitting in a bar asking whether life is just working and drinking and dreaming. The refrain declares that the secret of life is drinking a good cup of coffee or keeping your eye on the ball or putting up a poster of a beautiful woman. The bartender puts it another way: the secret of life is that there isn't one.

That point is most explicit in Churchman's comments about insight, understanding, or wisdom. He had started his investigation into the meaning of life with the assumed value of wisdom. It's where a scholar like Churchman would start. But if God gave human beings the instinct to try to discover the answer to that question in this way, then it was a joke that God was playing on us. The quest is a chasing after wind: you can never catch it or capture it. The poetic sentence about not being able to straighten something crooked (v. 15) may well be a saying that Churchman is quoting—hence I have put it in quotes. Typically, the point of such a saying lies in the second half. As you can't straighten something incurably crooked, so you can't count something that isn't there to be counted. There isn't a big picture (at least one accessible to us "under the sun"), so it's pointless to try to describe it. Seeking to make sense of life and the world involves trying to connect a small number of dots in such a way as to generate a big picture—or maybe like trying to turn a huge number of random-looking dots into a big picture that makes sense. Either way, it can't be done. All you achieve by the effort is to make yourself even gloomier. One of the guys in Gretchen Peters's song says, "I've been thinking"; the other replies, "That won't get you too far."

It's not that the exercise of wisdom is useless. Churchman declares that he has been directing his mind with insight even while testing enjoyment and so on. He didn't go in for his experiment with entertainment, wine, and achievement in a mindless way that abandoned control. He will talk further about enjoyment, food, wine, and achievement, and will not be referring to immoderate or irresponsible or sinful self-indulgence, only about enjoying the life in the world that God gives us. It was important to retain the capacity to think about his experiment while he was conducting it, because otherwise he would not be able to evaluate it. He has done so. Like wisdom itself, such expressions of self-indulgence (like the writing of commentaries on the Bible) are not to be despised, but they do not give life meaning. They do not contain the meaning of life. It is in this connection that they are empty, profitless. His testimony is especially forceful because as king he has been able to try all these things. It can be tempting to think, "Life would be different if only I could have this or try that; I would be able to discover the secret then." There is no such "if only" for Churchman; he has been there and done that.

ECCLESIASTES 2:12–26

What Legacy?

[12] So I turned to look at wisdom and madness and stupidity. Because what will the person [do] who comes after the king—that which people have already done? [13] I saw that there is value to wisdom over stupidity, like the value of light over darkness: [14] "The wise person—his eyes are in his head, but the stupid person walks in darkness." But I also acknowledged that a single lot comes to each of them. [15] So I said within myself, like the lot of the fool—so it will come to me, too. So why have I then been exceedingly wise? I spoke within myself: this is emptiness, too. [16] Because there's no remembering forever of the wise

person just like the stupid person, in that already in the coming days each will have been forgotten; and how can the wise man die just like the stupid person? [17] So I repudiated life because the action that occurs under the sun is evil to me, because everything is emptiness, a chasing after wind. [18] I repudiated all the labor that I've expended under the sun, which I shall leave to the person who will be after me [19] Who knows whether he'll be a wise person or a stupid person? But he'll control all the labor that I've expended and the wisdom that I've exercised under the sun. This too is emptiness. [20] So I turned to letting myself despair about all the labor that I've expended under the sun. [21] Because there can be someone whose labor was with wisdom, knowledge, and skill, and he gives his share from it to someone who didn't labor for it. This is also emptiness, something very evil. [22] Because what does a person have for all his labor and for his mind's chasing, which he has expended under the sun? [23] Because all his days, his undertaking is pain and vexation. By night, too, his mind doesn't rest. This is also emptiness.

[24] There's nothing better for a person [than] that he eats and drinks and lets himself see some good through his labor. I've also seen that this is from God's hand. [25] Because who eats and who worries apart from me? [26] Because to the person who is good in his sight he gives wisdom and knowledge and enjoyment, and to the offender he gives the task of gathering and collecting in order to give [it] to someone who is good in God's eyes. This too is emptiness, a chasing after wind.

I heard this morning of the death of someone whom I've known as a colleague, mentor, and friend. Every time I heard him preach, I gained from it. Everything of his that I read, it made me think. When he offered me insight or advice, it was always worth pondering. He lived on into his eighties and in his Christmas letter referred to the two theological papers whose publication he was looking forward to. He also spoke of his physical limitations and of the sadness of his wife's dementia that had necessitated her going into a nursing home. But in the midst of this sadness he spoke of how he has "leaned heavily on the love, presence and help of the God of the gospel in whom I have believed and tried to serve all these years, and he has in new, gracious, and gentle ways blessed me with his generous provision, and that has given me clear path through it all with a bright hope at the end." Not long after sending those Christmas greetings, he caught an infection that he could not throw off. "It's very strange to think he won't be around anymore," a mutual friend commented to me this morning.

A single fate comes to us all, Churchman notes. This morning I also read that in 1950 there were 2,300 people in the United States who were older than one hundred; by 2050, that number could hit half a million. But eventually, a single fate comes to all of them. This fate is a topic that recurs in Ecclesiastes. In general, the Old Testament is accepting of death. All being well, you are born, you grow up, you live your life, you grow old, you die, and you join your ancestors in the family tomb. That's OK. It gets vexed about death when the complete story threatens not to play out in that way—when people are threatened by death before their time (as happened to many more people in its context than is so in the West). Churchman's preoccupation is related. Wisdom may be valuable in enabling you to avoid stumbling in the short term, but death is going to get you in the end.

He makes the point by using a technique that will also recur in the book, by taking up an aphorism from regular wisdom teaching and raising questions about it. Here the aphorism is, "The wise person—he has eyes in his head; the stupid person —he walks in darkness." In other words, wise people can see where they are going and walk accordingly, whereas stupid people are like people walking in the dark without a flashlight; they are likely to stumble over something or fall into a hole. It's a saying that could have appeared in Proverbs. Churchman first anticipates the saying by putting the point in his own words: "there is value to wisdom over stupidity, like the value of light over darkness." But having lulled us into a false sense of security and/or having assured us that he really does accept the truth of wisdom's teaching, he follows up the aphorism by adding that he has come to face the fact that the same fate meets everyone, whether wise or stupid.

You can be the most profound philosopher or the best teacher in the world, but it won't ward off death. Maybe you'll live longer than the stupid person next door, but your good sense won't finally ward off death. You therefore can't control what happens after you die. In Solomon's case, the person who comes after him as king was Rehoboam; he was certainly stupid and brought out the dissolution of Solomon's kingdom (see 1 Kings 12). Churchman has no objection to the fact that there will be no reason to remember the stupid person for his achievements, but he objects to the fact that the wise person will also be forgotten. In one sense his statement deconstructs; we are in the midst of remembering Solomon and of remembering Churchman. But in the Old Testament, remembering implies more than a mere mental activity. Remembering implies keeping something in mind and living in light of it, and every teacher grieves over the fact that most pupils don't act in this way. In this sense, Rehoboam didn't emulate his father's wisdom (actually, 1 Kings suggests, he emulated his father's folly; but that's another story).

In the same way you could also say that Rehoboam squandered all the effort his father put into turning Israel into a state that could hold its head high in its world, with its administration and wealth. So what's the point of putting effort into something when your successor can undo all that you carefully put into place? Day and night you think and work and plan, but it can all be undone.

So don't get too focused on your achievements and your legacy, says "Solomon," to the extent that you fail to enjoy the ordinary good things of an ordinary life. These things come from God. Don't take me as your example, given that I've been a person who gives himself to eating and worrying instead of eating and drinking. Recognize how things often work out in ways that defy human calculation. It can be hard to see the moral or character reason why a particular person gets the gifts of wisdom, knowledge, and happiness and another person is able to acquire much wealth but turns out to do so for the benefit of someone else. Where Churchman speaks of being good in God's eyes or being an offender, he refers to the way we cannot see why one person gains God's favor while another fails to do so. If God has his reasons, we cannot know what they are or set about trying to make sure we are the ones who do well. It's another reason for being satisfied with those ordinary things of life and not aiming too high.

ECCLESIASTES 3:1–15

Everything Has Its Time

1   There is a moment for everything,
      a time for every matter, under the sun:
2   a time for birthing, a time for dying,
      a time for planting, a time for uprooting what is planted,
3   a time for slaying, a time for healing,
      a time for demolishing, a time for building,
4   a time for weeping, a time for laughing,
      a time for wailing, a time for dancing,
5   a time for throwing stones, a time for gathering stones,
      a time for embracing, a time for holding back from
         embracing,
6   a time for searching, a time for losing,
      a time for keeping, a time for discarding,
7   a time for tearing, a time for mending,
      a time for being silent, a time for speaking,
8   a time for giving oneself, a time for repudiating,
      a time for war and a time for peace.

9 To the man who acts, what is the value in what he labors over? 10 I have seen the undertaking that God has given human beings to be busy with. 11 He has made everything fitting in its time; he has also put permanence into their

mind, but not so that a person can find out what God has done from beginning to end. [12] I acknowledged that there is nothing good for them except to enjoy themselves and do what is good in their lifetime. [13] Also, everyone who eats and drinks and sees something good through all his labor—it is God's gift. [14] I acknowledged that everything that God does, it will be forever. To it there is nothing to add; from it, there is nothing to take away. God has acted so that people are in awe of him. [15] What has happened, already is; that which is to happen, has already happened; and God seeks out what has been driven away.

Relatively early in the Vietnam War, folk singer Pete Seeger wrote a song called "Turn! Turn! Turn!" with the closing line, "I swear it's not too late." Everything else in the song comes from the poem in Ecclesiastes 3, lightly rearranged. In the 1960s, when the war was escalating, the Byrds made the definitive recording of the song, which reached number one in the United States, though made only the top thirty in Britain. It was more obvious in the United States than in Britain that it was an antiwar song; indeed, as a seminary student in Britain at the time, I don't remember being aware of that aspect of its significance, because we were naturally less aware of the Vietnam War. There, it was just a neat song, puzzlingly based on the Bible. In the context of the United States, in the manner of the Prophets the song urged the country to "Turn, turn, turn" and promised that it was not too late to abandon war-making.

In itself, the poem is easily open to being applied in that direction. The teaching in Proverbs or Ecclesiastes sometimes comes to its real point in its closing line, with everything leading up to that last line, and in this case the significance of the last line is also underscored by the change in the form of the last line. Every other line has included two verbs; at the end of the poem, nouns take the place of verbs. Yet if the poem were designed as an exhortation to peace-making rather than war-making, one might have expected the move to be the other way around, from nouns to verbs, and one might have expected it to make clear that peace-making is preferable to war-making. Further, Ecclesiastes doesn't elsewhere go in for moral exhortation of the kind presupposed by this application of the poem. It's significant that the song needs to add the exhortation to "turn." Ecclesiastes doesn't issue one.

The context in which the poem is set underlines the point. The chapter begins with the declaration that there is a time or a moment for all the activities the poem describes, and it follows up the poem with the long reflection on the way God has made everything fitting in its time. Birth and death, weeping and laughter, silence and speaking, and so on, along with peace and war—they are all part of human life as God has created it, part of human life "under the sun," as we experience it. These are not exhortations but descriptions. (The allusion to stones perhaps refers to the deliberate ruining of an enemy's fields and the correlative clearing of the stones and/or the collection of them for use in building.) In most cases, perhaps in all, one of the pair of verbs denotes an activity that is preferable to the other, and one effect of the poem is then to rub people's noses into the reality of human life. Death is as integral to it as life, slaying as healing, **repudiating** as giving oneself (the latter are words commonly translated **hate** and **love**). The equal status of the positive and the negative is further suggested by the random order in which they appear—sometimes the positive comes first, sometimes the negative comes first. In other words, Ecclesiastes itself isn't evaluating them as positive and negative. They are just realities.

The evaluation comes in the prose reflection. The sovereign God's lordship lies behind all these activities, but he hasn't made it possible for humanity to make sense of them as aspects of some whole. Somewhat enigmatically, Churchman declares that God has put "permanence" into our minds. The Hebrew word appears in the common expression "forever," but that expression can refer merely to a person's lifetime rather than denoting something that lasts for eternity. Here, it suggests that God has put into our minds a yearning to understand the big picture about human life and about God's activity in the world. Churchman implies that there is such a big picture; but from our position within the context of earthly life "under the sun," we cannot perceive what it is. All we see is the apparently random collocation of the contrasting activities that the poem describes. Fortunately, we know that God knows what the big picture is and that we can trust him for it.

His realization doesn't make Churchman inclined to despair and suicide. Once more, it makes him urge people to settle for what we can have and do—enjoy our life, do what is good, eat and drink, enjoy the fruit of our labor, and accept the gifts God has given us but also the limitations God has placed on us. The enigmatic last phrase perhaps also refers to entrusting the past to God.

ECCLESIASTES 3:16–4:3

There's No Justice

[16] Further, I have seen under the sun: in the place of the exercise of authority, faithlessness was there; in the place of faithfulness, faithlessness was there. [17] I said within myself, God will exercise authority over the faithful and the faithless, because there will be a time for every matter and for every activity there. [18] I said within myself with regard to human beings, [it's] for God to differentiate them and [for them] to see that they are animals, for themselves. [19] Because the lot of human beings and the lot of animals is a single lot for them. Like the dying of the one, so is the dying of the other. Each has the same spirit. Advantage of humanity over animals—there is none, because each is emptiness. [20] Each goes to the same place. Each came into being from dirt, and each returns to dirt. [21] Who knows if the spirit of human beings goes up and the spirit of animals goes down beneath the earth? [22] So I saw that there is

nothing better than that a person enjoys his activities, because this is his share, because who can give him discernment to see what will happen after him?

4:1 I again looked at all the acts of oppression that were occurring under the sun. There were the tears of the oppressed, and there was no comforter for them; yes, in the hand of their oppressors was the power, and there was no comforter for them. 2 I congratulated the dead people, who had already died, more than the living people, who were still alive. 3 Better than both of them is the one who hasn't yet come into being, who hasn't seen the evil action that occurs under the sun.

I've just been invited to a baby shower, a party where you give gifts to a couple expecting a baby. The difference about this couple is that they spend the main part of their lives working to make known the plight of Darfuri refugees in Chad. These people have been in refugee camps for a decade after fleeing for their lives from a policy of ethnic cleansing on the part of the government of Sudan, partly instigated by the possibility of there being substantial oil reserves in the Darfuri area. What astonishes me isn't only the willingness of this couple to give their lives to opposing this act of genocide but their unwillingness to abandon hope for these people when powerful forces rage against them, and the world cares little for their fate. How can they not give up in hopelessness? For that matter, how can they not abandon hope for humanity in general—because in bringing their own child into this seemingly horrendous world, they are, after all, taking the most hopeful step humans can take.

You could sometimes think that Churchman needs to see a therapist, he's so depressed. But clinical depression implies a paralyzing gloom that is inappropriate to a person's situation. Churchman's gloom is quite justified by the phenomena he's reacting to. It's hard to look in the face the facts about oppression in the world. Of course Churchman is more fortunate than us in not having the resources of the media telling him every day about atrocities all over the world. He can look only at his own people. But that is enough to make him speak exactly like a prophet when he describes **faithlessness** occupying the place that should be occupied by the **faithful** exercise of **authority**. A community's life is designed to be based on people caring for one another, supporting one another, doing right by one another, and protecting one another; that's faithfulness. The people with power in a community are supposed to exercise their authority in a way that expresses and supports such faithfulness. But members of communities often care chiefly for themselves, and people in power commonly use their power to encourage the strong to take advantage of the weak rather than protecting them; authorities and people collude in faithlessness.

Churchman tells himself that God will eventually exercise authority in the lives of faithful and faithless. Doing so would imply rescuing the former from the latter. How could it be otherwise? (Of course even the faithful have an element of faithlessness in them, but the Bible assumes that nevertheless there's a difference between people whose lives fundamentally point in the direction of faithfulness and people whose lives basically work in the other direction.) But when he hard-headedly looks at how things are in the world, he comes to a more sardonic understanding of what is implied by God's exercising authority in the lives of faithful and faithless. It doesn't mean God rescues the faithful and puts down the faithless. It simply means that both faithful and faithless die. God thereby shows us all that the superiority over animals that means so much to us is a figment of our imagination. We may think we are godlike, being made in God's image. But God doesn't die, and we do. Death differentiates us from God. We may think we are godlike; God breathed his spirit into us. But God breathed his spirit into animals too, as Genesis 7 also

191

says. We are made from dirt and we return to dirt, as Genesis 3 says.

So there's no difference between human beings and animals. Genesis indicates that it was indeed God's intention that the human beings should live on with God and not simply die, but that intention was frustrated. Yet it's hard for human beings to believe that when you die, it's the end, so they convince themselves that they will live on. Churchman asks, who knows whether that is so? Is there any evidence? Until Jesus rises from death, there will be none. It doesn't make Churchman conclude despairingly that there's no point to life and work. Rather it makes him commend enjoyment of the work we have. Death will mean we can engage in it no longer, and we cannot know what will happen to our achievements after we die, but this doesn't rule out the possibility of committing oneself to them in the meantime.

Maybe neither he nor we are convinced. He goes on to imply a more lugubrious conclusion. Can you really give yourself to your work when you know how hopeless things look in the world? The oppressors have the power, and the oppressed have no comforter. Here his language resonates with that of Lamentations 1, where most of the Old Testament occurrences of the word "comforter" come, in descriptions of laments at Jerusalem's situation after it has been devastated by the Babylonians. The earlier verses' background may have been the faithlessness of one Judahite to another. Here the parallel with Lamentations may imply that the background is Judah's oppression by another superpower; in his day, the successors to the Babylonians are the Persians or the Greeks. Their oppression is also the background to the visions in Daniel, where Greek rulers are making martyrs of people who insist on staying faithful to God. They have no comforter. There are two aspects to the idea of comfort in the Old Testament. As is the case in English, it denotes offering solace and encouragement. In Hebrew it also denotes taking action to relieve the causes of distress. In neither respect do the oppressed receive comfort. It's so discouraging a fact that one might congratulate people who have died and escaped the oppression, or the people who have not even been born to see it.

Should Churchman have given himself to relieving the suffering of people rather than simply moaning about it? Maybe he did; we cannot know what he did with his time when he was not writing. Maybe the question presupposes he would be in a position to do so when it was not so; he isn't a citizen of the superpower but a citizen of the community it's oppressing. Either way, we need to thank him for rubbing our nose in facts and refusing us the option of not facing them.

ECCLESIASTES 4:4–16
If Two People Lie Together, They Can Be Warm

4   I've looked at all labor and skill in activity:
    it's [from] the envy of a person by another.
  This too is emptiness,
    a chasing after wind.
5   "The stupid person folds his hands
    and eats his own flesh."
6   Better a palm-full with rest
    than two fistfuls with labor,
    and chasing after wind.

7 I again looked at everything under the sun. 8 There is a person, and he has no second person, either son or brother. And there is no end to all his labor; nor is his eye ever full of wealth. "But for whom am I laboring and depriving myself of good things?" This too is emptiness, an evil undertaking. 9 Two are better than one, in that they have better return for their labor. 10 Because if they fall, one can lift up his associate; but alas for the single person who falls and has no second person to lift him up. 11 Further, if two people lie together, they have warmth, but for one person— how can he be warm? 12 Also, if someone overpowers him

(the one person), the two can stand up to him. And a triple cord doesn't break quickly.

¹³ Better a young man who is poor but wise than a king who is old but stupid, who doesn't know how to heed a warning, ¹⁴ because from the prison house [the young man] can come out to become king, even when he had been born poor in the [old king's] kingdom. ¹⁵ I looked at all the living, walking about under the sun with the youth, the second [king], who stands in his place. ¹⁶ There was no end to all the people, to all before whom he stood. Yet those who are after him will have no enjoyment in him. Because this too is emptiness, a chasing after wind.

A friend of mine lost his wife some years ago and got married again to a family friend within three months. I was both worried and sympathetic (he had been looked after too well by his first wife and had no idea how to cook), but it has worked out fine. When my own wife died, I knew I needed to get used to her being gone before I got involved with someone else. At first I hated coming home to a house that was empty of her, but eventually I got more used to that experience, though I was still aware that the house was empty of anyone at all. After about nine months there was an occasion when I took my bike to the beach and lay on the sand and realized, "I can do this thing. I can be on my own." I couldn't imagine meeting someone new, and I had a solemn conversation with another unattached person in which we agreed that the price of adjusting to living with someone else wasn't worth the benefits. With hindsight, I realize that it was pretty inevitable that I would subconsciously be looking for someone else (so it's as well that I bumped into someone who is ideal for me).

One reason it was pretty inevitable is the point that Churchman makes here. It's better to be with someone else than to be on your own. To put it at its lowest, if you're in bed with someone else, you're more likely to get warm. Churchman isn't thinking about marriage alone, or perhaps at all. The observations he makes about avoiding being on your own are surprising; one might have expected him to think that the general unreliability of life and other people would make it wise to take a more individualist view and rely only on oneself. Yet elsewhere, too, he commends enjoyment of everyday life rather than burdening oneself with big unsolvable questions. He isn't life-rejecting. The practical advice here fits that attitude.

His advice also makes for a nice match with his opening comments in this section about the link between labor and envy. We might reexpress it in terms of the link between ambition and the need to slog away at work. In the world of scholarship, an old guy like me can relax, but people at the beginning of their scholarly lives have to sweat away at writing papers and giving presentations not because they have something they are keen to say but because of the principle "publish or perish." Making it in the scholarly world means getting ahead of the other people who are trying to make it, because there are more people looking for the jobs than there are jobs available. Churchman grants the truth in the saying that the person who sits on his patio with his hands folded (that is, doing nothing) ends up with nothing to eat; you could almost literally say that people who starve and become emaciated eat their own flesh. But there's a happy medium between that level of laziness and ambition that makes a person consumed by work itself. It's consideration of this attitude that leads into the comments about the un-wisdom of an individualistic isolation from other people. Two are better than one. Three is better still.

The last verses look with characteristic acerbity at the realities of politics and the fickleness of people's allegiance. They also make one think again of Solomon, whom Kings describes as someone who abandons wisdom for stupidity in his later years. Ironically, thinking of Solomon in this connection would also remind one of Jeroboam (who took over most of Solomon's kingdom) as a young man such as

Churchman describes. And thinking of Jeroboam might remind one of the way the history of the northern kingdom in Israel involved a series of coups d'état. Whereas the whole nation might gather in support of a new ruler, the next generation might become disenchanted with his dynasty. There's no such thing as stability in politics.

ECCLESIASTES 5:1–7
Sell Your Tongue, and Buy a Thousand Ears

> [1] Watch your steps as you go to God's house. Drawing near to listen is better than the giving of a sacrifice by stupid people, because they don't acknowledge that they are doing something evil. [2] Don't be hasty with your mouth; your mind should not be quick to bring forth a word before God, because God is in the heavens and you are on the earth. Therefore your words should be few. [3] Because a dream comes with much business, and the voice of a stupid person with a multitude of words. [4] When you make a promise to God, don't delay to fulfill it, because he has no delight in stupid people. What you promise, fulfill. [5] It's better that you don't make a promise than that you make a promise and don't fulfill it. [6] Don't give your mouth to making yourself cause offense. Don't say before the aide, "It was a mistake." Why should God be angry at your voice and destroy the labor of your hands? [7] Because in a multitude of dreams is total emptiness, and [in] many words. So be in awe of God.

On Saturday we were at a jazz club where the ceiling bears a poem by the thirteenth-century Persian mystic Rumi that closes, "I should sell my tongue and buy a thousand ears when that one steps near and begins to speak." Rumi is referring to a voice that comes from inside us, but the words made a connection for me with words we were to read the next day in church, God's words at Jesus' transfiguration: "This is my Son, the beloved: listen to him." The exhortation confronts Peter, who has a bright, alternative idea regarding an appropriate response to Jesus' transfiguration. We were remembering that event because it was the weekend before Lent, a season when listening rather than speaking is appropriate.

There are people who are inappropriately fearful in relation to God and people who are inappropriately overfamiliar. Churchman suggests that some self-examination is appropriate when we come to worship. Stupid people are those who take no notice of God in their everyday life and need God to confront them about their lives. They don't recognize the evil in their lives. Like our own worship, the offering of sacrifice presupposes that things are reasonably OK between people and God. Christians often assume that the main point about sacrifice is the need to deal with sin but the Old Testament makes clear that its main point is that people need appropriate ways of expressing self-giving, worship, and fellowship in relation to God and in relation to one another. In effect, Churchman is pointing out to people in general that they could be offering the kind of worship that fools offer; they could be fools without realizing it. They need the self-examination that Lent encourages. They need to sell their tongues and buy a thousand ears.

Back in chapter 2, Churchman has expressed his conviction that all our physical and mental effort is not only pointless but inclined even to rob us of restful sleep. The first comment about dreams makes a similar point. Instead of our sleeping restfully, our daytime preoccupations find expression in our dreams. But Churchman's observation is one of those where the point lies in the second half. Maybe anybody would grant the opening point about dreams; Churchman's aim is to draw a comparison between the way our daytime preoccupations generate dreams and the way fluency with words generates stupidity. The closing line is enigmatically expressed, but perhaps restates the point. As dreams tend to be empty and pointless, so do words.

In between, Churchman refers to one form of words that people may address to God that can be stupid, words of promise. In the context, his warning relates to promises about making a sacrifice—the psalms often refer to such promises. First, he says, if you make a promise, fulfill it right away. It's the least you can do if you take God seriously. Making promises and not fulfilling them is stupid—that is, it's morally wrong and likely to lead to trouble, because not fulfilling promises does things to a relationship. So think twice before you make promises, and don't make them if you may not be able to fulfill them. We discovered at our church council meeting on Sunday that so far this year people are giving more than the pledges on whose basis we formulated our budget. Better that way around than the other. In church we don't have heavies to go around reminding people that they have not fulfilled their pledges, though it's not a bad idea, and it looks as if the temple had such aides. So watch it, Churchman says.

ECCLESIASTES 5:8–6:9

It's Not Enough, but It's Not Nothing

[8] If there's oppression of the poor person and violating of faithful exercise of authority in the province, don't marvel at the matter, because one who is higher watches over one who is high, and ones who are higher [watch] over them. [9] The benefit of the land in every way is this: a king for the countryside that is worked. [10] Someone who gives himself to money doesn't have his fill of money, and whoever gives himself to wealth doesn't have his fill of his income. This too is emptiness. [11] With the increase of his goods, the people who consume them increase, so what is [the result of] the skill of its owner except his eyes seeing [the things]? [12] The sleep of someone who serves is sweet whether he eats much or little, but the abundance of the rich person doesn't let him alone to sleep. [13] There is a sick misfortune I've seen under the sun: wealth kept by its owner to his

misfortune, [14] or the wealth perishes through an unfortunate undertaking; and he fathers a son but there's nothing in his hand. [15] As he emerged from his mother's womb, naked he returns when he goes, as he came; he carries nothing of his labor in his hand when he goes. [16] This too is a sick misfortune. Corresponding to the way he comes, so he goes, and what is the value to him that he labors for the wind? [17] Further, all his days he eats in darkness with much vexation, sickness, and anger.

[18] Here is what I've seen as good, that it's fitting to eat and drink and see what is good in all a person's labor that he expends under the sun for the number of days of his life under the sun that God gives him, because this is his share. [19] Further, each person to whom God gives wealth and possession and to whom he gives the power to partake of them and to take up his share and enjoy himself in his labor—this is God's gift. [20] Because he won't give his mind much to the days of his life, because God occupies him with the enjoyment of his heart.

[6:1] There's an evil thing that I've seen under the sun, and it's widespread among human beings: [2] a person to whom God gives wealth, possessions, and honor, and who has no lack regarding his appetite for anything that he desires, but God doesn't empower him to partake of it, but a stranger partakes of it. This is emptiness and an evil sickness. [3] If a man fathers a hundred children and lives many years, and however many are the days of his years his appetite cannot be full from the good things: then even if it was not buried, I say the stillbirth is better off than him. [4] Because it comes in emptiness and it goes in darkness, and its name is covered in darkness; [5] though it doesn't see or know the sun, that one has rest. [6] Even if he lives a thousand years twice over but doesn't see the good things, isn't each going to the same place? [7] "All a person's labor is for his mouth, but his appetite may not get full." [8] Because what benefit does the wise person have over the stupid person? What does the lowly person have, who knows how to walk before the living? [9] The eyes seeing is better than the appetite journeying. This too is emptiness, a chasing after wind.

One sunny January day some years ago I came home after a lecture and wheeled my disabled wife down to the row of shops where there was a magnificent ice cream parlor that alas subsequently closed down (evidently we didn't go there enough). I ordered a fabulous chocolate sundae and ate most of it; at that time Ann could also swallow a bit and took a spoonful or two. Afterward I pushed her back up the hill to our house, singing silly songs and joking that eating all that ice cream might mean I couldn't get to the top of the hill, and she giggled. When we got back into the house, I lay her on her side on the sofa to relieve the pressure on her rear, where she was inclined to get sores because her difficulty in swallowing meant she was not assimilating enough nutrition. On other similar days I would take her to sit by the pool near our apartment and we would sit in the sun; I might have a glass of wine. It was not enough, but it was not nothing. This realization became a kind of mantra for me.

It's not far from the conviction Churchman holds, which he expresses in the middle paragraph of this section. The three verses include a threefold declaration about God's giving. One of his favorite statements about God is that God is one who gives. Some of that giving has negative implications ("it's an evil undertaking that God gave human beings to be busy with," he has said in chapter 2); but elsewhere it's key to his positive understanding of God and of life. God gives us the (admittedly limited) span of our life, with our freedom to enjoy the basics of life, food and wine and the other things that can be the everyday fruit of our work such as ice cream and sitting in the sun. Don't let yourself think too much about the big questions to which you'll never find the answers, he says, offering advice he doesn't himself take. Enjoy the life you have. It may not be enough, but it's not nothing.

These declarations come in the midst of more statements about wealth, though he starts from poverty and a realistic awareness of the power structures that encourage it. People use power to feather their own nests at the expense of others, and the existence of a power structure, which might in theory be designed as regulatory, in practice encourages such self-indulgence. The enigmatic comment about the king perhaps qualifies the point, given that the king's vocation was to ensure that people could keep hold of their land, and thus not end up in poverty. Churchman goes on to underscore his comments on the futility of seeking to accumulate wealth. First, the strange thing about wealth is that you can never have enough; therefore seeking it will get you nowhere. One reason is that the more wealth you have, the more people will look to you for help, or otherwise relieve you of it. All the enjoyment you get from your wealth is seeing the figures in your bank account. The person who "serves" (that is, works for someone else) and thus has enough but doesn't live in luxury has less cares than the person who works hard in order to get rich. One background to that reality is that wealth is never secure. One mistake and you may lose your fortune, live the rest of your life "in darkness with much vexation and sickness and anger," die with nothing as you were born with nothing, and have nothing to pass on to your descendants. A stranger enjoys the benefits instead of you or your family. You're no better off even than a stillbirth, which doesn't even get a proper burial.

In the context, the comment about wisdom and stupidity relates to the question about wealth; a wise person may also lose everything through some misfortune. Being wise may bring no advantage to the wealthy person. In turn, in the context the comment about the lowly person takes up the point about the oppression of the poor at the beginning of this section. It adds that nothing is to be gained by suggesting that being lowly is better than being wealthy. The final comment about the seeing of the eyes takes up the point that seeing their wealth may be the only benefit that the wealthy gain from it.

ECCLESIASTES 6:10–7:22

Be Realistic

[10] What happens has already been called by name, and what a human person is has become known. He cannot contend with one who is stronger than him, [11] because the more the words are, the more is the emptiness. What is the benefit for a person? [12] Because who knows what is good for a person in life for the number of the days of his empty life? He spends them like a shadow. Who can tell the person what will happen under the sun after him?

[7:1] A good name is better than good oil, and the day of death than the day of birth. [2] Going into a house of mourning is better than going into a house of feasting, in that this is the end of everyone and the living person should take it into his thinking. [3] Vexation is better than enjoyment, because despite misfortune in the face, the heart may be fine. [4] The heart of wise people is in a house of mourning, the heart of stupid people in a house of enjoyment. [5] It's better to listen to the rebuke of a wise person than that one listens to the song of stupid people, [6] because the laughter of stupid people is like the sound of thistles under a pot. But this too is emptiness, [7] because extortion can make a fool out of the wise person, and a gift can corrupt the thinking. [8] The end of a matter is better than its beginning. Patience of spirit is better than loftiness of spirit. [9] Don't be quick to be vexed in your spirit, because vexation rests in the heart of stupid people. [10] Don't say, "Why were the old days better than these," because it's not out of wisdom that you ask about this. [11] Wisdom is good, like property, and a benefit to people who see the sun. [12] Because wisdom is a true shelter as money is a true shelter, but the value of knowledge is that wisdom keeps its possessor alive. [13] Look at God's activity, because who can straighten what he has twisted? [14] In the day when things are good, partake of what is good, and in the day when things are evil, see: God made both this one and that one, so that a person cannot find out anything after him. [15] I've seen each in my empty days. There's a faithful person who perishes despite his faithfulness and there's a faithless person who endures despite his faithlessness. [16] Don't be very faithful and don't show yourself exceedingly wise: why should you be devastated?

¹⁷ Don't be very faithless and don't be stupid: why should you die when it's not your time? ¹⁸ It's good that you take hold of the one but also not let go of your grasp of the other, because someone who is in awe of God will emerge in respect of each of them. ¹⁹ Wisdom makes a wise person stronger than ten officials who were in a city. ²⁰ Because there's no faithful human being on earth who does good and doesn't offend. ²¹ Further, don't give your mind to all the things that people say, so that you don't hear your servant belittling you, ²² because your mind also knows the many times that you too have belittled other people.

Reading the line in Ecclesiastes 4 about a triple cord not breaking quickly, I remembered an occasion in seminary when I gave our professor of preaching a hard time for using that line to support the idea that a sermon ought to have three points. I accused him of being exegetically irresponsible. I was right, but I was not very nice. As a professor myself, I am now reminded by the close of this section of how student evaluations of courses pierce professors to the heart. It's because we're stupid, of course. One of my colleagues comments that when you read fifty evaluations, you don't take much notice of the nice ones; it's the one critical report that gets to you. I feel obliged to read student evaluations, and I learn from them and change things in light of them. But I try to remember not to read them when I am about to go to bed and hope to sleep. I read them when I'm feeling OK and have a glass of wine in hand, and don't visit the website where students all over the country (all over the world, for all I know) rate their professors.

Professors are human beings with feelings like anyone else, but we are also people in positions of power over our students. That relationship is the link with Churchman's closing point, about the relationship of masters and servants. It issues from and connects with the preceding lines that face masters and professors among others with the fact that nobody always does well. No one always avoids falling short, even if one wise person can indeed be stronger than ten people with official positions in the community, and wisdom does offer better safeguards in life than money does. Masters and professors can forget that they inevitably make mistakes. I do remind my students that ten percent of what I say is wrong; the trouble is, I don't know which ten percent (I also suggest that it's probably not the ten percent they think). The mistakes may not be just over academic matters. Churchman has already noted that even a wise person can be led stray by money—by extorting money or yielding to a bribe.

The point about human fallibility connects with the scandalous comments about not trying too hard to be **faithful** or wise. While there's truth in the maxim that aiming at the moon may mean you hit the lamppost, which is better than nothing, unrealism about what you can achieve can be utterly disheartening. So accept the good with the evil, and accept that if God makes or lets things happen that interfere with the way you wish life would work out, you just have to deal with it.

While the latter part of this section is shocking, it's less gloomy than its opening, which nevertheless summarizes points Churchman made at the beginning of the book. Lying behind the opening words is the fact that the Hebrew word for a (human) person is *adam*, and Adam was made from *adamah*, earth. As a creature made from earth, a mere human being cannot argue with God and force God to reveal mysteries about life's meaning that God has chosen not to reveal; our wordy attempts to do so are futile. Churchman goes on to dwell further on one of his favorite themes: we are going to die. The subsequent point about vexation may then suggest that it's possible to combine some frustration about our life ending in death (and about those unanswerable questions) with some genuine inner gladness, but thereby to avoid mere frivolity; which is the stance the book as a whole takes. It does go on to note that there are other forms of vexation or bases for vexation that are unwise.

ECCLESIASTES 7:23–8:15

I Have Not Found a Woman

[23] When I tested all this with wisdom, I said "I am going to be wise," but it's far from me. [24] What happens is distant and deeply profound; who can find it out? [25] I turned with my mind to get to know, explore, and seek wisdom and explanation, and to get to know faithlessness as stupidity and folly as madness. [26] I find more bitter than death the woman who is all traps, whose mind is all snares, whose hands are all chains. The person who is good before God escapes from her, but the person who offends is caught by her. [27] Look, this is what I've found, Churchman said, adding one thing to another to find an explanation, [28] which my mind sought further but I didn't find. I found one human being among a thousand, but a woman among these I did not find. [29] Only, look at this, I found that God made humanity upright, but they have sought many explanations.

[8:1] Who is like the wise person, and who knows the meaning of a thing? "A person's wisdom brightens his face, and the hardness of his face is changed." [2] I [say], "Keep the king's word, on account of the oath to God." [3] Don't rush to leave his presence. Don't take a stand against an evil word, because he can do anything that he wishes, [4] in that the king's word rules, and who can say to him, "What are you doing?" [5] One who keeps a command will not know an evil thing. The mind of a wise person will know the time to make a decision, [6] because for every matter there is a time to make a decision, when what is evil for a person is heavy on him. [7] Because he doesn't know what will happen, because when it's going to happen, who can tell him? [8] There is no one who rules over the spirit, to restrain the spirit, and there is no one who rules over the day of death. There is no discharge in war, and faithlessness cannot rescue the people who practice it. [9] All this I saw as I gave my mind to every action that occurs under the sun,

205

the time when people ruled over one another with evil results.

[10] Then I saw faithless people buried, when they came from the holy place. They went and they were forgotten in the city where they had so acted. This too is emptiness. [11] When the edict for an evil deed doesn't occur quickly, therefore the mind of people is full of doing what is evil within them. [12] When an offender does what is evil a thousand times, he lives long. Because I know that it will be good for people who are in awe of God, because they are in awe of him, [13] and it will not be good for the faithless person and he won't lengthen his days, like a shadow, because he isn't in awe of God. [14] There is an emptiness that occurs on the earth, that there are faithful people to whom things befall in accordance with the action of the faithless, and there are faithless people to whom things befall in accordance with the action of the faithful. I said, "This too is emptiness." [15] So I praised enjoyment, because there is no good for a person under the sun except to eat and drink and enjoy himself. That can accompany him in his labor for the days of the life that God has given him under the sun.

I just had a message from a young friend who will be in town next week and wants to come to see us. It's only a few months since she emailed to tell us that she had maybe found the man of her dreams, a man whose instincts about Christian ministry match hers and who is as sporty as she is. It sounds a great match. Is that just a "girly" thing? Apparently not, because two weeks ago I had a touching message from a mutual friend who thinks that he has maybe found the girl of his dreams. He described her as someone who loves God and loves people, which is also a good description of him. He sees God's hand in the fact that they have both been drawn to each other.

So what's wrong with Churchman when he says the things he says about women? In chapter 9 he implies that he would understand my two friends' attitude, when he encourages his reader to enjoy life with the woman he loves. So his statements about womanhood here cannot be universal generalizations. Maybe he's telling us he hasn't found someone for him or that the person he found (or who was found for him) was a disaster. His own experiences of women were negative. So he urges men to avoid being caught by the wrong woman. We have noted some points at which Churchman has Genesis in the back of his mind, even the front of his mind, and maybe his comments about relationships with women are another example. Eve was designed to be a "helper" to Adam, sharing life and vocation with him, but the design didn't work out well and she led him astray (of course, he was just as responsible as she was). Maybe it's significant that Churchman says that he couldn't find a "human being" (not a "man")—he uses the word *adam*.

Churchman's point reminds us that the extra preoccupations of a sexual relationship make it easy for a man to be misled in his quest for wisdom by a woman he falls for. He loses his capacity for critical thinking. If Genesis may be in the back of Churchman's mind, so may Proverbs. It warns about the way women can lead men astray, and it sets its comments in the contexts of the search for an understanding of life. The woman who can lead a man astray is the embodiment of untruth; Ms. Wisdom is set over against Ms. Stupidity.

If you're a woman reading his gloomy statements, you'll need to turn their warnings inside out. For you, it will be hard to find a man you can trust. You have maybe found men to be traps, snares, and chains. For you, too, it may be easier to find one human being among a thousand, but it will be a woman you find, not a man. In addition, women have to recall how they can be traps for men and break their hearts or lead them astray, while men will have to recall the same fact about themselves.

Churchman goes on to comments on relating to the king. The person who receives an education in the teaching that appears in Proverbs and Ecclesiastes is someone who may be in government service, who then needs to be realistic about the power factors in such service. Wisdom can give someone a positive attitude to other people, but such a rule may not apply to people in power. The king's underlings will be wise to take into account the ease with which one can antagonize the king and risk losing one's position and one's head.

The subsequent comments on **decision** making and the exercise of **authority** make one feel sympathy for the king as the person with whom the buck stops. He has to make decisions even though he usually cannot know enough to be confident that his decision is right. His decisions may have fatal implications for himself and for other people; he has to make them without knowing what those implications may be. The final paragraph implicitly critiques people in a position of authority rather than sympathizing with them. There are circumstances when it's morally clear what should be done, and the authorities don't see that the right action gets taken. Churchman is characteristically grieved that God does nothing about such failures. In theory **faithfulness** and **faithlessness** are supposed to get their reward, but it often seems that things don't work out that way and God doesn't intervene. Once again, Churchman's only solution is to suck it up and settle for enjoying the ordinary down-to-earth enjoyments of life.

ECCLESIASTES 8:16–9:12

Remember You Are Going to Die, and It May Be Sooner than You Think

16 When I gave my mind to knowing wisdom and looking at the undertaking that is fulfilled on the earth (because even day and night one does not see sleep with one's eyes), 17 and looked at all the action of God: a human being cannot find out about the action that is undertaken under

the sun. When a human being persists in seeking, he doesn't find. Even if a wise person says he'll know, he cannot find out. [9:1] Because all this I took to heart, and sifted all this, that faithful and wise people and their deeds are in God's hands. Both [his] loving and [his] repudiating: a person doesn't know either beforehand. [2] Everything is as it is for everyone. A single lot comes to the faithful person and to the faithless, to the good and to the pure and to the polluted, to the person who offers sacrifice and to the person who doesn't sacrifice. As the good person so is the offender. The person who swears is like the person who is afraid of an oath. [3] This is the evil about everything that occurs under the sun, that there is a single lot for everyone. Further, the mind of human beings is full of evil and there is madness in their heart during their life, and afterward— to the dead. [4] Because whoever is joined to all the living— there is hope, because a living dog is better than a dead lion. [5] Because the living know they will die, but the dead don't know anything. There is no more reward for them, because their memory has been forgotten. [6] Both their loving and their repudiating, their passion, has already perished. They have no more share forever in all that occurs under the sun.

[7] Go, eat your food with enjoyment, drink wine with a good heart, because God already approved your actions. [8] At all times your clothes should be white and oil should not be lacking on your head. [9] See life with the woman you love all the days of the empty life that you have been given under the sun, all the empty days, because that is your share in life and in your labor that you expend under the sun. [10] Everything that your hand finds to do, do with all your energy, because there is no action, explanation, knowledge, or wisdom in Sheol, where you're going. [11] I again saw under the sun that the race doesn't belong to the swift people, the battle to the warriors, nor food to the wise people, nor wealth to the discerning people, nor favor to the knowledgeable people, because time and chance happen to all of them. [12] Rather, a person cannot know his time. Like fish that are taken in an evil net and like birds that are taken by a snare—like them, human beings are trapped by an evil time when it falls on them suddenly.

I'd like to finish writing The Old Testament for Everyone, but I'm not taking for granted that I will. I need another year, and who knows whether I'll get one? Yesterday I received a message from people at a Christian guest lodge where I once worked. A man who had been staying there in retirement came to reception as he did almost every day, "laughing and joking with people as always, when suddenly he complained about not feeling well," the message said. "Some of our staff came to help him and by that time he had lost consciousness." He had had a heart attack, and paramedics could not revive him. "It felt as if someone had just turned off the lights, quietly and peacefully." He was only a little bit older than me. Paul McCartney is the same age as me. A recent interviewer asked him what he thought about dying on stage, but he recoiled and asked, "What kind of question is that?"

Rather a good question, Churchman would say; death is a topic he keeps coming back to. This section is where he deals with the subject most systematically. He starts again from the magnitude of the task that people like him set themselves in seeking to get an understanding of the world and what goes on in it. He knows he's seeking to understand the entire purpose of God in the world, but even if he thinks about it all night as well as all day, he cannot do so. We are in God's hands. In other contexts, that fact would be good news, but in this context, not so. The comment's point is that we know that God is in control of the world, but we can't see the rationale of that control. We know God is in control of our life and thus of our dying, but we can't know when the moment will come when God will withdraw the life breath that he gave. While his **loving** and his **repudiating** of us might refer in general to when God makes or allows good things or bad things to happen to us, in the context it refers particularly to whether God gives life or withdraws life. We recently saw a movie whose premise was that time was like money in that you had a certain amount, you knew how much you had, and you could use it as a medium of exchange and thus add to your capital or spend it faster than was absolutely necessary. When their time was drawing near, people had to run all the time to pursue some way of acquiring more time. In real life, on any given day you cannot know beforehand whether God will give life or withdraw it. And it needn't make any difference what kind of person you are.

Badness and madness characterize human life. Churchman again agrees with the assessment in Genesis, this time in Genesis 6. You might think this observation is gloomy enough. He is even more appalled by the fact that the human life we have is all there is. "Afterward—to the dead." The austere reality of being dead means there is something to be said for being alive! Where there's life there's hope. One might think of being able to enjoy life in the way he elsewhere commends. The advantage he mentions is different and turns the positive statement into an irony. If you're alive, you know something—that you're going to die. If you're dead, you know nothing. You will not get anything out of existing when your existence is in **Sheol**. People will not be mindful of you, and you will not be mindful of anything. When you're alive, you have passions; it's part of being human. You love and you repudiate, like God. When you're dead, passion is over.

Facing the facts about death doesn't make Churchman reject life. Once again he does urge us to enjoy the lives we have with their real simple human pleasures as long as we have them. This time he includes the enjoyment of a relationship with the person one loves. God has approved our doing so—either by giving humanity in general such a life to live or by giving us as individuals the lives we have until God decides to terminate them. The fact that you will be able to do nothing in Sheol isn't reason to be paralyzed now; rather the opposite.

It was Ash Wednesday yesterday, and one of its themes is the importance of keeping in mind that you are going to die (*memento mori*). Eastern Orthodox Christian teaching is particularly inclined to emphasize the importance of thinking about this fact. With Ecclesiastes it affirms that facing death doesn't then inhibit you from enjoying life—again, rather the opposite. If I hide from the fact of death, it nevertheless sits there in my unconscious so that I may not be really able to enjoy life and to do in life what I would want to do, before it's too late. It means living in the present in the awareness that today might be the last day or week or month or year of my life. So I would be wise to do what I would not want to miss doing before I die rather than putting off what I would not want to miss or waiting until I am in the mood. Such an attitude brings depth and meaning to life. Jesus' death and resurrection has now made it possible for people to enjoy resurrection life, which takes the edge off the way death terminates the possibility of living a full this-worldly life, but it doesn't alter the fact that death does so.

I want to finish The Old Testament for Everyone.

ECCLESIASTES 9:13–10:20

The Distressing Dynamics of Wisdom and Power

13 This too I've seen as wisdom under the sun, and it seemed great to me. 14 There was a small city and a few people in it, and a great king came to it, surrounded it, and built great siege works against it. 15 There was found in the city a poor man, wise, and he rescued the city by his wisdom, but no one was mindful of that poor man. 16 I said, "Wisdom is better than strength." But the poor man's wisdom is despised, and his words are not listened to. 17 The words of wise people with calmness are listened to more than the crying out of a ruler among stupid people. 18 Wisdom is better than implements of war, but one offender destroys much good. 10:1 As dead flies putrefy, ferment the perfumer's oil, a little stupidity is weightier than wisdom, than honor. 2 The mind of a wise person goes to his right, the mind of a stupid person goes to his left. 3 Also, on a journey, when a stupid person walks, his sense is lacking, and he tells everyone that he's stupid.

⁴ If the spirit of the ruler arises against you, don't let go of your place, because calmness can let go of great offenses. ⁵ There is something evil that I've seen under the sun, the kind of error that has come from an official: ⁶ stupidity has been put in many high positions, and wealthy people sit in a lowly place. ⁷ I've seen servants on horses and ministers walking on the ground like servants.

⁸ The person who digs a pit may fall into it; the person who breaks down a wall—a snake may bite him. ⁹ The person who quarries stones may be hurt by them; the person who splits logs may be endangered by them. ¹⁰ If the iron has become dull and he hasn't sharpened the edge, he must exert more strength, so wisdom lies in the value of being skillful. ¹¹ If the snake bites when there's no spell, there's no value in having an expert with the tongue.

¹² The words from the wise person's mouth mean favor, but the lips of a stupid person swallow him. ¹³ The beginning of the words from his mouth is stupidity, and the end of his mouth is evil madness, ¹⁴ but the stupid person multiplies words. A person doesn't know what will happen; who can tell him what will happen after him? ¹⁵ The labor of stupid people wearies him, because he doesn't know how to get to a city. ¹⁶ Alas for you, country whose king is a youth and whose ministers eat in the morning. ¹⁷ The blessings of the country whose king is one born of nobles and whose ministers eat at the [proper] time, with control and not with drinking. ¹⁸ Through laziness the rafters sag, through idle hands the house drips. ¹⁹ For fun, people make a meal; wine makes life enjoyable; money answers everything. ²⁰ Even in your thinking don't belittle the king, and in your bedroom don't belittle a rich person, because a bird of the heavens may take the sound, a winged creature may report what is said.

Several days a week I find myself reporting to my wife something from the news with the explicit or implicit comment, "How can people be so stupid?" This week it's the fact that Western forces in Afghanistan had burned some copies of the Quran that they had taken from prisoners in detention as suspected Taliban members. Not surprisingly, this provoked riots by Afghanis outraged at the burning of their holy book, and army commanders and the U.S. president have been scrambling to bring about damage control. The cynic might ask whether the rioters were seizing an opportunity to riot rather than expressing their true religious outrage, but if that is so, then it makes the stupidity of the Quran burners more stupid. Similar sequences of events in the past surely mean that anyone could have predicted the result of their action.

Churchman is disheartened by such stupidity, which takes various forms. The verses about a particular city may be based on something that had been in the news in Churchman's day. Either an ordinary man had the insight that enabled the city to resist attack but was then forgotten, or someone had such an insight but no one took any notice of his idea because he was just an ordinary man. Either way the event illustrates how wisdom is more telling in military affairs than mere strength and that it can come from an apparently unlikely quarter but also that it may be ignored or forgotten or frustrated by the action of one stupid person, as a small amount of something rotten can ruin everything it touches. And if it's inevitable that some people in the military are not very wise, it's imperative that commanders make sure that wise people are spread around military units.

Since the section comes back to rulers in due course, the context suggests applying especially to rulers the comments about the mind of the wise person and the stupid person. It's often thought that the right is someone's lucky side, the left is the unlucky side; the saying about right and left starts from that assumption. The story goes that Napoleon would ask of a potential general "Is he lucky?" Maybe one implication is that people often make their own luck by means of their wisdom. Conversely, military commanders who lead their army the wrong way or fail to take a city that should have been vulnerable are the victims of their own shortcomings and not of mere bad luck. They reveal that they are stupid.

Their stupidity may turn them against you (Churchman goes on), but don't panic. Their volatility may also mean that they take a different attitude tomorrow. He closes his collection of sayings on the problem with people in authority with further expressions of frustration. Plato suggested that the state should be ruled by philosopher kings; maybe Churchman had read Plato. More obviously he's depressed by the way many rulers are not merely average with regard to wisdom but preeminent in stupidity. Perhaps wise people are also selfish and avoid becoming leaders. Churchman assumes here the regular rule that the wealthy people are the ones with power in society, as is the case in Western nations, and that turning the regular order upside down likely imperils the stability of the society as a whole. What if the wealthy are people who are stupid or who gained their wealth by unjust means? If you asked him that question, I imagine he would say he isn't talking about that kind of wealthy person.

Most of the sayings in the middle paragraph simply describe some unfortunate facts about life. Such sayings don't necessarily have implications such as, "So be careful." Their implication rather is, "If it happens to you, deal with it. That's just how life is." The exception might be the saying about the snake charmer, if its point is that you lose your opportunity to exercise your skill if you let things work out on their own.

The third paragraph returns to the interconnections of leadership and wisdom. The sayings about wisdom and stupidity would again be significant for someone working in the administration. The basic ideas are three: speak little; think before you speak; and don't sound as if you think you know what you don't actually know. In circumstances such as the ones the paragraph goes on to describe, when the king is young and his senior staff self-indulgent, it might be the more tempting to give them the benefit of one's wisdom, but discretion might be wiser. That discretion needs to extend to contexts where one is speaking in private; walls have ears. In the midst of these warnings, the context suggests it's the king and his ministers who especially need to be aware that negligence and self-indulgence are unwise and can cause them big trouble. But here, too, the sayings are describing how things are rather than suggesting that they could be otherwise.

ECCLESIASTES 11:1–12:7
Enjoy Your Life Mindful of Your Creator

[1] Send off your bread on the surface of the water, because in many days you may find it. [2] Give a share to seven or even to eight, because you don't know what evil thing may happen on the earth. [3] If the clouds fill, they will pour down rain on the earth; if a tree falls on the south or on the north, in the place where the tree falls, there it will be. [4] Someone who watches the wind will not sow, and someone who looks at the clouds will not reap. [5] As you don't know the way of the wind, like the limbs in the womb of a pregnant woman, so you don't know the action of God who does everything. [6] In the morning sow your seed and at evening don't let your hand relax, because you don't know whether the one will succeed or the other or if both of them will be equally good.

[7] The light is sweet, and it's good for the eyes to see the sun. [8] Because if a person lives many years, he should enjoy all of them but be mindful of the days of darkness, because they will be many. Everything that will happen is emptiness. [9] Enjoy yourself, young man, during your youth. Your heart should make you fine during the days of your youth. Walk about in the ways of your heart and in the sights of your eyes, and acknowledge that for all these things God will bring you to judgment. [10] So remove vexation from your heart and make evil pass from your body because youth and vigor are empty, [12:1] and be mindful of your creator in the days of your youth, before the evil days come and the years arrive of which you'll say, "There's no delight for me in them," [2] before the sun and the light, the moon and the stars, go dark, and the clouds return after the rain, [3] on the day when the keepers of the house tremble and the strong men stoop, and the women who

grind stop because they are few and the women who look through the windows grow dim, ⁴ and the doors to the street are shut as the sound of the mill becomes low, and one arises at the sound of a bird but all the daughters of song grow weak; ⁵ further, people are afraid of heights and there are terrors on the road, and the almond blossoms and the grasshopper becomes a burden and desire fails, because the person is going to his eternal home and the mourners are coming around in the street— ⁶ before the silver cord snaps and the golden bowl breaks and the jar shatters at the spring and the wheel breaks at the cistern ⁷ and the dirt returns to the earth as it came, and the spirit returns to the God who gave it.

I remember the first time I heard Ray Charles perform. Having been blind for many years, he had to be guided toward the piano, but he needed much more help than his blindness alone would have required. He was a frail old man (he died two or three years later). But as soon as his fingers touched the keys he was full of life, and it became clear that there was a big disparity between the inner man and the outer man. It was a moment that made me aware of the way a person can be still thrillingly alive inside but fragile and ailing outwardly. Paradoxically, the opposite can also be true. I have referred to my friend and mentor who died a few days ago, whose wife is in quite good shape physically, but who is seriously affected by dementia. Who knows what she will make of his funeral next week? Is it scarier to contemplate physical decline or mental decline?

In the Old Testament's world, the former is the more familiar reality, and as Churchman comes near the end of his book, he urges people to face it. Once again he does so not in order to inhibit people from enjoying life but in order to encourage them to do so in a way that doesn't ignore that other reality. It's an example of the Old Testament's "both-and" stance to life. The Psalms assume that when life is bad, you don't give in to the idea that it has never been good and can never be good again, but neither do you deny the grimness of present reality, and Churchman's attitude is similar. So he urges the young person to enjoy life and to remember that "God will bring you to judgment." He hardly refers to judgment after death, to which he hasn't otherwise referred; more likely he simply refers to death itself as a kind of judgment, the implementing of God's **decision** to terminate a life, which eventually comes to everyone. But the context may rather suggest that God's judgment is his evaluating whether we have made the most of enjoying our lives. In other words, the idea that the eventual approach of death makes youth and vigor empty and pointless should not make young people so vexed and unhappy that they fail to enjoy the youth they are given. Yet neither should they fail to keep their creator in mind during their youth, because he's eventually going to undertake that evaluation and bring about that judgment.

They need to be mindful in that way before they get old. It's a little as if Churchman is warning against the idea of deathbed repentance, or deathbed regrets and resentments, but the dynamics of his concern are different. He isn't saying that deathbed repentance is impossible or that death may take you before you get around to repenting, but that he wants people to live authentic human lives, and it's such lives that need to be characterized by enjoyment of what God gives but truthfulness in respect of where our lives will lead. He gives a vivid poetic description of the latter, focusing not on death itself but on old age. Many of the poetic images are ambiguous, but the general picture is clear. Old age is when you stop enjoying life because your physical frailty makes it impossible to do so. It's when gloom falls on your life. It's when your arms fail, your legs grow weak, your teeth fall out, your eyes grow dim. It's when your ears become deaf and your voice becomes faint. It's when you wake up with the birds because you can't sleep, but you can't properly hear girls singing. It's when you're afraid of heights and of the danger of going out. It's when your hair grows white like almond blossom and you shuffle along like a grasshopper and your desires fail. All these experiences indicate you're on your way to your eternal home in the grave, in **Sheol**; indeed the mourners are already gathering like rival undertakers looking for business. It's the moment when the thread of life snaps, or like a bowl breaking. It's when dirt and spirit return whence they came.

The opening part of this section deals with the more general need in life to live with uncertainty and not be paralyzed by it. Maybe these verses comprise advice for adulthood rather than for youth or old age. In trade, you have to be prepared to take a chance. It's no good being like the man in Jesus' parable who hides his bag of gold in the ground. There are laws of nature that God works by and that we have to live with, even though we may not be able to understand them (any more than we can understand how a baby grows in the womb) or predict how they will work out on a given day.

ECCLESIASTES 12:8–14

One Ecclesiastes Is Good, but One Is Enough

> [8] "Utter emptiness," said Churchman, "everything is empty." [9] But further: because Churchman was wise, he also taught the people knowledge. He weighed and examined, set in order many sayings. [10] Churchman sought to find pleasing words, and what was written was upright. Truthful words, [11] wise words, are like goads; the masters of collections are like fixed nails. They were given by one shepherd. [12] But further, beyond these, my son, beware. Of the making of many books there is no end and much study is a wearying of the body. [13] The conclusion of the matter; everything has been heard. Be in awe of God and keep his commands, because this is [for] everyone. [14] Because God brings every action to a decision, concerning everything hidden, whether good or evil.

219

Yesterday a student came to see me because he's having a hard time with my course on the Psalms and with his academic work in general. He wasn't concerned to make excuses but just wanted me to understand what was going on. He has almost completed his degree and is finding it difficult to concentrate on his work. It's partly because he has been in education for too long; he came to seminary straight from his undergraduate degree at a Christian college where he also studied some theology. He needs to get out into the world, though another problem he has is that he isn't sure what he should be doing after graduating. He also has another classic problem. He came to seminary thinking he would find answers to questions, and he has found some but has also discovered many more questions.

The closing paragraph of Ecclesiastes recognizes his problem and offers him advice, though maybe advice isn't what he most needs. He also needs friends and relaxation and prayer (I did pray with him) to help him simply get through the next three months and start breathing. This closing paragraph begins by repeating the mantra with which the book began, whose key word it has repeated many times along the way. Everything is totally empty. The repetition of the phrase makes clear that Ecclesiastes isn't a book that makes progress or comes to a conclusion or finds resolution for the problems and questions it raises. Everything is as empty at the end as it was at the beginning. The implication isn't that life itself is empty; Churchman has made that conviction clear by his exhortations to enjoy the everyday delights of life such as food and drink and relationships. But he does face us with the fact that "under the sun" there's no answer to the big questions about how the world works and what it means, and about how the world doesn't work.

To find the answers to those questions, you have to look elsewhere. Churchman's declarations implicitly fit with a basic presupposition of the Bible as a whole. The answers lie in the account of what God did in the story of God's involvement with Israel that begins with the exodus and leads up to the story of Jesus. The reason the Bible has authority is that it alone can tell us this story. Churchman submits himself and us to a thought experiment. What happens when you leave out this story and confine yourself to what you can discover empirically? "Everything is empty" is the answer. Why does he go in for the thought experiment? Possibly it's that the exodus is a long time ago, and in more recent centuries God's involvement with Israel has been harder to perceive. Okay, people say that one day God will send the Messiah, but does that idea help in the present? On what basis do we live now? Churchman's answer is to look to what we can see now and to live in light of those facts. He may thus be an encouragement to people in the twenty-first century for whom Jesus' story may seem a long time ago and his return also theoretical and remote.

The book's last paragraph offers its own attempt to square the circle of acknowledging the worth of Ecclesiastes yet setting the book in the context of Israelite faith. It speaks about Churchman in the third person, suggesting that it is a conclusion by someone else, perhaps the people who wanted to make sure that Ecclesiastes became part of the Scriptures, as the book's opening verse was their introduction to the book. In case readers question whether they should take seriously a collection of teaching that ends where it began with that comment about emptiness, the conclusion affirms that Churchman was indeed someone wise who wrote insightfully and well. Then it offers an observation about the nature of its wisdom. Churchman's wise words are like spurs. When horse riders dig their spurs into their horses, this isn't a pleasant experience for the horses, but it's an important experience. Many of Churchman's statements make one say "Ouch, I wish you hadn't said that," but one knows that it was true and it was therefore something one needed to face rather than hide from, if one is to move forward in life. To put it another way, Churchman operates like a craftsman banging nails into a wall and making sure they are firmly fixed. Each time he bangs, we say "Ouch," but we know the banging is necessary if there is to be proper construction. So, the conclusion affirms, these painful sayings come from a shepherd. The shepherd might be a human leader of Israel or might be Israel's divine shepherd; either way, the comment affirms that they comprise teaching that is edifying and nourishing for the sheep.

On the other hand (the conclusion goes on), while one Ecclesiastes is a good thing, it would be of no use for the Bible to be full of books like Ecclesiastes. The theology student's favorite verse about the making of many books and the wearying nature of study thus applies specifically to books that are stronger on questions than on answers—which may be the nature of most theological books, I reflect as I think about it in light of my discussion with that student. So the closing verses advise, don't lose track of the basics. They don't point the reader to those basics of Israelite faith that distinguish the Old Testament, the story of God's promises to Israel's ancestors, the exodus, Sinai, the gift of the land of Canaan, **Yahweh's** commitment to David, the building of the temple, the drama of the monarchy, the exile, the restoration, and the activity of Ezra and Nehemiah. They stick with the basics of the faith expressed in Proverbs and Job. Be in **awe** of God. Express that commitment by doing what God says. And remember Churchman's own words about God's judgment.

SONG OF SONGS 1:1–17
Alone Together

1   The Song of Songs, which is Solomon's.

2 May he give me some of the kisses of his mouth!—
     because your love is sweeter than wine.
3 Your fragrance—your oils are sweet,
     your name is flowing oil.
   Therefore girls love you;
4   draw me after you, let's run.
   The king has brought me into his apartments;
     let us rejoice and exult in you.
   Let us commemorate your love more than wine;
     rightly they love you.
5 I am dark but lovely, Jerusalem daughters,
     like the tents of Qedar, like Solomon's curtains.
6 Don't look at me because I am dark-skinned,
     because the sun has stared at me.
   My mother's sons were angry with me,
     they made me one who guards the vineyards.
   My vineyard, the one I had,
     I did not guard.
7 Tell me, you whom I love with my whole being,
     where do you pasture, where do you rest at midday?
   Why should I be like someone covering herself
     by the flocks of your companions?

8 If you don't know for yourself,
     loveliest of women,
   get yourself out in the tracks of the flock,
     pasture your goats by the shepherds' dwellings.
9 To a mare among Pharaoh's chariots
     I have compared you, my dear.
10 Lovely are your cheeks with earrings, your neck with
     necklaces;
11 we will make gold earrings for you, with studs of silver.

12 While the king was on his couch,
     my nard gave its fragrance.
13 My love to me is a bag of myrrh
     that lies between my breasts.
14 My love to me is a cluster of henna
     in the vineyards of En-gedi.

15 There you are, so lovely, my dear;
     there you are, so lovely, your eyes doves.

223

> [16] There you are so lovely, my love,
>   yes beautiful, yes our couch is verdant.
> [17] Cedars are the beams of our house,
>   cypresses are our rafters.

A couple of years ago, when we were planning to get married in the month of December, I initially assumed we would honeymoon somewhere tropical like Bali. Instead we went to Scotland, where it turned out to be the coldest and snowiest December for two hundred years, but it had been from there that some of my fiancée's ancestors had been expelled to the American colonies in the seventeenth century. Bali or Scotland, there was no doubt we would honeymoon somewhere. A couple who are coming together to start a new life need to get away from everyone. We were fortunate that we met no opposition in doing so. (When you are young, you have to get your parents' goodwill to get married; when you are old, you have to get your children's goodwill.)

The couple that speak in this first part of the Song of Songs want to get away, though the getting away is more a part of their courtship. There's no particular reason to think that the whole book concerns the same couple any more than all the Psalms are spoken by the same person, and it solves some problems about understanding the Song if we assume it's a collection of separate love poems rather than a single poem. This idea fits the fact that the Song begins "in the middle of things" and ends in the same way; it doesn't have a linear structure. The title "Song of Songs" could then mean "A Song made up of songs," though it may mean "The most tuneful song" (compare the phrase "emptiness of emptinesses, that is, "utter emptiness," in Ecclesiastes).

Most of the poems involve a dialogue between a man and a woman. In the Hebrew it is usually easier to tell who is speaking, because it has different words for when a man says "you" from when a woman says "you," as English has different words for male and female, such as "he" and "she." I have divided the translation into paragraphs according to who is speaking, and you can see easily enough how the alternating works. You'll also see that there can be big differences in the length of the sections, as happens in real conservations. The woman sometimes speaks of her man as "he," sometimes as "you," and she can switch between the two in one line; though it reads oddly in English, it's not uncommon in Middle Eastern poetry. In addition, we need not take all the occurrences of "we" too literally. Sometimes it's like the royal "we," when a British monarch says "we" but means "I."

So the first two paragraphs are partly concerned with how the woman and man can make sure they are able to be together for some time during the day. In the poet's imagination at least, they are both shepherds, which is a common occupation for young men and women. The woman wants to know where she'll be able to find her man, particularly during his lunch break and siesta. She doesn't want the embarrassment of having to negotiate her way through other groups of shepherds, veiled in order not to be caught. So he tells her which track he intends to follow as he finds pasture for his sheep, so she can follow with her goats.

Each tells the other how lovely they are. In their imagination (but perhaps also in reality) all the women recognize how handsome he is and all the men recognize how attractive she is. The woman herself doesn't think she is lovely, but the poem recognizes how someone who loves sees the beloved differently from other people. To the woman, in a culture that values fair skin, she's unattractive because her skin has been darkened by the sun, as a result of the way on other occasions she has been sent to keep guard in the vineyard, to chase off animals and/or raise the alarm when people tried to steal the grapes. Maybe her brothers' anger results from her desire to spend time with this young man. But in the Song a vineyard can be an image for a woman's personal self, especially her sexual self, and the ensuing comment implies that having to look after the literal vineyard has meant she hasn't been able to look after her physical self.

At the same time as picturing them as shepherds or vineyard keepers, the poems picture them as a king and a princess—or rather, that is how they picture themselves. In each other's eyes, it's what two lovers are. They are sitting outside in the shadow of the trees, but it's as if they are reclining in the royal apartments. Little girls have often thought of their weddings as coronations or royal-like ceremonies, as the time when they get to be "queen for a day." The appearance of this new image reminds us to be wary of taking even the first image too literally. The poems are not simply describing an actual shepherd and shepherd girl. They are poetry.

In the Song as a whole the woman speaks first and speaks at greater length than the man, which might be one possible indication that it was written by a woman or that parts of it were. It contrasts with the idea that a woman should not take the initiative in a relationship or in speaking. The description of the Song as "Solomon's" in the opening line need not imply the idea that Solomon is its author. The picture of Solomon (with his harem) in 1 Kings doesn't give the impression that he was someone who would write love poetry. As is the case with Proverbs and Ecclesiastes, the reference to Solomon indicates that the book's contents are Solomonic in the sense that they express real wisdom.

One implication of the presence of the Song in Scripture is a recognition that natural human love is God's gift, including the love of ordinary people like a shepherd girl and a shepherd boy. Our instinct to love, our sexuality, and our sexual enthusiasm are part of the way God created us, and something God rejoices in. The boy and girl in these poems are on the way to marriage and looking forward to it rather than already married, but that fact doesn't stop them from rejoicing in their sexual enthusiasm for each other. Maybe the assumption is that it's appropriate for this aspect of their relationship to grow as they get near marriage. Without it, the marriage may be less likely to work. The poems don't actually talk about marriage, though in the context of the Scriptures it would be assumed that their relationship will lead to marriage. The Old Testament would not be working with the idea that a man or a woman might be involved in some temporary sexual relationship in whose context such poems might belong, and the poems imply that the relationship they describe involves this relationship being the love of their life for each of them. But marriage has all sorts of more solemn aspects than love and sex, and it's these latter that the Song is interested in.

SONG OF SONGS 2:1–17

My Love Is Mine, and I Am His

1 I am a crocus of Sharon,
   a lily of the valleys.

2 Like a lily among thorns,
   so is my dear among the girls.

3 Like an apricot among the trees of the forest,
   so is my love among the boys.
   In its shade I delighted to sit,
   and its fruit was sweet to my palate.
4 He brought me into his house of wine,
   and love was his standard over me.
5 Refresh me with raisins, revive me with apricots,
   because I am sick with love.
6 His left hand would be under my head,
   his right hand would hold me.
7 I adjure you, Jerusalem girls,
   by the gazelles or the wild deer,
   Don't awaken, don't arouse love,
   until it wishes.

227

⁸ The sound of my love!—there, he's coming,
  leaping over the mountains, bounding over the hills.
⁹ My love is like a gazelle
  or a young stag.
There, he's standing, behind our wall,
  gazing from the window, peering from the lattice.
¹⁰ My love spoke up and said to me:
"Get yourself up, my dear,
  my lovely one, and get yourself going!
¹¹ Because there—the winter has passed,
  the rain has stopped and taken itself off.
¹² The blossoms have appeared in the country,
  the time of singing has arrived,
  the voice of the pigeon has made itself heard in our
    country.
¹³ The fig tree has ripened its fruit,
  the vines in blossom have given their fragrance.
Get yourself up, my dear,
  my lovely one, and get yourself going!
¹⁴ My dove, in the clefts of the crag, in the hiddenness of the
    cliff,
  let me see your appearance, let me hear your voice.
Because your voice is sweet,
  your appearance is alluring."

¹⁵ Catch the foxes for us, the little foxes,
  ruining the vineyards, when our vineyards are in
    blossom.
¹⁶ My love belongs to me, and I belong to him,
  the one who pastures among the lilies.
¹⁷ While the day blows and the shadows flee,
  turn, be like a gazelle, my love,
  or a young stag on the mountains of Bether.

One of my best friends when I was a teenager, having exhausted the dating possibilities in our youth fellowship, started going out with a girl from another church, and I commented that she was rather plain compared with some of the girls he had gone out with. He knew what I meant, but he commented that when you are going out with someone and you come to love them, they become more attractive in your eyes. Indeed, I later recognized, his new girlfriend became more attractive in my eyes, too, and I realized that when you are loved, it adds a sparkle to your face. We were pretty sophisticated sixteen-year-olds, don't you think? And my friend and that new girlfriend have now been married for nearly fifty years; further, nowadays my own wife sometimes says I'm handsome, and I look in the mirror and think, "Not so much."

That motif in the first chapter of the Song reappears in the second chapter. Traditionally translations have the woman describing herself as a rose of Sharon, a phrase that has become an image for beauty. But Sharon is the marshy coastal area of Israel, and the crocuses there are just common wild flowers. Likewise there would be nothing special about lilies in a valley. The man accepts the image of lily, but he makes her a lily among thorns. No offense intended to the other girls, but the image points to her specialness to him over against them.

Conversely, he's no huge cypress like the one they sat under in chapter 1, no cedar of Lebanon. He's a homely apricot tree. But even an apricot tree has enough shade for them to sit under, and it has the great advantage of producing refreshing fruit. To put it another way, it's as if he takes her into a wine bar; she finds his love intoxicating. To put it yet another way, he's like a warrior who puts his battle standard over her and protects her.

In this section, within the drama of the poem the woman is speaking to other people (in Hebrew you can also tell whether "you" refers to one person or to a group of people; she isn't just speaking to her love). It eventually becomes clear that it's the other Jerusalem girls that she's addressing. Once more she's separated from her man, and it hurts. She needs them to provide her with the refreshment she might have if she were with him. So apricots feature again, along with raisins; they would be an equivalent revitalizing indulgence when fresh fruit was not in season. Her exhortation not to arouse love until the proper time links with the poem's presupposing that the two of them can't be together at the moment. Maybe she needs her girlfriends to take her mind off her romance and not to want to hear every detail about it, because she needs not to think about it too much when they are not yet in a position to be together all the time. Or maybe it's only in her imagination that she addresses the Jerusalem girls, urging them not to let themselves get overwhelmed by love when it cannot reach its goal, because that is the ache she feels (as if one has any choice!); she's really speaking to herself and processing that ache. Either way, her words could be a comfort to the people who are hearing the poem read, who have the same ache and are wondering if they are the only one for whom "love hurts." It would come home in different ways to young people learning about love for the first time and to older people remembering their young love; it might even help renew their feelings for their longtime spouses.

In the longest paragraph she imagines her lover coming and speaking. She thereby ignores her own advice, which she perhaps thereby acknowledges to be unrealistic. From inside her parents' house she pictures him coming and calling through the window, urging her to come and join him. "In the spring a young man's fancy lightly turns to thoughts of love" (Alfred Lord Tennyson), and so do hers. As he is inaccessible to her, in her imagination (and no doubt in reality) she is inaccessible to him. In her parents' home she's as inaccessible as the kind of cleft in a rock where a bird takes refuge, and he wants to see her and hear her voice as she wants to hear his voice and see him.

The line about the foxes takes up the image of a vineyard and issues an appeal that their love may not be attacked and harmed, but it's not clear who is addressed; maybe we don't have to identify addressees. It's common for someone to worry that the lover will be stolen away when they are apart.

The background to the appeal is the straightforward but profound description of their mutual commitment, "My love is mine, and I am his." If the Old Testament spoke only of a wife as belonging to her husband, one might infer that it had a property understanding of marriage; but it speaks of "her husband" as well as "his wife" (literally, "her man" and "his woman"). Its ideal is a relationship in which each person owns the other; the man gives himself to his wife, the woman gives herself to her husband (and, incidentally, they therefore surrender the right to give themselves to anyone else). Although they are not yet married, that is already the nature of this couple's mutual commitment. They no longer belong to themselves. There isn't a lover and a beloved, as if the man were the head and the woman were the submissive one (the Old Testament never tells wives to obey their husbands). The relationship is a radically mutual and reciprocal one.

The chapter closes with an appeal taking up the imagery of her earlier imaginative description of her lover, urging him (as if he could hear) to come to her, and to come *now*!

SONG OF SONGS 3:1–11

Nightmares and Dreams (1)

1 On my bed by night, I looked for the one my heart loves;
 I looked for him but didn't find him.
2 "I'll get up, then, and go around the city,
 through the streets and through the squares.
I'll look for the one my heart loves,
 because I've looked for him but not found him."
3 The watchmen found me as they went around the city:
 "Have you seen the one my heart loves?"
4 Scarcely had I passed them
 when I found the one my heart loves.
I took hold of him and would not let him go
 until I had brought him to my mother's house,
 to the room of the one who conceived me.

5 I adjure you, Jerusalem girls,
      by the gazelles or the wild deer,
   don't awaken, don't arouse love,
      until it wishes.

6 What is this coming up from the wilderness,
      like columns of smoke,
   perfumed with myrrh and incense,
      from every powder of a merchant?

7 There—Solomon's carriage,
      around which are sixty warriors, of the warriors of Israel.

8 All of them are girded with a sword,
      trained in battle,
   each with his sword on his side,
      because of the terror of the night.

9 King Solomon had made himself a carriage,
      of wood from Lebanon.

10 He had made its posts of silver,
      its base of gold, its seat of purple;
      its inside was inlaid with love by the Jerusalem girls.

11 Go out and look, girls of Zion, at King Solomon,
      in the crown with which his mother has crowned him,
   on his wedding day,
      on the day of his heartfelt joy.

A student of mine from southern Africa once gave me an account of aspects of her life at home. In homestead life in her grandparents' day, her grandfather had eleven wives; each had six to ten children. His wives' huts stood in a half-moon, his in the center so he could monitor and control his family. If another man angered him and he could not fight the man, he would beat one of his wives. When one wife got pregnant and he thought another man was the father, he beat her in front of the other wives till she aborted. The wives fled but returned in fear of wild animals, and as the ringleader the student's grandmother was beaten. The situation hasn't changed so much in succeeding decades. She had just heard about the death of a friend after being beaten by her husband. She knew a woman who used to run away to her brother's house because her husband beat her. The husband would always come to get his wife back, and the brother would always surrender her because the husband had the right to do what he liked with her, as his property. If she had run back to her parents' home, she would invite a lecture from her mother on submission to her husband. Eventually he hit her on the head with an iron bar, and she died. The same property understanding of marriage means that women have no right to withhold themselves sexually from their husbands when the latter have contracted AIDS or HIV through their promiscuity, so that many of the countless women who have died from AIDS were infected by their husbands.

Such stories have equivalents in the different cultural contexts of the West. One aspect of a remedy is for men to have something more like the attitude to their wives that is suggested by the Song. Maybe this possibility points to another aspect of the significance of the way the woman's viewpoint and words dominate in the Song. This chapter begins with her relating a dream as she speaks of lying in bed but looking for the man she loves. Her description has a dream's surreal quality as she wanders about the city looking for him but unable to find him. Even the city police, whose job is to know everything that is going on and to know who is wandering about in the middle of the night and potentially up to no good, don't know anything about his whereabouts. But she finds him, takes his arm, and drags him off to her mother's house. In referring to her mother's house and room she implies at least that her father and mother had separate personal space within the family dwelling or perhaps had separate actual houses, as could specifically be the case where the man had more than one wife. Once more the dream indicates how she's longing for the time when she and the man she loves can be together all the time. Once more she urges the actual or figurative Jerusalem girls not to make her mistake of falling in love before you're in a position to do something about it (not that she would have things change for a moment!). It's evidently an important motif; any love you can't do something about is just pain and longing.

The second paragraph is another quite separate highly imaginative poem. It pictures the arrival of a carriage bearing Solomon, surrounded with a military escort that is partly ceremonial but also has a practical significance; if there's any possibility of a night attack, it's the escort's job to protect the king. Solomon is acknowledged not only by the young men with their fighting ability but also by the young women of Jerusalem who have contributed in their love for him to making his carriage a suitably splendid affair. The last line indicates that the carriage carries him in his wedding procession. The crown it refers to isn't his regular kingly crown but a wedding crown that his mother has made him.

Now the rest of the Song suggests that it concerns the relationship of an ordinary couple on their way to being able to spend their life together. It doesn't suggest a king and a princess or a potential princess or queen, certainly not any of Solomon's actual seven hundred princesses and three hundred secondary wives who are mentioned in 1 Kings 11. So why does the Song include an imaginative poem about one of Solomon's weddings? In Song of Songs 1, "king" seemed to be the woman's way of referring to her man—he's a king to her, as she's a princess to him. So here, the woman again lets her imagination loose as she formulates her description of an actual king's splendid arrival in a way that expresses her wonder at the man she loves and pictures him coming to her on their wedding day. It won't literally be a procession like this one when he comes from his house for the wedding, but to her, it will be just like it. Once again she draws the other young girls of Jerusalem into her admiration of her beau; once again it's another way of expressing her own feelings about him.

SONG OF SONGS 4:1–5:1

Crazy for Love (2)

1 There you are, so lovely, my dear, there you are, so lovely;
    your eyes are doves behind your veil.
  Your hair is like a flock of goats
    that stream from Mount Gilead.

2 Your teeth are like a flock of shorn ewes
    that climb up from the pool
  that are all twinning,
    and there's none bereaved among them.

3 Like a crimson ribbon are your lips;
    your mouth is lovely.
  Like the splitting of a pomegranate
    is your brow behind your veil.

4 Like the Tower of David is your neck,
    built in courses,
  hung with a thousand shields on it,
    all the armory of warriors.

5 Your two breasts are like two fawns,
    the twins of a gazelle pasturing among the lilies.

6 While the day blows and the shadows flee,
    I'll get myself to the mountain of myrrh, to the hill of
      incense.

7 Every part of you is lovely, my dear;
    there's no flaw in you.

8 With me from Lebanon, my bride,
    with me from Lebanon, come!
  Come down from the peak of Amana,
    from the peak of Senir and Hermon,
  from the dens of the lions,
    and from the mountains of the leopards.

9 You have captured my heart, my sister, my bride,
    you have captured my heart,
  with one [look] from your eyes,
    with one jewel from your necklace.

10 How sweet is your love,
    my sister, my bride!
  How much sweeter is your love than wine,
    the fragrance of your oils than all perfumes!

11 Your lips drop honey, my bride;
    syrup and milk are under your tongue.
  The fragrance of your robes

235

is like the fragrance of Lebanon.
¹² You are a locked garden, my sister, my bride,
    a locked fountain, a sealed fountain.
¹³ Your shoots are an orchard of pomegranates,
    with splendid fruit,
henna with spikenard,
¹⁴   spikenard and saffron,
cane and cinnamon, with all the incense trees,
    myrrh and aloes, with all the best of perfumes.
¹⁵ You are a garden spring, a well of living water,
    flowing from Lebanon.
¹⁶ Awake, north wind, come, south wind,
    blow on my garden so that its perfumes may spread.

May my love come to his garden
    and eat its splendid fruit!

^{5:1} I've come to my garden, my sister, my bride.
    I've plucked my myrrh with its perfume.

Eat, my friends, drink,
    get drunk on love.

I was amused when a friend who (like me) had fallen in love when he was of mature age asked me for advice about his sexual relationship with his fiancée, who was also of mature age. Like me, he had been brought up to assume that kissing was the most that people who were not yet married ought to do, but we now live in a culture where people usually don't wait to get married before they have sex. My friend and his fiancée would find it natural to make love, but they feel inhibited about doing so. It's not just a legalistic inhibition. They want to preserve something for their wedding night. They want there to be synchronicity between their position in relation to their church, their families, and their society, which relate to them as people who are not quite married; and they want this synchronicity in the way they relate to each other. On the other hand, they feel it's natural for there to be a growing sexual intimacy between them, though one that comes short of full-on sex.

That seems to fit with the Song. Whereas so far, the woman has dominated the poems, for this chapter the man does so. Maybe it's significant that he talks more about the visual than she does; it's said that men tend to be more visual than women. Maybe it's also significant that she talks more about fragrances, but I mustn't generalize from the fact that I personally don't have much of a sense of smell. Maybe it's the fact that he talks more about the visual that gives a more overt sexual tone to his lines, and thus raises the question about how a man and a woman relate sexually before they are married.

I imagine that Middle Eastern readers would be puzzled by the imagery of Western love poetry ("My love is like a red, red rose," Robert Burns; "Drink to me only with thine eyes," Ben Jonson). Likewise the imagery of the Song of Songs can be puzzling to Western readers. We don't know why dovelike-ness would be an appropriate compliment for eyes, but it's slightly clearer why a flock of dark-haired goats streaming down a mountain would provide an image for flowing hair. Like sheep, the woman's teeth are white and well-matched, with none missing—more remarkable in a culture where there are no dentists' offices. A split pomegranate has both dark and light colors, which perhaps suggests the light aspect to the visible part of a woman's brow and the dark aspect hidden under the veil. She has a long neck covered in jewels, like armor. Her breasts have the gracefulness of fawns or gazelles. Evidently her man isn't lacking in his sense of smell; he wants to savor the fragrance that he imagines her body wafting.

They are not able to be together, and for practical purposes it's as if she's in the far northeastern mountains, where wild animals live; she's inaccessible to him and he longs for her to come to him as his bride (calling her "sister" suggests the closeness of a relationship, like that within a family). At the moment she's a locked garden or fountain, sexually unavailable even to him, yet an exotic garden, full of delights, and a garden whose door he eagerly anticipates entering. Thus he urges the winds to come and blow her fragrances so that they will be there for his inhaling.

His long and passionate declaration of his admiration and longing totally wins over the woman, who responds with her own expression of longing that he may indeed come to her, as he wishes her to be brought to him. He in turn says he has come. Thus the two of them in the imagination of the poet delight in the joy of making love, and the poet himself or herself, or their friends (maybe the Jerusalem girls), encourage them to do so.

SONG OF SONGS 5:2–6:10

Nightmares and Dreams (2)

2 I was sleeping, but my mind was awake;
    the sound of my love, knocking!
  "Open for me, my sister, my dear,
    my dove, my perfect one;
  my head is covered in dew,
    my hair with the moisture of the night."
3 "I've taken off my robe; how can I get dressed?
    I've bathed my feet, how can I get them dirty?"
4 My love put his hand through the [latch] hole;
    my heart sighed for him.
5 I myself got up to open to my love;
    my hands dripped with myrrh.
  So my fingers were flowing myrrh
    on the handles of the bolt.
6 I myself opened the door for my love,
    but my love had disappeared, flown.
  My spirit had gone [from me] at his speaking;
    I looked for him but I didn't find him,
    I called him, but he didn't answer me.
7 I found the watchmen as they went around the city;

they hit me, injured me.
They took my coat from upon me,
   the watchmen on the walls.

8 I adjure you, Jerusalem girls, if you find my love:
   what are you to say to him?—that I am sick with love.

9 "How is your love better than [any other] love,
   loveliest among women?
How is your love better than [any other] love,
   that you adjure us so?"

10 "My love is radiant and ruddy,
   outstanding among ten thousand.
11 His head is gold, fine gold;
   his hair curly, black as a raven.
12 His eyes are like doves by streams of water,
   bathing in milk, sitting by a full pool.
13 His cheeks like a bed of perfume, towers of spices;
   his lips are lilies, dripping flowing myrrh.
14 His hands are rods of gold, covered in Tarshish-stone;
   his stomach is a plate of ivory, adorned with sapphires.
15 His legs are alabaster pillars, set on sockets of gold;
   his appearance is like Lebanon, choice as the cedars.
16 His palate is total sweetness; all of him is desirable;
   this is my love, this is my darling, Jerusalem girls!"

6:1 "Where has your love gone,
   loveliest among women?
Where has your love turned,
   so we may look for him with you?"

2 "My love has come down to his garden, to the beds of
      perfume,
   to pasture in the gardens and pick lilies.
3 I belong to my love and my love belongs to me,
   the one who pastures among the lilies."

4 You are as beautiful, my dear, as Tirzah,
   as lovely as Jerusalem,
   as awe-inspiring as the bannered [cities].
5 Turn your eyes away from me; they—
   they overwhelm me.

239

Your hair is like a flock of goats
   that stream from Mount Gilead.
6 Your teeth are like a flock of shorn ewes
   that climb up from the pool
that are all twinning,
   and there's none bereaved among them.
7 Like the splitting of a pomegranate
   is your brow behind your veil.
8 There are sixty queens,
   eighty secondary wives,
and girls without number;
9   my dove, my perfect one, is the one.
She is the one belonging to her mother,
   she is special to the one who bore her.
Girls have seen her and called her blessed;
   queens and secondary wives have praised her.
10 "Who is this who gazes down like the dawn,
   as beautiful as the moon,
special like the sun,
   as awe-inspiring as the bannered [cities]?"

My wife and I both have recurrent features of our dreams. Kathleen's dreams tend to be frightening—yesterday in her dream she fell under a car. In my dreams, more often than not an incidental feature is that I am pushing my first wife, Ann, in her wheelchair. We both know that we are processing tough events from the past in our dreams; for Kathleen, it's some traumatic events she went through before we met; for me it's the sadness and stress of Ann's illness. We both hope that over time this processing may eventually fade, not least through the healing that our relationship brings us.

The woman in the Song is processing as she dreams. I have assumed that she is doing something of this kind in her imagination in chapter 2. It's more clear that she is relating an actual dream in chapter 3 as she speaks of lying in bed but looking for the man she loves, and again in this chapter, where her description has not only the surreal character of a dream but also a more marked nightmarish quality. She describes dreams as issuing from the mind being awake while we are sleeping, rather a neat if also extraordinary way to describe it. In this state she thinks she hears her love arriving, and she reacts with some slightly irrational objections, the kind of thing that happens in a dream. He nevertheless seems to be coming in, and she gets up to open the door, but her hands slip on the bolt, and by the time she gets it open, he has disappeared. She goes out to look for him as she did in the previous dream, but this time the watchmen are not only unhelpful, but they attack her, as if she's a robber up to no good in the night.

Her plea to the Jerusalem girls leads to their asking what is so special about this man that they should bother themselves with her concern to find him. Their reaction in turn gives her the opportunity to give an equivalent description of him to the one he gave of her in the previous chapter, though one whose description is more straightforward. She convinces the girls, and they agree to join in the search.

Again with the disorienting logic of a dream, the sequence comes to completion with her suddenly being in his company, or rather his being in her company, and with the two of them in a loving sexual embrace. In her imagination she's the perfumed garden where he pastures, the flower bed where he picks lilies. The nightmare, the watchmen, and the girls have disappeared. It's what happens when you find your true love; your fears and nightmares and other people's opinions are overshadowed by the other person's love. She can thus reaffirm the earlier declaration about their mutual commitment ("I belong to my love, and my love belongs to me"), though she of course reverses it and thereby underlines the mutuality it expresses. There's no leader and no led in this relationship.

The last paragraph is one of the man's rare contributions, in which he describes the one he loves. Much of his language simply applies to her the imagery she has applied to him. Tirzah was for a period the capital of Ephraim and was thus a powerful city, like Jerusalem. Thus both are impressive and "bannered"; they are like an army bearing its standards. He continues in the same vein as he speaks of her overpowering him, using an unusual verb that lies behind the name Rahab, which appears elsewhere as the name of a powerful sea monster (not the Rahab in Joshua, whose name is spelled differently in Hebrew). Just one look can reduce him to putty. A man could have all the women in the world, but none would compare with her.

SONG OF SONGS 6:11–7:13

I Belong to My Love, and His Desire Is toward Me

11 I went down to the garden of nut-trees
    to see the blossoming in the wash,
to see the budding of the vine,
    the blooming of the pomegranates.
12 Though I didn't recognize,
    my heart set me with the chariots of Ammi-nadib.

13 Turn, turn, Shulammite; turn, turn,
    so we may look at you!

    Why do you look at the Shulammite,
    like the dance of two camps?

7:1 How lovely are your feet in sandals,
    noble woman!
The curves of your hips are like rings,
    the work of a craftsman's hands.
2 Your navel is a round bowl;
    mixed wine will not be lacking.
Your stomach is a heap of wheat,
    encircled by lilies.
3 Your two breasts are like two fawns,
    the twins of a gazelle.
4 Your neck is like a tower of ivory,
    your eyes are pools at Heshbon,
    by the gate of Bath-rabbim;

242

your nose is like the Lebanon tower,
    looking toward Damascus;
5 your head upon you is like Carmel,
    the locks on your head like purple;
    a king is captivated by your tresses.
6 How lovely you are, how beautiful you are,
    love with delights.
7 This, your stature, is like a palm,
    your breasts are clusters.
8 I've said, "I'll climb the palm,
    I'll take hold of its stems."
    Your breasts will be like the clusters of the vine,
    the fragrance of your breath like apricots;
9 your palate like good wine, going rightly to my love,
    gliding over the lips of sleepers.

10 I belong to my love,
    and his desire is toward me.
11 Come, my love, let's go out into the countryside,
    let's lodge in the villages.
12 Let's go eagerly to the vineyards,
    let's see if the vine has flowered,
    the blossom has opened, the pomegranates have bloomed;
    there I'll give my love to you.
13 The mandrakes have given fragrance,
    and at our doors are all splendid things.
    Fresh and also old things, my love,
    I've kept for you.

I once had to review a commentary on the Song for a journal. The author assumed that the Song is about the relationship between a man and a woman and dismissed the idea that under the surface it's about the relationship between Christ and us, which has been a traditional Christian understanding. I noted this fact and simply approved of it. I then received a forthright letter from a nun who was convinced that the traditional understanding is right (and was writing a PhD on the subject) and upbraided me for dismissing it. She pointed out that whereas it's sometimes assumed that people interpret the Song in that way because they have a hang-up about sex, there's no more evidence for that conviction than there is for the view that it's our sex-obsessed society that generates the view that the Song is simply about sex. We had an amicable correspondence and the next time I was in her town I went to her convent for tea.

I have several sorts of reasons for continuing to affirm the view she questioned and for thinking that it's important to emphasize it. One is that there's no hint in the Song that its surface meaning (that it's about the relationship between two people) isn't also its real meaning. Another is that the church needs to talk about sex and not leave it as a subject that people can think is unrelated to God, nor confine its conversation to the link between sex and sin. Another is that in isolation the Song would give us a weird impression of the nature of our relationship with God and a different impression from the one we get elsewhere in Scripture.

Chapter 7 includes the third occurrence of a phrase that recurs three times in the Song in slightly different formulations: "I belong to my love, and his desire is toward me." Desire can be both a positive and a negative word, in Hebrew as in English, not least in connection with sex. The word comes only twice elsewhere in the Old Testament, in Genesis 3 where it refers to Eve's desire for Adam and in Genesis 4 where it refers to sin's animal-like desire for Cain. In the last of these occurrences it's negative; in Genesis 3 it's ambiguous. Here in the Song there's nothing in the context to suggest that it's negative; the context rather suggests it's a variant on the different expressions the Song uses for the mutual attraction of the man and the woman. The lines that follow refer to the couple's shared desire to be able to make love. In the imagery of the Song the city has negative connotations; it's where the woman has been beaten up when she was looking for her man. The countryside has positive connotations, and the imagery of nature such as the vineyard and the pomegranates specifically has the connotation of lovemaking. Mandrakes contain hallucinogens, which might explain the tradition that they are aphrodisiacs; but in Hebrew it's more significant that the word for mandrakes is almost the same as one of the words for love; they are in this sense "love plants." In this context, the new and old things are maybe familiar and also innovative ways of making love.

The sensual nature of the love relationship in itself would make it an odd way to speak indirectly about the relationship between God and us. The Bible does not speak of that relationship in romantic terms. The Bible rather portrays this relationship as like that between parent and child or teacher and pupil or king and subject or master and servant. All these relationships can involve affection and mutual commitment, but they are essentially hierarchical relationships. God is God and we are human beings. We are not equals, like the man and the woman who speak in the Song. While the Old Testament doesn't tell wives to obey their husbands, a patriarchal culture would likely have that expectation, and when the Bible uses the husband-wife relationship as a metaphor for God's relationship with us, it doesn't then speak in terms of the egalitarian relationship reflected in the Song.

In the opening paragraphs in this passage, the woman is going out into the countryside in her imagination, but the garden, the blossom, and the vine are again metaphors for lovemaking. The reference to surprise hints that she is again relating something strange and unpredictable that happened in a dream, in which she is apparently transported into "the chariots of Ammi-nadib." The expression suggests excitement with a hint of danger and pairs with the man's description of her having the power of bannered cities. It's perhaps the Jerusalem girls who then bid her turn around so that they can look at her in her impressiveness. Her reply again takes up the military imagery. Looking at her is like looking at the excitement of two armies "dancing" as they confront each other. Here alone the woman is referred to as the Shulammite;

the man is a kind of Solomon (*Shelomoh*) and she is a kind of
female equivalent.

SONG OF SONGS 8:1–14

Love Is as Fierce as Death

¹ O that someone could make you like my brother,
   one who was nursing at my mother's breasts.
When I met you in the street I could kiss you;
   further, people would not condemn me.

² I would lead you, I would bring you,
   to the house of my mother, the one who taught me.
I would get you to drink some spiced wine,
   some of my pomegranate juice.

³ His left hand would be under my head,
   his right hand would hold me.

⁴ I adjure you, Jerusalem girls, don't awaken,
   don't arouse love, until it wishes.

⁵ "Who is this coming up from the wilderness,
   leaning on her love?"
Under the apricot tree I aroused you;
   there your mother conceived you,
   there the one who bore you conceived you.

⁶ Make me like a seal on your heart,
   like a seal on your arm.
Because love is as fierce as death,
   passion as tough as Sheol.
Its darts are darts of fire,
   a supernatural flame.

⁷ Much water could not quench love,
   nor rivers drown it.
If someone gave all his household's wealth for love,
   they would totally condemn him.

⁸ "We have a little sister;
   she doesn't have breasts.
What shall we do for our sister
   regarding the day when she is spoken for?

⁹ If she's a wall, we'll build on it a silver battlement;
   if she's a door, we'll enclose it with cedar paneling."

¹⁰ I am a wall but my breasts are like towers;
   thus I've become in his eyes one who brings peace.

¹¹ Solomon had a vineyard in Baal-Hamon;
   he gave the vineyard to guards;
   someone gives a thousand silver pieces for its fruit.
¹² My vineyard is before me;
   the thousand are for you, Solomon,
   and two hundred for the guards of the fruit.

¹³ You who live in the gardens, with friends listening:
   let me hear your voice.

¹⁴ Hurry, my love, be like a gazelle or a young stag
   on the mountains of spices.

A recent movie tells the story of Edward VIII, who reigned as king of the United Kingdom for 325 days in 1936. Before coming to the throne he had fallen for a woman called Wallis Simpson who had not only committed the sin of being an American but also had two divorces behind her. There was no way that leaders of church and state would accept the king's marriage to such a person. After long agonizing, Edward told the nation, "I have found it impossible to carry the heavy burden of responsibility and to discharge my duties as king as I would wish to do without the help and support of the woman I love." My wife comments, "Women dream of being loved this much, that a man would give his kingdom for her." Edward abdicated the throne, married Ms. Simpson, and they lived together happily for thirty-five years until his death in 1972.

Love is as fierce as death, passion is as tough as **Sheol**. It's quite a comparison. When death gets hold of you, it doesn't let go. Sheol or Hades (the equivalent term in Greek) has gates that a person cannot burst open in order to get out. They can be broken through only from outside, Jesus says in Matthew 16. Love has the same power. It's like an archer who shoots burning arrows at you, arrows that burn so ferociously that you could never find enough water to put them out. It's as if they shoot a supernatural flame. Literally, they are "a flame of

Yah" (the name is a short form of the name **Yahweh**—or maybe Yahweh is a long form of the short name). It's the only time God is named in the Song of Songs. Love is stronger than any other earthly force. When love comes along, you're done for.

You don't mind, the Song implies, or at least you may not mind the fact that you are overwhelmed. You just want this other person to be clearly marked as yours, soul and body: the seal goes on the heart and on the arm. The double reference implies that the poem isn't referring to a literal seal, and we don't know of any material marker (analogous to the Western wedding ring) that indicated an Israelite was married, but the image of a seal that was outward as well as inward suggests a reference to marriage. In this connection, once again the Song excludes the idea that marriage means the man henceforth owns the woman in any way except as one side of an arrangement whereby the woman also owns the man. Her seal of ownership is on his inner being and on his body for all to see. Cultural assumptions might presuppose that she belongs to him, as is implicit in the tradition in Western culture that a father gives away the bride to the groom so that she passes from the ownership of one man to that of another man. This woman disputes that idea. He belongs to her as much as she belongs to him.

Yet a couple like this one who are prepared to make that mutual commitment may well not be able to marry right away, and waiting to do so is agonizing; hence the impossible longing expressed in the opening line of this final chapter. If her man were her brother, she could express her affection for him by kissing him and embracing him, but such a display would be unacceptable in her culture except between members of the same family. Or she could take him home; the way she speaks of their embrace there suggests that the refreshment she speaks of is a metaphor for the lovemaking she longs for. How long may they have to wait until the families have completed their negotiations and the arrangements for the celebration have been completed? The woman repeats once more the exhortation not to arouse love until it wishes. A couple needs not to get too overwhelmed by love when they are not yet in a position to act on their feelings and spend their lives together. Yet the fierceness of the flame makes such a declaration useless,

The ferocity of love may put you into an even more difficult position than King Edward. Maybe the person you fall for is married to someone else, or maybe you are. You may not merely have to wait a while but may have to face the fact that you're never going to be able to act on your feelings. Maybe you would be prepared to ignore your commitments to your family and dedicate its entire resources to a new love; but you would then end up an object of shame in the entire community. Maybe the person you fall for is simply not interested; maybe you would give up everything for this person, but if the love is unrequited, there's simply nothing to be done. "Money can't buy me love." Or if the person you fall for cynically agrees that it's in her best interests to accept your offer and you do give up everything for her, you become a laughing stock. For such reasons, further importance attaches to that exhortation with its contradiction of the principle that love has irresistible power. There's no way out of the conflict between the two principles.

Presumably the girls whom the woman exhorts are the ones who ask the question that follows the exhortation, to which she then replies with an ironic admission that she had in fact aroused her man when they were out together in the countryside, where they can be less restrained than in the city to which they are now returning. While the Song implies that her mother colludes with the relationship between her daughter and the young man, in the city one of her problems is that her brothers are not reconciled to it. We know from the very first section of the book about the tension in their relationship with her. She now quotes from them. They say she's not old enough to be thinking about a boy and that she needs to be kept sexually safe for her wedding day. Her response is that she remains a wall—that is, she remains sexually intact. For all the talk about lovemaking through the book, she hasn't been breached. The talk about lovemaking is all imagination and anticipation, as the Song has often indicated. On the other hand, her brothers haven't noticed that actually she has grown up. She is a wall and she has towers, and therefore (she wittily argues) she embodies peace and can bring peace to the man who recognizes both facts.

With more wit and bite, she takes the point further by means of a sardonic comment concerning Solomon and his "vineyard." As usual, the vineyard is a metaphor for a woman, and we have noted that 1 Kings 11 tells us that Solomon had a thousand women. There are so many, she observes, he has to employ guards to ensure that they are under control or protected. "He can keep his thousand partners," she says. "I'm in control of my vineyard, and I know who I am going to invite into it." Maturity implies she can protect her wall, and she knows she needs to do so until she's married and can rely on the man she loves in a new way.

The last two verses form a closing exchange between the man and the woman, who are still separate, not able to be together. The Song ends the way it has been all the way through, with longing, not fulfillment. She still belongs to her friends; he wants to hear her voice. He is still far away from her, and she can't wait for them to be together.

GLOSSARY

authority

Leaders are people who "exercise authority" in Israel. The Hebrew word for someone who exercises such authority is traditionally translated "judge," but such leadership is wider than this word implies. The exercise of authority implies the making of decisions in any area of life. It can include deciding matters of conflict in the community ("judging") but also any other proper exercise of authority or government. It's the job of leaders to exercise authority in accordance with **faithfulness** to God and people, and thus to protect powerless people.

awe

Hebrew uses the same words for being afraid of someone fearsome and for respecting someone whom it's appropriate to revere. Occasionally it's hard to be sure which sort of attitude is designated by the word. I have used "awe" where the context implies the second sort of attitude, which also implies submission and obedience. In the Wisdom books, awe is seen as a key aspect of a relationship with God, of crucial importance to understanding God and life. Awe for God has been described as the Old Testament expression for spirituality.

commitment

The word *commitment* corresponds to the Hebrew word *hesed*, which translations render by means of expressions such as "steadfast love" or "loving-kindness" or "goodness." It's the Old Testament equivalent to the special word for love in the New Testament, the word *agapē*. The Old Testament uses this word to refer to an extraordinary act whereby a person pledges himself or herself to someone else in some act of generosity, allegiance, or grace when there is no prior relationship between them and therefore no obligation to do so. It can also refer to a similar extraordinary act that takes place when there is a relationship between people but one party has let the other party down and therefore has no right to expect any continuing faithfulness. If the party that has been let down continues being faithful, they are showing this kind of commitment.

decision, see authority

faithfulness
In English Bibles this Hebrew word (*sedaqah*) is usually translated "righteousness," but it denotes a particular slant on what we might mean by righteousness. It means doing the right thing by the people with whom one is in a relationship, the members of one's community. Thus it's closer to "faithfulness" than "righteousness."

faithless
A word for sin that suggests the opposite of **faithfulness**, an attitude to God and to other people that expresses contempt for what right relationships deserve.

give oneself
I use this expression in many passages to translate the Hebrew word traditionally translated "love," because whereas the latter word in English easily suggests an emotion, the Hebrew word denotes an attitude and action as much as it does an emotion.

hate, see repudiation

love, see give oneself

repudiation
This word is the opposite of **giving oneself**. Traditionally the word is translated "hate," but like the word for "love," it denotes a term for an attitude that expresses itself in action and not so much an emotion.

Sheol
The most frequent of the Hebrew names for the place where we go when we die. In the New Testament it is called Hades. It is not a place of punishment or suffering but simply a resting place for everyone, a kind of nonphysical analogue to the tomb as the resting place for our bodies.

Torah
The Hebrew word for the first five books of the Bible. They are often referred to as the "Law," but this title gives a misleading impression. Genesis itself is nothing like "law," and even Exodus to Deuteronomy are not legalistic books. The word *torah* itself means "teaching" or "instruction," which gives a clearer impression of the nature of the Torah and of its significance in Proverbs.

Yahweh
In most English Bibles, the word *Lord* often comes in all capitals thus, as does sometimes the word *God* in similar format. These represent the name of God, Yahweh. In later Old Testament times, Israelites stopped using the name Yahweh and started to refer to Yahweh as "the Lord." There may be two reasons. They wanted other people to recognize that Yahweh was the one true God, but this strange foreign-sounding name could give the impression that Yahweh was just Israel's tribal god, whereas anyone could recognize a term such as "the Lord" or "God." In addition, they did not want to fall foul of the warning in the Ten Commandments about misusing Yahweh's name. Translations into other languages then followed suit in substituting an expression such as "the Lord" for the name Yahweh. Unfortunately this practice obscures the fact that God wanted to be known by name and the fact that often the text refers to Yahweh and not some other (so-called) god or lord. It also gives the impression that God is much more "lordly" and patriarchal than actually God is. (The form "Jehovah" is not a real word but a mixture of the consonants of Yahweh and the

vowels of that word for "Lord," to remind people in reading Scripture that they should say "the Lord," not the actual name.)